There Are No Mansions in Heaven

A fresh look at life, the universe, & eternity.

Stan & Margie Osterbauer

Cover image: *Tree of Life in Realms of Light*, by Heather Petersen.

D4 Publishing
Sequim, WA 98382
info@d4publishing.com

Acknowledgments

We owe a debt of gratitude to the many people who gave of their time to proof and review this book. We sought a wide range of viewpoints. Our readers included those at various points in their walk of faith, from "regular" Christians, to pastors, Bible study teachers, doctors, and college students. Thank you to all who helped.

For I know that my Redeemer lives,
and at the last he will stand upon the earth.
And after my skin has been thus destroyed,
yet in my flesh I shall see God,
whom I shall see for myself,
and my eyes shall behold, and not another.
My heart faints within me!

Job 19:25-27

Contents

Footnotes are located at the end of each section.

Beginnings

Road Map | Where We're Going With This

While the overall theme of this book is heaven and how you can change what life will be like there, we also look at how we get there. There's a progression to history from the first singularity to the New Heavens and New Earth.

Our purpose is threefold:

Apologetic. To those who believe there is a God, but are not quite sure how Jesus fits into all of this. We wish to present reasoned arguments in justification of the claims of Christianity. We wish to provide a counter-narrative to the materialistic and naturalistic worldview in which we are daily saturated.

Informative. To new believers. To believers who find their faith stagnant, yet instinctively know there must be more. There seems to be a great lack of Biblical literacy in American culture. We wish to present some of the astonishing truths of the Bible in a fresh way. We wish to lay out a framework for a vigorous faith.

Motivational. To mature believers. To disciples of Jesus Christ. We wish to look at the foundations of our faith. We wish to motivate believers to shift their focus, and begin storing up more treasure. We really do have a hand in designing what life in eternity will be!

We have folded these three purposes into one book because, wherever we are in our journey of faith, it is good to see where we've come from and where we're going. It's good to hear the counter-narrative. It's good to be reminded of those astonishing truths. It's good to shift our focus toward eternity.

To all who seek God. We wish to provide ammunition for the battle of the mind.

Romans 12:2a
*Do not be conformed to this world, but **be transformed by the renewal of your mind**...*

So here's a road map. The book is laid out in seven main sections. Each section has six or seven short chapters.

Section One | In Your Skin
What are our skewed perceptions of heaven? What is a soul? What are those mansions? How can we change what life will be like in eternity? What exactly happens when you die? What will it be like to see God face to face?

Section Two | Design
The New Heavens and New Earth will be birthed from what is present now, so how is everything designed? Who designed it and how. DNA, atoms, quantum mechanics, and more.

Section Three | Deception
The original design got messed up. How, and by whom? What is the source of truth and lies? We'll look at undeniable evidence from DNA, the laws of probability, and Darwin himself. And Scientific Naturalism's last desperate hope: the illogical improbable multiverse.

Section Four | Dominion
Where is God when disaster and evil prevail? What happened to the original dominion (control) which God gave to Adam and Eve? How does that change, and where does that leave us now?

Section Five | Citizenship
With dominion restored, how can you be a part of the new kingdom? What does it really take to get into heaven? How can you be sure? What does it look like to be a disciple of Jesus Christ?

Section Six | The Non-Existent Now

According to Augustine of Hippo, the present does not really exist. Before it can become "now", the future flies into the past in an infinitely small spec of time. *That's* where you meet God. *That's* where you live out the life which leads to eternity. *That's* where you learn spiritual discipline, and how to abide in Jesus.

Section Seven | Eternity

How the world ends. How the universe is remade. What life looks like without sin and death. Life on the New Earth. Traveling to the New Jerusalem. What you'll be doing, and what you'll be in charge of. The best party in all history...the Great Wedding Feast.

Get ready for the journey of a lifetime.

Preface | Letting Scripture Speak

All Scripture is breathed out by God...
2 Timothy 3:16a

There are a few things you should know before launching into this book. Our goal is to let the holy scriptures speak for themselves as we look at what they say about life in eternity.

It is more than a choice between heaven and hell. What happens now drastically changes where and how and with whom you will live in eternity. It affects the authority you will be given, and the abilities you will have, and the level of beauty you will reflect.

Before we begin there are some basic assumptions we must make.

First, there is a God. He calls Himself "I AM", or "Yahweh" (sometimes pronounced "Jehovah"), which means "Self-Existent Cause". He is self-contained. He exists independent of any other person or thing. He caused everything which is not Him to be. Everything. To quote Jason Petty from his brilliant rap anthem *G.O.S.P.E.L.*[1]:

> "...trying to prove God is like defending a lion homie. It don't need your help, just unlock the cage".

Second, the Bible describes itself as the Word of God...His very breath. If there is any part of it we cannot trust as entirely accurate and truthful, then we are left with nothing. It would be foolish to think that a God who could create the vast universe could not preserve His words intact. If we must pick and choose which verses to believe, then it is all up to human opinion, and we are left rudderless. You might as well make up your own god. That god will invariably resemble its creator.

Third, the words of the Bible were written in such a way that they can be understood by plain people. The scriptures were originally given to farmers and goatherds. While we don't need an academic or priest to explain them, there is a great cloud of witnesses who have gone before us. Many Christian classics can help point the right direction.[2] But you are going to have to pick up a Bible and read it for yourself, trusting the Holy Spirit to reveal truth. If you aren't doing that already, a good place to start might be the Gospel of John.

Fourth, the promises laid out in this book are not for everyone. There are specific things we will look at which are essential for entering into heaven. The Bible never promises universal salvation. God is calling. Are you listening?[3]

Fifth, not much in this book is new. Most of what can be said about scripture has already been said over the last 3,500 years. What we're trying to do is take a fresh look at some very old ideas, and perhaps view them from a different perspective. The idea that what happens in this life profoundly affects life in eternity, and that you really can "lay up for yourselves treasures in heaven", is very compelling. Something with such massive consequence deserves a fresh look.

Sixth, we should not flinch at letting self-interest be a motivation. At least five times in the Gospels, Jesus tells His followers to "lay up treasures in heaven" for themselves.[4] In the parable of the talents, Jesus says that if you have been faithful over the little you've been given in this life, He will "set you over much" in eternity.[5] That's an appeal to self-interest.

If we don't want God first and foremost, then we don't want heaven. God is the center. But we would be fools to pass up what Jesus is offering just because we don't think it's "spiritual" enough. These treasures are a reflection of Him. He's offering us *Himself*.

Seventh, we are acutely aware of our own inadequacy. We approach the writing of this book with humility. Based on their understanding of scripture, the crowd in John 8:59 was right when they sought to stone Jesus. He had the audacity to say "Before Abraham was, I am". That's claiming to be God.

What the crowd didn't realize was that God was standing right in front of them.[6] We are very much aware that the more we think we know, the greater chance we can miss the simple truth that God is right here. That is why we always try to approach scripture with a certain child-like simplicity.

Lord, may we not be blinded by what we think we know, and miss You standing right in front of us!

A note about Scripture quotations in this book:

We abhor the practice of quoting the Bible out of context when the result is a misrepresentation of the meaning of the text. However, to quote the entire chapter surrounding a verse is impractical.

We will always give the verse reference, and encourage you to look up the context. When quoting a partial verse, we will always signify this with an "a" or "b", to indicate that we are quoting the first or last part of the verse. We do this for space considerations, not in an attempt to conceal the full context.

Introduction | The Magic Jacket

For this perishable body must put on the imperishable,
and this mortal body must put on immortality.
1 Corinthians 15:53

What if someone of immense power and wealth offered to give you a jacket worth several billion dollars? We'll call it the "Magic Jacket", but it has nothing to do with the occult or witchcraft. It is "magical" in the sense of being so powerful, so extraordinary and transcendent and amazing, that it is truly miraculous.

The trillionaire has sent a foreign-speaking ambassador with an interpreter to make the offer and explain the terms. He reveals that this extraordinary jacket has been engineered to work with your body's systems to radically improve every part of you.

With this jacket you are better than Superman. You can leap farther, see better, and think with clarity and intelligence far beyond that of Einstein or Hawking.

There are only two conditions. One is that you will not have full use of your new jacket for a period of undetermined length; it could be five years, it could be thirty, perhaps longer. The other condition is that your jacket is unfinished.

In fact it's just an empty shell compared to what it could be. The foundation of something with unlimited potential.

You can add anything you like to your Magic Jacket. As you learn more about how it works you can add more power and ability. You can expand the authority it will bestow. You can extend it until it covers your entire body in dazzling beauty. Your wealthy benefactor will even send an engineering designer to guide you every step.

As you go, you begin to see that the more you work on your jacket, the more you learn about the trillionaire. Everything amazing and glorious and powerful and beautiful you add to the jacket is actually a reflection of him. And so over time your motivation becomes less and less about what you get in the jacket. Your motivation becomes more and more simply to know him.

But in the end you get both. To intimately know this amazing trillionaire, and to put on this powerful jacket, which is a reflection of him. Even more amazing, with the jacket, the trillionaire is sharing his authority and his wealth. You will command many of his servants and be in charge of some of his vast creative enterprises. It all depends on how much you add during the waiting period.

All of us have a creative spark. For some it is hidden deep inside. With your Magic Jacket, that spark will be fanned into a blaze of creative brilliance, with unlimited resources and intelligence and wisdom behind it. The more you add to your jacket, the greater the level of creativity you will have.

So what would you add to your Magic Jacket? Where would your focus be? What would you be willing to give up in terms of time and money to gain such an amazing thing? Would you start in with single-minded purpose, or would you go on as you always have? Is there something you're not willing to let go of?

He is no fool who gives what he cannot keep to gain that which he cannot lose.[7]

And so at the end of the undetermined waiting period, what would your jacket look like? What power and authority would it impart? What level of beauty would it reflect? Would your Magic Jacket be glorious and intricate? Would it have creative powers beyond imagining? Or would it be less than one billionth of what it might have been? A mere shell.

Sound far-fetched?

What we have just describe is real. It is not some fairy tale. The offer is genuine. In the following chapters we will unpack this. There are treasures beyond imagining ahead. Please don't miss out.

One more thing. That immensely powerful and wealthy trillionaire has invited you to a party. It will be the greatest in all history, with joys you can't even imagine. You get to hang out with the most fascinating, loving, creative person who ever lived. You get to speak with him face to face and learn things which will amaze you.

But you can't get into the party without your Magic Jacket.

¹ Video: https://youtu.be/jyYFxp7apl4

² There are some modern classics as well, such as the works of J. I. Packer and A. W. Tozer. There is also a great deal of misguided rubbish out there. See also our Recommended Reading section.

³ Romans 10:17: *So faith comes from hearing, and hearing through the word of Christ.*

⁴ Matthew 6:20, Matthew 19:21, Mark 10:21, Luke 12:33, Luke 18:22. The idea that we can store up treasures in heaven for ourselves is also discussed by the Apostle Paul in 1 Timothy 6:19 and Colossians 3:23-24.

⁵ Matthew 25:23.

⁶ This insight into John 8:59 is not original with us. We know we've heard it in a sermon or read it in a book somewhere, we just can't remember where.

⁷ Paraphrased by missionary Jim Elliot from an earlier quote by Philip Henry (1631-1696), father of commentary-writer Matthew Henry.

Section One | In Your Skin

Pemberly

In my Father's house are many mansions: if it were not so,
I would have told you. I go to prepare a place for you.
John 14:2 (KJV)

There are no mansions in heaven.
There are no personal castles of individual sovereignty and isolation. That may strike some as incorrect. What about the verse we just quoted above from the 1611 King James Version of the Bible? Didn't Jesus say, "In my Father's house are many mansions"?

In the original Greek, the word translated "mansions" here is *moné*. It means "abode" or "dwelling place". It could be a hut or an apartment or a mansion...or just a tent. It's the place you live. It's the place you call home.

The word "mansion" creates a picture in our mind of a huge structure with dozens of rooms, maybe a hundred. It has tens of thousands of square feet, and vast open spaces. It is ostentatious. Showy. You know, fluted Grecian columns and elaborately decorated ceilings. Mr. Darcy's Pemberly in *Pride & Prejudice*.

Picture yourself rambling about the place in idleness like the aristocrats of the nineteenth century. Maybe once in a while you'll host a fancy ball and invite all your friends. Maybe on Thursdays you'll take one of the purebred horses from your vast stables for a leisurely ride. If there are Thursdays in heaven.

But for the most part you wander around your big mansion with nothing in particular to do. For thousands of years. For eternity.

Sound like fun?

If the picture of heaven we just painted is not appealing to you, there's a reason for that. *It's not true!*

Here's the truth:

2 Timothy 2:12a
If we endure, we will also reign with him...

It is an amazing thought that you could someday be *reigning* with Jesus Christ. Do you grasp what that actually means? You will have royal authority, power, and control over some aspect of heaven. That's the definition of "reign".[1]

This is not just some fairy tale. Get that out of your head. This is *real!* More real than the ground you walk on.

You have an astounding inheritance waiting for you. You will have a magnificent new body. No more aches and pains. No more fear. No more tears. No more death. No more sin!

Sometimes the enemy of truth is not a lie. Sometimes the enemy of truth is an almost-truth.

The truths of heaven and eternity can be so muddled by our skewed concepts that they are lost altogether.

Our goal in this first section is to expose those skewed concepts, and discover the thrilling truth that we *can* live forever with God, and that what happens now, on this planet, drastically affects the richness of that eternal life.

One more thing...

The whole idea that there will be no *time* in heaven is pure bunk! Is that blunt enough for you? Our culture, and even our Church, so often minimizes what heaven will be like. Without *time*, how could we move in and out of the New Jerusalem, as Revelation 21 tells us? Without *time*, how could we explore a marvelous, regenerated New Heavens and New Earth? Why would God have even created them?

There is something essential and wonderful we may be missing here. And *that* is what this book is all about!

An Image of Heaven Spun From The Stuff of Earth

T hese "mansions" are sitting in a heaven of which the Bible only gives fleeting glimpses. In a later chapter we will look in detail at how scripture portrays what heaven will be like. But first we need to look at our skewed perceptions. Many of us have a kind of cartoon image of our life in heaven. Feathery wings and a halo, sitting on a cloud strumming a harp.

A quick survey[2] of opinions on heaven reveals some interesting, and often odd concepts:

I think of it as a sort of resort. A really huge resort. Every family would have their own section of the resort. Each individual has their own room. This room is a personal paradise where you could have everything you wanted on Earth.

I'm finally doing all the cool stuff I've always wanted to do on Earth.

Just like our entire existence now...only without the bad stuff.

I expect my area in heaven will be high on a mountain overlooking other stunning mountains.

I will be sitting on a cloud in a white smock for all eternity, strumming a harp.

God will create a Heaven for each of us that is perfect and it will have everything that makes us completely happy.

Crystal castles and crystal fountains, glowing illuminated streets with purple-blue skies.

In the musical theater production *Les Misérables*[3], there's a scene where young Cosette sings a solo while sweeping the floor at the Thénardier's inn. Copyright restrictions prevent us from quoting the lyrics. But the song's title, "Castle on a Cloud", ties in neatly with the picture most of us have of heaven and mansions. Cosette see's her imaginary cloud-castle as a place to escape the drudgery and hopelessness of her existence. It's a place where no one shouts at her, where there's no crying, and where she's told that she is loved.

Cosette's song echoes what many of us feel. A longing for hope, peace, and to be truly loved. There seems to be an empty spot deep inside each of us which nothing of this world can completely fill. C.S. Lewis expressed a similar sentiment:

If I find in myself a desire which no experience in this world can satisfy, the most probable explanation is that I was made for another world.[4]

That other world, that castle on a cloud, is a longing which seems to be found in every culture in every time in history. Hope for something better than what we see around us. Peace with others, and especially peace within. And love.

But there is another side to this longing. There seems to be a fear of what might replace the emptiness. The familiar, however bad, is often better than the unknown. It is ironic that the author of the novel *Les Miserables*, Victor Hugo, is quoted as saying,

"An intelligent hell would be better than a stupid paradise."[5]

Another quick survey reveals some rather negative opinions about heaven:

Christian "heaven" is not my liking because worshiping God for eternity, having chores, not remembering earth memories or loved ones sounds depressing to me.

Eternal existence and freedom from care sounds more like a description of hell to me.

The heaven concept kind of sickens me though. If God is so great and goes on about free will, why is he bribing us in order to accumulate groupies?

Our picture of life in heaven is often so skewed that to some, hell looks appealing by comparison. Hell is where the party is, right? All your friends will be there. The picture of hell we manufacture is often as skewed as our cartoon visions of heaven. To quote Mark Twain,

Go to Heaven for the climate, Hell for the company.[6]

Or Issac Asimov,

For whatever the tortures of hell, I think the boredom of heaven would be even worse.[7]

Even if our picture of heaven is a "better place", a place where life basically resembles what it is here and now only better, we are still missing something. What is familiar is safe. It's comfortable. The concept of a mansion we can get our minds around.

In a place that's kind of like here, only better, a mansion might come in handy. We may like the idea because it provides a place to be quiet by yourself. To be "me". Those of us who are introverts can get "peopled out", and it's nice to have a cozy place of refuge. A retreat. Maybe your idea of a mansion isn't Mr. Darcy's Pemberly. Maybe it's more of a quaint cottage by a lake, with beautiful flowers all around.

But a mansion, whether it's Pemberly or a cottage, walls us off from others. It isolates us in a personal space where we are "king". The idea of one's home as a castle dates back to at least 1628, when Sir Edward Coke wrote,

"A man's house is his castle and fortress, and each man's home is his safest refuge."[8]

But in heaven, what do we need to take "refuge" from? Why would we need to retreat to our mansion for safety? A fortress holds back the attacking hordes, and preserves our sovereignty in this space we call "mine".

So what do *you* think of when you think of heaven? What pops into your mind? Don't analyze it. What's your first impression?

The view we have of heaven may be colored by a hodgepodge of books, movies, and various cultures and religions.

Janna, Arabic for "paradise", is depicted in the Qur'an as a garden of everlasting bliss, home of peace, and home of the righteous. There, the righteous will find "rivers of milk of which the taste never changes, rivers of wine, a joy to those who drink; and rivers of honey pure and clear".[9]

The Hindu concept of heaven consists of several realms that have no suffering. The kingdom of heaven is ruled by a god named Indra. Pleasure is experienced continually and you are surrounded by beautiful celestial beings. To get to heaven, you must have accrued high amounts of good karma and performed many religious activities. Time in heaven is temporary. Once the merit you earned on earth is used up, you must leave heaven to incarnate as a human again.[10]

In Buddhist thought there is no reality. *You* create reality and the universe around you simply by being. When you achieve Nirvana you have let go of all thought, all desire, and the illusion of "self". You become one with ultimate "Truth". According to Musila, a disciple of Buddha, "Nirvana is definitely not annihilation of self because there is no self to annihilate. If at all, it is the annihilation of the illusion, of the false idea of self."

There is a concept in Catholic teaching called the "beatific vision". It is described as the "final end" of the believer. The saved will gaze into the face of God for all eternity. Though it may not be taught as such, some understand this as your disembodied soul gazing with unblinking spiritual eyes upon the face of God forever.[11]

A disembodied existence devoid of thought and self may seem alien, but these ideas have crept into our modern culture and form the background noise amid which our ideas of heaven float.

Even more so, our modern Western cultural notions of heaven are shaped by novels and movies. "We will meet again" or "he's looking down on us" are common themes. Even in many secular stories, a child who dies is often spoken of as being "an angel now". Nowhere in scripture is it written that when humans die they become angels. But somehow this idea gained traction, particularly in the 20th century.

Angel Second Class Clarence Odbody is a prime example. Born in May, 1653, and having long since died and gone to heaven, Clarence has been trying to get his angel wings for over 200 years. We meet Clarence in Frank Capra's *It's a Wonderful Life*, where he is sent to earth to rescue George Bailey.

> *Look, Daddy. Teacher says, every time a bell rings an angel gets his wings.* [12]

Even if we recognize the pure fantasy of such tales, these perceptions seep into our concept of what eternity will be like. More recent cultural depictions are a little more subtle, if no less skewed.

In Mitch Albom's novel *The Five People You Meet in Heaven*, heaven is described as a place "for understanding your life on earth". This is said to be "the greatest gift God can give you: to understand what happened in your life. To have it explained. It is the peace you have been searching for."

The Lovely Bones, by Alice Sebold, depicts heaven as a place which "includes all my simplest desires", where there are "cakes and pillows and colors galore".

These visions of heaven, like most popular concoctions, are very self-centered. Understanding your life on earth. Cakes and pillows and comfort, and "all my simplest desires". It's about fulfillment and self-revelation and *me*. A little more nuanced than Cosette's Castle on a Cloud or Clarence Oddbody's angel wings, but still casting an image of heaven which is spun from the stuff of earth. Like making shadow puppets with your fingers in front of a candle and hoping they are somehow real.

The picture many of us have of life in heaven, if we have a positive view of it at all, is basically a new and improved "you" in a new and improved place. The "Garden" of the Qur'an. The continual pleasures of the Hindu "heavenly spheres". The self-fulfillment and self-revelation of modern popular myths. You get to do all those wonderful things you missed here on Earth.

And your Heavenly Father will even throw in a fancy new house, just for you.

I, Zombie

Most modern translations of the Bible have "abode" or "rooms" in place of "mansions" in John 14:2. Before we move on to look more closely at what our heavenly "abode" might look like, it would be good to examine exactly what or who will be residing in these "rooms".

We live inside bodies which have been described as "ugly giant bags of mostly water"[13]. Your are made up of water (57%), carbon (18%), hydrogen (10%), calcium (1.5%), and dozens of trace elements. But where is "you" in all of that? Is the essence which is "you" in your brain?

The human brain is composed of about 100 billion nerve cells interconnected by trillions of connections, called synapses. Each connection transmits about one signal per second. Somehow, that's producing thought.[14]

Try to imagine 100 billion neurons all chattering back and forth through trillions of synapses. Is the real "you" hidden somewhere in all those trillions of little "signals"? Is the essence of who you are just an electro-chemical stimulus between neurons?

I think, therefore I am.[15]

Is that what constitutes "you"? Your thoughts? But what is a thought? Are thoughts just a vapor? Just an electrical charge between two neurons? Can you touch a thought?

The Buddhist idea is that there is no "self". It is the thought that thinks...there is no thinker behind the thought. Is that what you are? A figment of your own imagination? Oh wait, if there is no self then there is no one to have an imagination.

The materialist would reduce you to a biological machine with a computer-like brain. The Buddhist would reduce you to an illusion. What, then, is a "sentient" being?

sentient: responsive to or conscious of sense impressions[16]

To be "sentient", then, is to be conscious of your senses and responsive to them. So the next question would be, "What is consciousness?"

The problem of what constitutes consciousness has stumped philosophers, psychologists, and scientists for centuries. There are two basic schools of thought: physicalism and dualism. Physicalism holds that consciousness is entirely physical. Dualism is the theory that consciousness somehow falls outside the realm of the physical.

This is somewhat similar to the debate between Darwinian evolution and Intelligent Design. Is all there is to life and consciousness the physical? Are you the sum total of all of your molecules and nothing more? Would that make you a robot or a zombie?

Or is there something beyond the physical, from which intelligence is applied to the physical? In the case of Intelligent Design, is there an intelligence being applied to the physical to produce life? In the case of consciousness, is there an intelligence being applied to your physical structure to produce consciousness?

An article in *Psychology Today*[17] describes a "thought-experiment" by David J. Chalmers.[18] In it, he tells us to imagine a molecule-by-molecule replica of ourselves, exact down to each individual neuron and its firing state. He asks us to consider whether this creature is a philosophical zombie. A creature that is behaviorally indistinct from us but lacking consciousness. Even though on the outside a zombie appears conscious just like you and me, is it possible for it to be "dark" inside?

We hold that Chalmers' human replica would be a zombie. A walking pile of molecules and neurons without consciousness. It would react to its environment in a robot-like manner, coldly processing data, analyzing information from its senses, and selecting a logic path. You might call this "thought", but it would not be "consciousness". There would be no "self".

Philosopher Frank Jackson has another thought-experiment. He imagines a scientist named Mary, who is forced to investigate the world from a black and white room via a black and white television monitor. She discovers which wavelengths of light from the sky stimulate the retina, and how this produces, via the central nervous system, the contraction of the vocal cords resulting in uttering the words "The sky is blue". But when she is let out of the black and white room, she learns what it is like to see a brilliant blue sky in person, in glorious living color. Jackson says Mary will not say "ho, hum". It will make her say "wow".[19]

These thought-experiments demonstrate that consciousness is something more than just the physical. If there is anything which a physical being can learn which cannot be provided by purely mechanical processes, then physicalism must be false.

What if the zombie suddenly awoke from its dark state and experienced love. Would it say "wow!"? What made Mary say "wow!? It is the experience of a quality which has value totally apart from any physical properties. Love. Seeing a blue sky for the very first time.

When Adam first laid eyes on Eve, the first thing he said was "at last". A very loose translation might be "Wow!". A bull doesn't look at a cow and think, "wow". A stag doesn't look at a doe and think, "wow". The bull and the stag are drawn to the cow and the doe from an instinct to reproduce, but there's no appreciation of beauty. Any more than an amoeba can savor the flavor of the bacteria it eats.

We get some spectacular sunsets here in the Pacific Northwest. If we were to sit on our porch with a dog, watching an amazing sunset, with pinks and purples and orange hues splashed from one end of the sky to the other, the dog might be aware of the waning light, but it could in no way recognize the beauty before it.

We on the other hand, would say, "Wow!".

It is that higher level of consciousness we are talking about. The ability to think, "Wow!" It's not just self-awareness. It's existence-awareness. The ability to be aware not only of the fact of your existence, but the ability to experience qualities which have value totally apart from any physical properties.

This is an important question. For an atheist to have any claim to intellectual honesty, they must come up with an answer. What constitutes human consciousness and personality?

Some behavioral scientists would say we are nothing more than the sum total of heredity plus environment. If that is so, then imagine this. One day advances in artificial intelligence will produce an android brain capable of mimicking every function of the human brain. At that point, what would separate it from humans?

If we are just a collection of neurons responding to behavioral stimuli, then we are indeed nothing more than zombies. But every human being who ever walked this planet knows instinctively that this is a lie. If you really believe that, then you might be a zombie. But you'll have to prove it first. So far, nobody has been able to.

Let's be honest here. What we are describing, what Chalmers and Jackson stumble into with their thought-experiments, though they would likely not admit it, is what we call the "soul". So here's the inescapable truth:

You either have a soul, or you are a zombie.

There is no other alternative. Science can only take us so far. The sum total of your parts cannot account for consciousness. You have a soul, and it will continue on after your body has ceased to function.

But there is more. The apostle Paul speaks of the soul and spirit as two things which are tightly knit, but which can be "divided", indicating that they are indeed two separate entities.

Hebrews 4:12
*For the word of God is living and active, sharper than any two-edged sword, piercing to the division of **soul and of spirit**, of joints and of marrow, and discerning the thoughts and intentions of the heart.*

Your soul and spirit are tightly linked. So tightly linked, in fact, that only the "word of God" can divide them. Paul also speaks of your spirit as being dead, if it has not been regenerated, or "born again" by the Resurrection power of the Holy Spirit:

Ephesians 2:1
And you were dead in the trespasses and sins

You were literally a "dead man walking". You are a soul which has consciousness. But you also possess a spirit, which is dead until it is regenerated by God. Your spirit came from God, and it can be made alive again. You were created in the image of God, who is spirit.

Genesis 1:27
*So God created man **in his own image**, in the image of God he created him; male and female he created them.*

You were created as what the Bible calls "a living being".

1 Corinthians 15:45
*Thus it is written, "The first man Adam became a living being"; the last Adam became a **life-giving spirit**.*

There are three Greek words which come into play when looking at what is meant by "living being": *psyche*, the animal sentient principle only; *pneuma*, spirit, the rational and immortal; and *zōē*, which is mere vitality, even of plants.[20]

A plant possesses *zōē*, mere vitality. Animals posses *psyche*, they are self-aware conscious beings. But only humans posses *pneuma*, an immortal spirit. All three make up the totality of who you are, and each is uniquely yours: body, mind, and spirit. There is only one you, and you are precious. You are an "image-bearer of the Most High God"[21]. That image may be dead, but it can be "born again".

The purpose of this examination of what constitutes "you" has been to determine what exactly is going to inhabit the "mansions" or "rooms" Jesus promised. The Bible indicates that all three parts of what make up "you" will inhabit your heavenly dwelling. The vitality or *zōē*, the sentient or *psyche*, and the spirit, *pneuma*.

Job 19:25-27
*For I know that my Redeemer lives, and at the last he will stand upon the earth. And after my skin has been thus destroyed, yet **in my flesh** I shall see God, whom I shall see for myself, and **my eyes shall behold**, and not another. My heart faints within me!*

Job is going to see God in a body of "flesh". That's *zōē*. Job's eyes "shall behold" God. That's *psychē*. Job, along with all descendants of Adam, was created "in the image of God". That's *pneuma*.

The apostle Paul also speaks of these three parts of mankind, and shows that they will all three be present "at the coming of our Lord Jesus Christ":

1 Thessalonians 5:23
*Now may the God of peace himself sanctify you completely, and may your whole **spirit and soul and body** be kept blameless at the coming of our Lord Jesus Christ.*

Like Job, when we at last see our Redeemer face-to-face, we will stand in a body, think and perceive with a rational mind, and be alive with an eternal spirit.

But there is one more thing you will need to take with you when you enter heaven. Something more than *zōē*, and *psychē*, and *pneuma*. Job said that even after his "skin has been thus destroyed" he would see God.

If Job's "skin" has been destroyed, then he's going to need something else to wear. So will you. That's what the "last Adam" supplies. In our introduction we called this the "Magic Jacket". We'll have much more to say about it later.

The Big Sleep

So, are you looking forward to your mansion? Do you have your ticket to heaven? Are you ready to go today? No? Not quite yet? Depending on your current age, will you be ready in twenty, forty, or sixty years?

Many of us have an unspoken, even unconscious thought: "Give me some time to enjoy life, Lord. When I'm old and decrepit You can take me to that castle on a cloud."

We can't dictate how long we will live. None of us can know how much time we have left on this earth. The only thing you can be sure of is that one day death will come. You will cease breathing. Your heart will stop beating. Your brain functions will come to an end.

Exactly what happens then is debated. There are three basic schools of thought: soul-sleep, instant heaven, and intermediate paradise. We can from scripture unequivocally rule out one of these right away: instant heaven.

You will not go to heaven and receive your *final* reward immediately after death. Certain things must happen first. The body and the spirit part company at death, but the Resurrection won't happen until Jesus comes back. There may be a long interval between being "absent from the body" until you finally step into your heavenly "mansion". We're making a distinction between "heaven" and "paradise", which we'll explain shortly.

This idea of instant "heaven" is usually based on the phrase, "to be absent from the body is to be at home with the Lord". This is an inexact quotation of two statements by the apostle Paul. In both, Paul is talking about his *desire*.

2 Corinthians 5:8
Yes, we are of good courage, and we would rather be away from the body and at home with the Lord.

Philippians 1:23
I am hard pressed between the two. My desire is to depart and be with Christ, for that is far better.

"Away from the body and at home with the Lord". "Depart and be with Christ". This certainly sounds like it is instantaneous heaven. But, as always, we need to look at the rest of scripture. Looking closer, there seems to be a sequence to this. No one will be at their final "home" before the rest of us. We all get there together.

1 Thessalonians 4:15:
*For this we declare to you by a word from the Lord, that we who are alive, who are left until the coming of the Lord, **will not precede those who have fallen asleep.***

Ecclesiastes tells us that at death, the body and the spirit part ways. The body returns to the earth, and the spirit to God.

Ecclesiastes 12:7
And the dust returns to the earth as it was, and the spirit returns to God who gave it.

But for a spirit without a body, a "mansion" wouldn't be of much use. Are we talking about two separate things? One, your spirit returning to God? Two, finally arriving at your eternal dwelling place on the New Earth? Is there an "in-between" place?

The answer lies in understanding one concept which is repeated over and over and over in scripture: *resurrection*.

John 5:28-29
*Do not marvel at this, for an hour is coming when all who are in the tombs will hear his voice and come out, those who have done good to the **resurrection of life**, and those who have done evil to the resurrection of judgment.*

When will "those who have done good" receive the reward of eternal life?

Luke 14:14
*And you will be blessed, because they cannot repay you. For you will be **repaid at the resurrection** of the just."*

When will you be blessed? *When* will you be repaid?

Matthew 16:27
*For the Son of Man is going to come with his angels in the glory of his Father, and then he will **repay each person** according to what he has done.*

When will the Son of Man repay each person?

There is some sort of interval between death and our final "home" on the New Earth. Our final reward won't come until the *Resurrection*, and we will not precede those who have gone before.

But, as Ecclesiastes 12:7 said, the body and the spirit part ways at the moment of death. The body goes back to the "dust" of the earth. Many cultures try to retard the process, but after hundreds or thousands of years, most humans, except for a few mummies, will return to the earth. Their molecules will be scattered among the dust. An exchange in *Hamlet*[22] illustrates the point:

Hamlet: A man may fish with the worm that hath eat of a king, and eat the fish that hath fed of that worm.

Claudius: What dost you mean by this?

Hamlet: Nothing but to show you how a king may go a progress through the guts of a beggar.

After death, your physical body does not face a glorious prospect. But what of your spirit? Where does your spirit go? There are two basic and opposing viewpoints on this question:
Soul-sleep.
Paradise.
Here we're making a distinction between "heaven", which in our context we define as our *final* home on New Earth, and "paradise", which is an in-between place.

33

Let's look at soul-sleep first. The idea is that between death and the resurrection, your body and soul "sleep". You are not aware of anything at all until the moment you are resurrected. From the point of view of the person who has died, one moment they died, and the next moment they are being resurrected.

Thus, according to this viewpoint, the time between the apostle Paul being "away from the body" and when he is "at home with the Lord" would appear to Paul as but an instant of time.

One group supporting soul-sleep puts it this way:

"Therefore, God's Word refers to the dead as being asleep. For example, upon learning that his friend Lazarus had died, Jesus Christ told His disciples 'Lazarus our friend has gone to rest, but I am journeying there to awake him from sleep.'"[23]

However, the quotation above of John 11:11 is incomplete. We need the rest of the quotation for the full story:

John 11:12-14
*The disciples said to him, "Lord, if he has fallen asleep, he will recover." Now Jesus had spoken of his death, but they thought that he meant taking rest in sleep. Then Jesus told them plainly, "**Lazarus has died.**".*

Clearly Jesus was using the common euphemism of the time, referring to death as "sleep". The quotation above using John 11:11 to support soul-sleep leaves out verse 14. Jesus told them plainly, "Lazarus has died".

Just because there are Bible verses referring to death as "sleep" does not mean that the soul sleeps between death and the resurrection. Most Bible dictionaries note the metaphorical use of "sleep", and agree that it should not be taken as the literal sleep of the soul:

That the body alone is in view in this metaphor is evident, (a) from the derivation of the word koimaomai, from keimai, to lie down...; (b) from the fact that in the NT the word resurrection is used of the body alone.[24]

Along with Martin Luther, John Calvin is known as one of the leaders of the Reformation. Writing in 1532, Calvin has some harsh words for the doctrine of soul-sleep. Calvin felt that this was no mere quibble over words. His main point is this:

For those who admit that the soul lives, and yet deprive it of all sense, feign a soul which has none of the properties of soul, or dissever the soul from itself, seeing that its nature, without which it cannot possibly exist, is to move, to feel, to be vigorous, to understand.[25]

When your body sleeps, you are still alive. Not so with your soul, according to Calvin. A soul which sleeps is no longer a soul, for its very nature and essence is to move and feel, to be vigorous, and to understand. When your body sleeps, your soul is still awake. It is still feeling and understanding and vigorous. Perhaps that's where dreams come from. A soul which cannot do any of those things is not asleep according to Calvin. It is dead. And that's not you. When your soul leaves your body, you will still be alive!

Most early church fathers agree that the soul does not sleep after death. Most of the great preachers of the 18th and 19th centuries also agree. And most modern evangelical preachers seem to also agree, including John Piper, David Platt, John MacArthur, and Billy Graham.

There is one place in scripture where we get a vivid picture of "souls" who have died. In John's vision of heaven we see "the souls of those who had been slain for the word of God". These souls are "under the alter". They are not residing in mansions, and they do not seem to be "at home". They are simply described as "souls".

Revelation 6:9-10
When he opened the fifth seal, I saw under the altar the souls of those who had been slain for the word of God and for the witness they had borne. They cried out with a loud voice, "O Sovereign Lord, holy and true, how long before you will judge and avenge our blood on those who dwell on the earth?"

These souls are in an in-between place. They are definitely not in their final home. But they are not "asleep". They are communicating with God, and they are aware of what is (and is not) happening on earth. This is often referred to as "paradise".

This brings us to the question of what our existence in this intermediate paradise will be like.

Will we have some sort of intermediate bodies? There are hints in Scripture that we may. Those souls who are waiting under the alter in Revelation 6 were "each given a white robe and told to rest a little longer" (Rev. 6:11). A disembodied spirit doesn't put on a robe.

We also get a glimpse of the intermediate paradise in Luke chapter 16, where Jesus tells the parable of the rich man and Lazarus. After they both die, Jesus describes the rich man as in "Hades", and Lazarus by Abraham's side in paradise. But they definitely do not seem to be disembodied spirits.

The rich man can *see* Abraham and Lazarus, even though "a great chasm has been fixed" between him and them. Jesus speaks of various body parts: Lazarus' *finger*; the rich man's *eyes* and *tongue*.

From these two passages, we believe that we *will* have some sort of intermediate bodies in paradise. We will be with Jesus. We will be communicating with God. We will recognize friends and family. We will be comforted and at rest. We will be aware of events on earth.

The truth is, we are all going to be surprised when we get there. Remember, the more we think we know, the greater chance we can miss the simple truths.

Here's the simple truth:

If you are a believer, when you die your spirit will depart your earthly body and go to be with Jesus in "paradise", where your spirit will be clothed in a temporary body. When He is ready, whenever that is, Jesus will return, resurrect your physical body, transform it into an eternal body like His, reunite your spirit with that eternal body, and take you to be with Him on the New Earth.[26]

Until then we must wait.

A Movable Mansion

When at last Jesus returns, when the long wait is done, when our bodies are resurrected, when they are transformed, when they are reunited with our spirit, what then?

This is personal conjecture, but for us, when that time comes, we don't think we'll be paying much attention to mansions or castles on clouds or angel wings or self-fulfillment. First and foremost, we will see God face to face. We will see Jesus, and we will be like Him.

1 John 3:2
*Beloved, we are God's children now, and what we will be has not yet appeared; but we know that **when he appears we shall be like him**, because we shall see him as he is.*

Let that sink in.

If a blue sky made Mary say "Wow!", if seeing Eve for the first time made Adam say "Wow!", if a spectacular sunset makes us say "Wow!", what then will we have to say when we see God, the maker of all of these, face to face?

But not only will we see Him, "we shall be like Him". What will you say to *that*? "Wow!" just doesn't cut it. No word can. Ten billion words couldn't begin to express it. In fact, you will spend all eternity expressing the wonder and joy of seeing Him.

After the resurrection, scripture says you will receive your "reward". You will lay your hands on all of those "treasures in heaven" Jesus told you to store up. You will go to the "place" Jesus said He was preparing for you. You will finally get the title deed to your mansion. So it's time to look at what these "mansions" actually are. Here's the "mansions" quote in the ESV:

John 14:2-3
In my Father's house are many rooms. If it were not so, would I have told you that I go to prepare a place for you? And if I go and prepare a place for you, I will come again and will take you to myself, that where I am you may be also.

This is one of the foundational promises of the Bible. Jesus is preparing a place for us. He will one day come again and take us to be with Him.

But what will that look like? What kind of place, what kind of room is Jesus talking about? As we mentioned before, the Greek word means "abiding places". It's where you live.

So let's ask a question. Where do you live *now*? If you answered something like, "555 Elm Street", then you're missing the point. We're not asking for the street or town or state or country you live in. Where is the essence of "you"...right now?

That's right, you live in your body right now. You are living "in your skin". And that's a clue. It's a link. Ponder that Greek word, *moné*. If it means "where you live", and where you live now is in a body, then could it be that where you live in heaven isn't going to be a mansion after all? Could it be that Jesus was talking about your new heavenly body?

A mansion is a building, right? In Second Corinthians Paul also talks about a "building". But in the same verse he compares this building with the "tent that is our earthly home".

2 Corinthians 5:1-2
*For we know that if the **tent** that is our earthly home is destroyed, we have a **building** from God, a house not made with hands, eternal in the heavens. For in this tent we groan, longing to **put on our heavenly dwelling**.*

The "tent that is our earthly home" is our body. It's where we live. Paul says that this "tent" will be replaced by a "building". But look at how he phrases it: "longing to *put on* our heavenly dwelling". You don't "put on" a house. You put on clothes. In this case, you put on a new body. It's a body transformed from your earthly body. It's not something totally different. It's a body, not a mansion.

From these verses it is clear that the rooms Jesus spoke of and the building Paul talks about are not houses or "mansions" as we would commonly think of, any more than the tent that is our earthly home is a structure of canvas and poles.

It is obvious that the tent is our body, and so is the room Jesus is preparing, and so is the "house not made with hands". We are going to live in a perfected, glorious body, the like of which we have never seen or even imagined. But it will be a body, not a mansion.

1 Corinthians 15:40; 49; 53
*There are heavenly bodies and earthly bodies, but the glory of the heavenly is of one kind, and the glory of the earthly is of another...Just as we have borne the image of the man of dust, we shall also bear the image of the man of heaven...For this perishable body must put on the imperishable, and **this mortal body must put on immortality**.*

Earthly bodies and heavenly bodies. The image of the man of dust (Adam) and the image of the man of heaven (Jesus). We bear one image now. We will bear the better image then, when "we shall be like him, because we shall see him as he is".

Notice that phrase again , "put on". It's like Paul is talking about putting on clothes. We'll meet this imagery frequently in the coming chapters. But let's look now at a story which Jesus told about the importance of putting on the right clothes.

Fashion Police on Steroids

In our present life on Earth our immortal spirit is clothed with a body of flesh and bone and sinew. It is a corruptible, perishable tent. But one day — praise God — this mortal body must put on immortality. The imagery is that of changing your clothes... exchanging filthy rags for glittering wedding garments.

Jesus told a parable which has perplexed some. On the surface, it appears that the king, who obviously represents God, is being rather petty. Why be nit-picky about wearing exactly the right clothes to a wedding. The important thing should be that this poor guy answered the invitation and showed up. Right?

Let's listen in as Jesus spins the yarn.

Matthew 22:11-13
But when the king came in to look at the guests, he saw there a man who had no wedding garment. And he said to him, "Friend, **how did you get in here without a wedding garment?"** *And he was speechless. Then the king said to the attendants, "Bind him hand and foot and cast him into the outer darkness. In that place there will be weeping and gnashing of teeth."*

What a shock! Could you imagine being cast into the "outer darkness" simply because you didn't wear the right clothes? And "weeping and gnashing of teeth"? That's a bit extreme, don't you think? Let's look at how this story starts out:

Matthew 22:2-3
The kingdom of heaven may be compared to a king who gave a wedding feast for his son, and sent his servants to call those who were invited to the wedding feast, but they would not come.

41

So the king gives a wedding feast and invites folks, but those who were invited blow him off. What happens next?

Matthew 22:4-5
Again he sent other servants, saying, 'Tell those who are invited, "See, I have prepared my dinner, my oxen and my fat calves have been slaughtered, and everything is ready. Come to the wedding feast."' But they paid no attention and went off, one to his farm, another to his business...

Hmm...business as usual. Who cares about the king's wedding feast. We've got to make money while the sun shines. Gotta get more stuff. The mall closes in an hour. Sorry, gotta go.

So the long-suffering king sends his servants out into the streets to invite as many as they could find. The wedding hall was filled with guests.

But this one poor schmuck comes in without wedding garments, and the king tosses him out on his ear. What's up? Keep in mind that this is a parable of the Kingdom of God. Jesus starts out by saying, *"The kingdom of heaven may be compared..."*. The wedding invitations are obviously God's invitation to heaven.

The poor guy answered the call. He raised his hand and said a prayer. He's got his "fire insurance". Doesn't that count? Why did the king toss him into the outer darkness, just for a lack of spiffy duds? These wedding garments must be pretty special. What are they?

As usual, looking elsewhere in scripture provides the answer. The best way to interpret scripture is with other scripture. So let's see if we can find somewhere else where wedding clothes are mentioned:

Revelation 19:7-8
Let us rejoice and exult and give him the glory, for the marriage of the Lamb has come, and his Bride has made herself ready; it was granted her to clothe herself with fine linen, bright and pure — for the fine linen is the righteous deeds of the saints.

The wedding garments, the means by which you are admitted to the wedding feast, turn out to be "the righteous deeds of the saints".

We need to stop right here and highlight that salvation is by grace through faith, not of "works".

Ephesians 2:8-10
*For by grace you have been saved through faith. **And this is not your own doing; it is the gift of God, not a result of works,** so that no one may boast. For we are his workmanship, created in Christ Jesus for good works, which God prepared beforehand, that we should walk in them.*

So why are "righteous deeds" described as the wedding garments which are required for the feast? The answer is that true faith will *always* produce "works". If your faith has not changed you, then something is wrong.

James 2:17
So also faith by itself, if it does not have works, is dead.

The faith of the guy at the wedding feast was dead. He had no wedding garments. His "faith" had produced nothing.

So if the garments which seem to be a prerequisite for the wedding feast of the King, with which we will be clothed for all eternity, are "righteous deeds", then we are somehow joining Jesus as He prepares a place for us. We have a hand in "weaving" our own wedding garments.

The imagery of a building and clothing keeps switching back and forth, but it is clear that the Bible is talking about the same thing. Jesus has gone to prepare a place for us. But that's just the beginning. We need to build on what Jesus has started. Paul lays this out in vivid detail. First, he talks about a foundation:

1 Corinthians 3:11
For no one can lay a foundation other than that which is laid, which is Jesus Christ.

The foundation is the "place" Jesus is preparing for us. It's the foundation of our wedding garments. The process starts when you turn to Him and surrender. Jesus starts right then to build your "house". He's the foundation. That is solid, and can never be taken away from you. Then Paul talks about us building on that foundation. Somehow we're joining Jesus in this process:

1 Corinthians 3:12-13a
Now if anyone builds on the foundation with gold, silver, precious stones, wood, hay, straw—each one's work will become manifest, for the Day will disclose it...

It seems what Jesus is preparing is not complete. He's only laying the foundation. It's up to us to build on that foundation. It's up to you to complete your wedding garments, which are "the righteous deeds of the saints". Let your faith produce something that will last...something you can wear for all eternity...your Magic Jacket.

You can join Jesus in weaving wedding garments with fine linen, bright and pure, fashioning the heavenly clothes in which you will explore and serve and reign with Christ for all eternity! But what you build with, that which your faith produces, must pass through a grueling quality-control inspection. It will be tested by fire.

1 Corinthians 3:13b-14
*...it will be revealed by fire, and the fire will test what sort of work each one has done. **If the work that anyone has built on the foundation survives, he will receive a reward.***

This may seem like an impossible task. How can you possibly do good enough? How can you be sure you're not wasting your time with wood, hay, and straw? In Section Six we look at this in detail. Here's the short answer, in the words of Jesus:

John 15:5
*I am the vine; you are the branches. Whoever abides in me and I in him, he it is that bears much fruit, **for apart from me you can do nothing.***

Those of us who came to faith a little later in life may feel remorse for all the missed opportunities to store up treasure in heaven. It's fine to regret the years of rebellion, but it is never too late to start storing up treasures. You never know how much will be waiting for you. Just start, and let God the Spirit guide you! In God's economy, it is often the quality, not the quantity that counts.

The point is this: God will decide how to reward us. Whether we start young, or later in life, we all must depend on the Spirit of God in us, guiding us as we store up treasures in heaven. Let your faith produce "righteous deeds", and leave the rest to God.

There's one more you thing you need to know about your new body and those awesome wedding garments. They intimately connect you with others in heaven.[27] Our lives on earth are often lived out in isolation and loneliness. That's not how humans were originally created. We were created for intimate connection with others and with God. Your awesome new body is not a standalone creation. You're going to be wired into the Source of everything!

Your new body will exist in what the Bible calls the "New Heavens" (Universe) and the "New Earth"[28]. There will be places to explore and create and serve and rule and worship and fellowship.[29] The "New Jerusalem" will be at the center of it all, a place to meet with God, and join every culture and ethnic group from all history in worshiping and learning and discovering what real joy is all about.[30]

These treasures are real. Your heavenly body will be a real walking, talking, seeing, feeling, laughing, thinking, creating, loving masterpiece. Your wedding garments are real.

Make them shine!

Like Melted Wax

S o what are you going to do about it? If all this is true, then how should the rest of your life look?

What is really important, and what is just a distraction? We all want to be comfortable and safe. But what if you knew the reward was worth it, and the chances good? Would you take some risks, make some sacrifices, to gain something of great value?

Imagine you're in a science fiction movie about time travel. You've gone into the future two years, and discovered that developers plan to build a major shopping mall on a certain piece of land, and the land will sell for $200,000,000. Now you've come back in time two years. The land where the future shopping mall will be built is on the market for just $50,000.

What would you be willing to give up, what would you be willing to sacrifice, in order to purchase that piece of land? The scripture we've given you about the treasures of heaven are far more certain, and the reward infinitely more valuable. How much are you willing to give up for *that*?

We'll have much more about this later. For now, here's one last point before we close this section. At the Resurrection you will see God face-to-face. That could be a very dangerous proposition if you aren't prepared with the right body and the right clothes.

Moses once asked God if he could "see his glory". God came back with a frightening reply:

Exodus 33:20
"But," he said, "you cannot see my face, for **man shall not see me and live.***"*

If you were to see God right now, you would melt like wax heated in a furnace.[31] Just like Dr. René Belloq at the end of *Raiders of the Lost Ark*. He opened the Ark of the Covenant, and melted like wax.

Here's an example which might put this into stark perspective:

All life on earth depends on the warmth and light of our sun. From about 93 million miles away, the sun is a life-sustaining gift from God. But a closer encounter would prove disastrous.

If you were to have a "face-to-face" encounter with the sun, say about 300 miles above its surface, you would be blinded by light billions of times brighter than a 100 Watt light bulb. You would be crushed by massive gravity, in which you would weigh about 56 million pounds. Intense radiation would nuke every cell in your body. And you would instantly vaporize in heat over three million degrees Fahrenheit.

A face-to-face encounter with God would be trillions of times more intense. No heat shield ever devised could protect you.

You're going to need a drastically different body, and drastically different clothes!

You are going to need a Magic Jacket!

NOTE: When quoting other authors, we have done our best to vet the sources, and have tried to avoid the questionable practice of "Quote Mining". When possible we have gone to the original source, and practice the old precept: "text without context is pretext".

[1] Merriam-Webster.

[2] This was a quick non-scientific survey of some online forums.

[3] The 1985 musical is based on the novel *Les Misérables* by Victor Hugo.

[4] C.S. Lewis; *Mere Christianity*.

[5] Victor Hugo, from *Ninety-Three*.

[6] Between May 1889 and August 1890 Mark Twain wrote this witticism in one of his notebooks.

[7] Isaac Asimov, as quoted in *Philosophy on the Go*.

[8] Sir Edward Coke - *The Institutes of the Laws of England* (1628).

[9] Sura 47:15.

[10] Bhagavad-Gita 9:21.

[11] Pius XII; *Mystici Corporis*, 1943.

[12] ZuZu Bailey, speaking to her father; *It's a Wonderful Life*, Liberty Films, 1946.

[13] A microscopic non-organic alien life form, describing humans; *Start Trek: The Next Generation*; "Home Soil" episode; 1988.

[14] Per Charles Jennings, director of neurotechnology at the MIT McGovern Institute for Brain Research.

[15] René Descartes, *Discourse on the Method of Rightly Conducting the Reason, and Seeking Truth in the Sciences*, 1637.

[16] Merriam-Webster Dictionary.

[17] *What is Consciousness?*; Psychology Today, March 1, 2013.

[18] *The Conscious Mind: In Search of a Fundamental Theory*; David J. Chalmers; Oxford University Press, 1996.

[19] *What Mary Didn't Know* by Frank Jackson; *The Journal of Philosophy*, Vol. 83, No. 5 (May, 1986). These quotes were pieced together from two different sources. Jackson went back on his original premise a few years after the original "What Mary Didn't Know" article, but later reconsidered, and wrote of Mary seeing the blue sky for the first time, "it made her say 'Wow!'".

[20] From Strong's Dictionary of the Bible.

[21] *Hinds' Feet On High Places*, by Hannah Hurnard ;Christian Literature Crusade, 1955.

[22] *Hamlet*, Act 4 Scene 3; William Shakespeare.

[23] *Knowledge That Leads to Everlasting Life*, Watch Tower Bible and Tract Society of Pennsylvania, a Jehovah's Witnesses publication.

[24] *Vine's Complete Expository Dictionary*; in reference to the usage of the Greek word *koimaomai*; "to sleep".

[25] *PSYCHOPANNYCHIA* by John Calvin, 1532.

[26] You may wonder why we say nothing about the "Millennium". There are too many different ideas bouncing around out there. There just is not enough evidence in the Bible to be dogmatic. We're not even going to go there. What we're focusing on in this book is the New Heavens and the New Earth and the New Jerusalem and *Eternity*.

[27] This is based on the Greek word *koinōnia*, which is often translated "fellowship". See John 17:20-23 & 1 John 1:3.*

[28] Isaiah 65:17, 2 Peter 3:12-13, Revelation 21:1.*

[29] Gen. 1:26, Exodus 35:31, Matthew 25:23, 1 Corinthians 6:3.*

[30] Revelation 5:9-10, Revelation 7:9-10, Revelation 21:2-4.*

[31] Psalm 68:2, Psalm 97:5, Micah 1:4.

* See Section Seven for a deeper look into these ideas.

Section Two | Design

For his invisible attributes, namely, his eternal power and divine nature, have been clearly perceived, ever since the creation of the world, in the things that have been made. So they are without excuse.
Romans 1:20

Present Gives Birth To Future

T his book is about heaven. Before we can look at what heaven will be like, we need to see how it all started. The Bible makes it clear that there will be a "new heavens and a new earth"[1], but that they will not be so different from the present heavens and earth as to be unrecognizable[2].

All creation, the entire universe, was cursed with Adam and Eve when they rebelled.[3] And the entire universe will share in the rebirth at the Resurrection.[4] Just as our physical bodies will be resurrected and transformed "in the twinkling of an eye"[5], so too shall the earth and the entire universe.

Just like the the present earth, there will be cities.[6] There will be land to farm.[7] There will be travel and learning and singing and feasting.[8] There will be productive, creative work, which will require supervision by those who have been appointed.[9]

And there will be treasure...all that you have stored up for yourself...that which has not burned up.[10]

All of this is very much like the world we live in now.

So since the future New Heavens and New Earth will be very much like the present ones, only redeemed and transformed just as our resurrected bodies will be, we need to first look at the original *design*. Much of that design will carry over into eternity. What did God first put in place? How is everything designed so that it all fits together to "declare the glory of God"[11]?

How your body was engineered, how the interconnected ecology of our planet works, how sub-atomic particles and the vast structures of the universe and the fundamental forces of physics are all intricately designed and fine-tuned and balanced...it is all a glimpse of what is yet to come in eternity.

Present gives birth to future. The new heavens and the new earth will be born of what is already here.

So let's look at *Design*.

E.T. Phoned Home!

Anytime you encounter information, you can be certain that there was some form of intelligence which created it. Information does not create itself. Information is essential to any design. So we first need to see where *information* came from.

If you are walking along a beach and come upon the words "George loves Martha" drawn in the sand, you don't need to study it very long before you determine that some form of intelligent being created it. The odds are very much against the words in the sand being the result of random action by wind and waves.

In the same way, researchers looking for evidence of alien life on other star systems look for information coded into radio signals. Like storm-tossed sands on a beach have thousands of ripples, the "sands" of the universe are filled with random microwave signals, thought to be the remnants of the Big Bang. But so far searchers have found only static and noise...no message in the sand.

If verifiable information in an interstellar radio signal were ever detected, we can be certain that intelligent alien life is behind the message. That's because scientists know that there is always intelligence behind information. That's the basic assumption driving the Search for ExtraTerrestrial Intelligence (SETI).

Imagine the worldwide impact if intelligent life were discovered on another planet! The news would flash around the world in minutes. It would be the greatest discovery in all history. It would generate both awe and fear, as the human race grappled with the implications.

Just such a scenario was described in the 1985 novel *Contact* by Carl Sagan. A repeating series of 26 prime numbers is discovered in a signal coming from the Vega system 25 light years away. Further analysis reveals *information* in the polarization modulation of the signal.

55

After studying the information, it turns out to be detailed plans for an advanced machine. But there is no way of decoding the 30,000 pages of cryptic instructions, until the scientists in Sagan's novel eventually uncover a primer, which allows the construction of a colossal trillion-dollar machine.

Sometimes real life is more fantastic than a novel. Here's a true story which is more amazing than fiction. As you read this, keep in mind that this *actually happened*. This is not made-up.

In 1953, coded information was discovered which could not have been created by humans. Let that sink in. Highly complex coded information was found, which could *absolutely not* have been created by humans.

Just like the prime numbers in Sagan's novel, at first only basic components of the information were understood. Also mirroring the novel, further analysis revealed detailed plans for the design and construction of complex machines. And like Sagan's SETI scientists, researchers working on this discovery at first did not understand how the information could be decoded and used for the construction of these amazing machines.

There are, however, some drastic differences between the novel *Contact* and the actual 1953 discovery. In the novel there are 30,000 pages of instructions in the E.T. message. In the actual discovery there are as many as 3 billion coded instructions. In the novel the blueprints in the message produce a single-purpose machine. In the actual discovery, the tightly-packed information held construction designs for a vast array of amazingly complex machines.

In the novel, scientists at first could not find the "primer" necessary to decode and actually use the information. In the actual "E.T." discovery, the information code discovered in 1953 used a four-character "alphabet". A complex transcription process was found, whereby this "four-bit" code could be translated into a twenty-letter "alphabet", which was then used to construct the huge array of components for thousands of different kinds of complex machines.

This mysterious information obviously did not have a human origin, but any efforts to trace its source would have been futile. There was no microwave signal from an alien planet which carried the information to earth. It just appeared from out of nowhere...as if it had always been there, just waiting to be discovered.

As we said before, this story is absolutely true. The amazing discovery was announced in a paper just one page long, published April 25, 1953, in the British scientific weekly *Nature*. But no one outside of elite academic and scientific institutions took much notice.

There was no worldwide fanfare. There was no awe and fear. The human race was not driven to grapple with existential implications. Major news organizations of the day paid little attention, focusing instead on more "newsworthy" stories, like the Yankees defeating the Dodgers in the World Series, or that new gadget called a "television".

Why?

Because the coded information which was discovered in 1953 by James Watson and Francis Crick was embedded in the double helix structure of DNA. Even though this was clearly *information*, and even though it was detailed instructions for the construction of every form of life on Earth, including human life, no scientist was willing to admit that this information must have an intelligent source. No one was willing to apply the same criteria used to determine intelligence in SETI research to the information coded into DNA.

But the probability that the information in DNA somehow assembled itself by mere chance is statistically impossible. The odds against it are far greater than for our "George loves Martha" message in the sand being the result of random action by wind and waves. The odds against it are literally beyond astronomical.

It would be many trillions of times easier for you to find one marked sub-atomic particle among all of the sub-atomic particles in the entire known universe (10^{86}), than for the DNA information which defines the creation of the simplest one-cell amoeba to have arisen by pure chance $(10^{40,000})$[12].

The coded information in DNA actually *does* have an intelligent source. It is impossible for that source to have originated on earth. It is by definition, therefore, *extraterrestrial*. It originated outside of planet earth. In fact, it originated outside of our universe.

That intelligent source is, of course, God.

Rewind

L et's rewind now, and look at how this all began. In looking at design, we need to understand who the Designer was; that "extraterrestrial intelligence". The first four words in the Bible are the most important:

Genesis 1:1a
In the beginning God...

There was a beginning. There was God. Before that "beginning" there was nothing and no one else. Not angels. Not demons. Just God. Everything and everyone else came from Him.

The first six words of the Gospel of John open up additional detail:

John 1:1a
In the beginning was the Word...

There was a beginning. There was the "Word". Since we have already established that before the "beginning" there was only God, then what or who do you suppose this "Word" is? John makes it very clear:

John 1:14
And the Word became flesh and dwelt among us, and we have seen his glory, glory as of the only Son from the Father, full of grace and truth.

The "Word" became a human being. He was the Son of God. John saw him. That, of course, was Jesus. So Jesus was there "in the beginning". And according to Genesis 1:1, God was there "in the beginning". John goes on to reveal with grammatical precision the relationship between these two:

John 1:1b
...and the Word was with God, and the Word was God.

"The Word was God". Let's review some fifth-grade grammar. "God" is the predicate nominative of a definite subject ("the Word"). That means there's an equal sign between them: Word=God.[13]

Some mis-translate this, "the Word was a god"[14], but John, being a Jew and strict monotheist, would never say that there was another god besides Jehovah. The Word WAS God. The Word was NOT "a god".

And since we know for a certainty that the Word was Jesus, then we have this undeniable equation:

$$JESUS = GOD$$

Because Jesus is often spoken of in the Bible as the "Son of God", some people mistakenly think that means Jesus came after God. Fathers come before sons, right? Not in this case. "Son", when referring to Jesus, is describing *relationship*, not sequence.[15]

The prophet Isaiah, writing more than seven hundred years before Jesus "became flesh and dwelt among us", described His coming with some very precise terms:

Isaiah 9:6
For to us a child is born, to us a son is given; and the government shall be upon his shoulder, and his name shall be called Wonderful Counselor, **Mighty God,** **Everlasting Father**, *Prince of Peace.*

Mighty God. Everlasting Father. Jesus IS God. We will see that this is an absolute essential truth when we get to the means of salvation in Section Four.

So in the beginning, before there was anything or anyone else, there was God and Jesus. And there was one more. We are told in Genesis that in the beginning, the Spirit of God was there:

Genesis 1:2b
And the Spirit of God was hovering over the face of the waters.

This is called The Trinity. God the Father, God the Son, God the Spirit. All three equal, absolutely the same, yet somehow distinct in relationship and Person. And all three were involved in what happens next:

Genesis 1:1
In the beginning, God created the heavens and the earth.

God created. Going back to the Gospel of John again, we see even more detail:

John 1:1-3
*In the beginning was the Word, and the Word was with God, and the Word was God. He was in the beginning with God. All things were made through him, and **without him was not any thing made that was made.***

Nothing was made without Jesus. Nothing. As if to put it in bold italics, a few verses later John repeats it:

John 1:10
*He was in the world, and **the world was made through him**, yet the world did not know him.*

The Apostle Paul repeats this three times. Jesus created the universe and everything in it.[16]

And as we have seen, God the Spirit was also involved in Creation, as "the Spirit of God was hovering over the face of the waters".

God in three Persons created all of the galaxies and stars and planets of the universe. Before we move on to look at this design, let's take a moment to look at *purpose*.

Purpose

Dibrah is an old Hebrew word, rarely used in the Bible. It means cause, reason, order.[17] Roll them together and you have *purpose*. What caused something? What is the reason behind its being? How is it ordered (or designed)? In other words, what is it *good* for?

Six times during the creation account in Genesis, God declared that what He had just made was "good".[18] And in the final verse, when He has completed His work, God declares it again, adding, "it was *very* good".[19]

If the universe which God created was very good, that begs the question, "What is it good for?". Glad you asked. Four things come to mind: revelation, representation, dominion, and habitation.

Revelation

The universe is good as a revelation of who God is (His "glory").

Psalms 19:1
The heavens declare the glory of God, and the sky above proclaims his handiwork.

"Handiwork" is defined as "something impressive that someone has done or created".[20] You can tell a great deal about someone by what they have made. So what can we learn about God from the universe He has created? Here's a short and non-exhaustive list:

1. self-existent
2. timeless
3. wise
4. unbounded by place
5. unlimited in power
6. unlimited in knowledge
7. orderly

Representation

But the centerpiece of the revelation of God is...you.

Genesis 1:26a

Then God said, "Let us make man in our image, after our likeness..."21

The Hebrew word translated "image" here is *tselem*. It means the statue of a god in its temple.[22] Adam and Eve were God's revelation of Himself in the "temple" of the earth.

As a descendant of Adam and Eve, you too are a statue in the temple of the earth. You were made in the image of God, and in His likeness. Notice the repetition: "image" and "likeness". God does not want you to miss this. You are like Him, and you are His revelation and representative in the universe. Humbling thought, eh?

Dominion

Looking a little closer at our job description, we find this:

Genesis 1:26

*Then God said, "Let us make man in our image, after our likeness. **And let them have dominion** over the fish of the sea and over the birds of the heavens and over the livestock and over all the earth and over every creeping thing that creeps on the earth."*

Dominion. As Creator, God has the right of ownership and control of the universe. But from the start, God delegated some of that "dominion" to human beings. That was our job description: to take care of planet earth. But that's not all. God goes on to expand our marching orders:

Genesis 1:28

*And God blessed them. And God said to them, "**Be fruitful and multiply and fill the earth** and subdue it, and have dominion over the fish of the sea and over the birds of the heavens and over every living thing that moves on the earth."*

Multiply. God wanted lots and lots of "statues", all revealing and representing Him, all filling the earth and having dominion over it. Multiplication, Dominion, Revelation, Representation. These were our original purpose. What a massive delegation of power and authority! How sad that we gave it away with the bite of an "apple".

Habitation

This is related to reasons two and three, since it's about us. The universe is good as a habitation for humans. Physicists have recognized for decades that certain parameters seem to be fine-tuned. Renowned physicist Stephen Hawking put it this way:

*The laws of science, as we know them at present, contain many fundamental numbers, like the size of the electric charge of the electron and the ratio of the masses of the proton and the electron...The remarkable fact is that **the values of these numbers seem to have been very finely adjusted to make possible the development of life.**[23]*

Arno Penzias, who won a Nobel prize in physics, also sees a fine-tuning going on in the universe:

Astronomy leads us to a unique event, a universe which was created out of nothing, one with the very delicate balance needed to provide exactly the conditions required to permit life...[24]

So what are some of these fine-tuned values? What follows is another short and non-exhaustive list.[25] The ratio to the right of each parameter is the maximum deviation from acceptable values which would either prevent the universe from existing, not having matter, or being unsuitable for any form of life:

1. Ratio of Electrons to Protons $1:10^{37}$
2. Ratio of Electromagnetic Force to Gravity $1:10^{40}$
3. Expansion Rate of Universe $1:10^{55}$
4. Mass Density of Universe $1:10^{59}$
5. Cosmological Constant $1:10^{120}$

Remember that all of the sub-atomic particles in the entire known universe add up to 10^{86}. That is a 10 with 86 zeroes after it. It is an enormous number. Now look at the ratios above. For instance, if the mass density of the universe were different by just one part in 1,000,000,000,000,000,000,000,000,000,000,000,000,000,000, 000,000,000,000,000 no life would be possible. Get the picture?

There are literally hundreds more examples of fine-tuning in creation.[26] Many relate to the atomic structures and basic laws of physics. Others relate to the makeup of our planetary and biological systems. Carbon-based lifeforms (that's you) require a very delicate balance. Astrophysicist Sir Fred Hoyle leaves little doubt:

A common sense interpretation of the facts suggests that a super-intellect has monkeyed with physics, as well as with chemistry and biology, and that there are no blind forces worth speaking about in nature. The numbers one calculates from the facts seem to me so overwhelming as to put this conclusion almost beyond question.[27]

So these four things which the created universe is "good" for give us a clue as to its purpose, both now, and in eternity: revelation, representation, dominion, and habitation.

Going back to that old Hebrew word dibrah, the universe had a cause, it has a reason, and it has order. The cause is God. The reasons are (in part) revelation, representation, dominion, and habitation. The order, or design, is what this whole section is about.

Stretch Marks

W e have seen how the present gives birth to the future. We've seen the importance of understanding design and purpose. We've looked at information and intelligence, and the Who of creation. Let's look now at *how* the universe was created.

What "tool" did God use when He created the heavens and the earth? What part of Himself did He use? God is often spoken of in the Bible in anthropomorphic terms. Anthropomorphic is defined as "considering something such as a god, animal, or object as having human features or qualities".[28] So how does this relate to the creation of the universe? What mechanism did God use? Let's take a look:

Genesis 1:3
And God said, "Let there be light," and there was light.

God *said*. He used His mouth. Seven times in the first chapter of Genesis, God speaks, and something comes into being out of nothing. Poof! God spoke, and our entire space-time universe popped into existence *ex niblo*...out of nothing.

This is consistent with the cosmological theory called the Big Bang. We know from measurements that the universe is expanding. If you wind the clock backwards, reversing that expansion, you come to a point where all of matter and space are crushed into an infinitely small dot.

In 1907, German mathematician Hermann Minkowski proved that our universe is made up of four dimensions: length, width, height, and time.[29] Time was created in the same instant with matter and space. Time is inextricably bound to space. In that first micro-instant, all of space and matter and time popped into existence as a microscopic pinprick.

That pinprick is called a "singularity". It is similar to a black hole, which is also called a singularity, but this was the mother of all singularities. Everything...all matter, all space, all time...crushed into an infinitely small point. Here's how Stephen Hawking explains it:

Extrapolation of the expansion of the universe backwards in time using general relativity yields an infinite density and temperature at a finite time in the past.[30]

Hmm. How curious. An infinitely small point is what we would call "nothing". Everything came from nothing. How Biblical!

But something very odd was going on as everything was popping into existence from nothing. It's called the "Horizon Problem". The universe has about the same temperature everywhere, but different regions could not have transferred energy and heat between each other because of the great distances. In order for that to have happened, the energy would have had to travel at a speed 10^{60} greater than the speed of light.

Two theories which attempt to solve the Horizon Problem are Cosmic Inflation, and Variable Speed of Light.

Cosmic Inflation theorizes that "in the moments following the Big Bang, space expanded faster than the speed of light, growing from smaller than a proton to an enormity that defies comprehension."[31] It is generally considered to have occurred between 10^{-36} and 10^{-32} seconds after the big bang. This is an extremely tiny period of time.

Variable Speed of Light theory suggests that light may have propagated as much as 60 orders of magnitude faster, but only in the very early universe.[32]

Both theories have massive problems, which we will look at in Section Three, but they are the only viable candidates so far which could solve the Horizon Problem.

We mention all of this scientific information because the Biblical record of Creation generates its own Horizon Problem. In order for the light from galaxies billions of light years away to have reached earth during the time period described, either light must have traveled much much faster, or space-time itself must have been rapidly stretched.[33]

As it turns out, the Bible seems to describe something like a Cosmic Inflation model:

Isaiah 40:22
*It is he who sits above the circle of the earth, and its inhabitants are like grasshoppers; who **stretches out the heavens like a curtain**, and spreads them like a tent to dwell in.*

The Hebrew word translated "stretches out" is *natah*. It means extending something outward until it reaches a goal.[34] This would be vastly different from the Cosmic Inflation described above, which lasted a fraction of a microsecond. There are at least ten places in scripture where God is described as "stretching" out the universe.[35]

This is just speculation, but after God spoke the entire universe into being from nothing, could it be that He then blew very very hard? Did God inflate the "balloon" of the universe and cause it to expand faster than the speed of light? Or did God cause the speed of light itself to be 60 orders of magnitude greater in the beginning?

All of these theories introduce a "Wrinkle in Time"[36]. Minkowski proved that time is inextricably bound to space. And Einstein proved that time is also inextricably bound to the speed of light.[37] So when you start monkeying with rapidly stretched space or radically faster light-speed, you are also monkeying with time. When that happens, could billions of years appear to some observers as mere thousands?

One way or another, both physicists and theologians have a Horizon Problem. But this much they both know for certain: In less than an instant all of matter, space, and time were created out of nothing in a colossal burst of light.

You can call it the Big Bang if you want. We prefer this:

Genesis 1:3:
And God said, "Let there be light," and there was light.

And now...here you are. Able to look up into the starry night in wonder and observe it all declaring the glory of God.

Of Quarks, Quantum, and You

G od in three Persons created all of the galaxies and stars and planets of the universe. With this came the laws of physics and the four fundamental forces: the strong and weak nuclear force, electromagnetism, and gravitation, all delicately fine-tuned and balanced.

The basic workings of physics are called "laws" for a very good reason. If you break a human law, such as robbing a bank, you will eventually suffer the consequences. The laws of physics are the same. If they are broken there are enormous consequences.

Many of these physical laws were first codified by Sir Isaac Newton.[38] They include his Laws of Motion, Gravity, and Thermodynamics. Einstein's Theory of Relativity[39] gave us the law of Conservation of Energy, expressed in the famous equation $E = mc^2$.

All of these physical laws reveal a design throughout creation which is breathtakingly beautiful to behold. They express an immense care in the creation of the universe. Like a master clock maker gently placing each gear.

Scientists often call these laws "elegant". In fact, there's a principle in physics and mathematics called the "Beauty Principle", or the "principle of mathematical simplicity".

Paul A. M. Dirac was one of the leading theoretical physicists of the 20th century. He pioneered the development of Quantum Mechanics. Dirac is quoted as saying:

God used beautiful mathematics in creating the world.[40]

Dirac described the Beauty Principle thus:

*The research worker, in his efforts to express the fundamental laws of Nature in mathematical form, should strive mainly for **mathematical beauty**.*[41]

Elegant, beautiful, finely tuned laws don't just write themselves. The universe would cease to work without these "beautiful" laws. Somewhere there must be a Lawgiver at work.

Let's drill down now in this beautiful law-aiding creation, and see how it was designed at the tiniest level.

Consider a glass of water. What's in the glass? "Why, water, you fool", might be your answer. Our reply would be, "Not exactly". If you drill down a little farther...well actually a *lot* farther...you will see that there is something going on at the microscopic level.

A water molecule is made up of two atoms of hydrogen and one atom of oxygen. If you drill down even farther you find that an oxygen atom is made up of 8 protons, 8 neutrons, and 8 electrons. If you break open a proton or neutron (which are identical except for electrical charge) you will find that they are made up of three quarks each. When you reach the quark you have reached the end of the line according to many physicists, although some propose something even smaller which they call a "preon".

While it may be possible in the future to slice and dice quarks into ever smaller bits, eventually you come to a fundamental question. What's it all made of? Fortunately we don't have to wait for the Large Hadron Collider[42] to keep smashing sub-atomic particles until it finds the answer. It was given to us over 100 years ago[43]:

$$E = mc^2$$

What's it all made of? Energy. A really, really, really *huge* amount of Energy.

You probably already know this, but we'll unpack Einstein's equation just to be sure nobody misses it. Energy (E) is equal to mass (m) times the speed of light (c) squared. Energy and mass are interchangeable. They're the *same thing*. Restated in plain English:

What you think of as solid matter is really just an enormous amount of energy.

How much energy? If you could release the energy in one gram of matter with 100% efficiency, it would be enough to keep a 100 watt light bulb running for 30,000 years. If you released that energy all at once, it's about the same as the energy released by the atomic bomb which destroyed the entire city of Hiroshima in 1945.

One person commenting on the physics blog *Quantum Diaries* asked a very interesting question:

> *If matter is merely a fancily arranged portion of energy tweaked and tuned so it takes on the shape of an atom with all of its inner parts fully functioning, then **what is this "energy" which is capable of wearing a wide variety of costumes** and playing many roles?*[44]

The answer to this blogger's question is, of course, *God*. The origin of the universe is God, and therefore everything in it was designed by God, and has its source in God. God is supplying the energy, and it is God who has "fancily arranged" it, and "tweaked and tuned" it so that it "takes on the shape of an atom".

These things are a profound mystery to scientists, but it should not be so. The mystery was explained thousands of years ago in the Bible. The profound mystery is the design of God, and it is pouring forth speech.

But not only is energy tweaked and tuned so it takes on the shape of an atom, there is also an enormous amount of energy required to hold that atom together. It's called the Strong Nuclear Force.

Have you ever played with a child's magnets? If you put a *positive* and a *negative* together they'll stick. Opposites attract. If you put *positive* and a *positive* together they'll push apart. Like repels.

Inside the nucleus of an atom you'll find protons (which always have a *positive* charge) stuck together. And inside of protons and neutrons you'll find quarks of the *same electromagnetic charge* stuck together. How can this be? Why don't the like charges repel?

The nucleus of an atom sticks together because of the Strong Nuclear Force, which is 100 times stronger than electromagnetism and 10^{38} times stronger than gravitation.

So not only is matter made up of huge amounts of pure energy, but a huge amount of energy is bound up in that matter just to hold the internal bits of atoms together.

Scientists have no idea what causes the Strong Nuclear Force or where it came from. These things are a profound mystery to them, but it should not be so. The mystery was explained thousands of years ago in the Bible. The profound mystery is the design of God, and it is pouring forth speech.

But things get even more strange when you look at the mass (weight) of matter. It seems the basic constituents of an atom, it's protons, neutrons, and the quarks from which they're made, have no mass. They weigh *nothing*.

This was a perplexing problem for physicists until 1964, when Belgium's Francois Englert and Britain's Peter Higgs independently theorized the existence of a subatomic particle that came to be known as the Higgs Boson. It was key to explaining how things acquired mass.

Until 2012 the Higgs Boson (sometimes called the "God Particle") was only theorized. But in that year the Large Hadron Collider (LHC) in Switzerland confirmed its existence. The Higgs Boson is very generous. It "imparts" mass to every other constituent of matter.

The Higgs Boson is called the "God Particle" because it seems to have god-like powers. It hands out mass like lollipops from an inexhaustible storehouse. Without the Higgs Boson the universe would not exist. Without mass there would be no gravity. Every atom in the universe would fly off into the vast reaches of nothingness.

This god-like power mystifies scientists, but it shouldn't. The mystery was explained thousands of years ago in the Bible. The profound mystery is the design of God, and it is pouring forth speech.

But the mystery deepens. *How* the Higgs Boson imparts mass is a tale even stranger yet. It's called the Higgs Field. Here's how physicist Kate Lunau describes it:

> *The Higgs particle tells us something very basic and fundamental about why we're here. It is evidence of the Higgs field, **an invisible force field that stretches across the universe**, encasing us like a Jell-O mould, and giving mass to elementary particles within it.*[45]

An "invisible force field" stretching across the entire universe? They've got to be kidding, right? Nope. The Higgs Field has been proven by subsequent tests at the LHC. It is indeed "encasing us like a Jell-O mould".

This seems preposterous. It's more science fiction than science. Where could such an invisible force field stretching across the entire universe come from? You know our answer: God.

These things are a profound mystery to scientists, but it should not be so. The mystery was explained thousands of years ago in the Bible. The profound mystery is the design of God, and it is pouring forth speech.

But it gets even stranger yet. All the stars, planets and galaxies in the known universe make up just 4.9% of the total mass-energy. The other 95.1% is made of stuff astronomers can't see, detect or even comprehend. It's called Dark Matter and Dark Energy.

Dark Energy is an unknown form of energy which permeates all of space, making up 68.3% of all the energy in the universe. It does not interact through any of the fundamental forces other than gravity. It's the most accepted hypothesis to explain recent observations indicating that the universe is expanding at an accelerating rate.[46]

Dark Matter is a kind of matter that cannot be seen with telescopes or detected directly, but would account for 84.5% of the total mass in the universe. The existence of Dark Matter is inferred from its gravitational effects on visible matter. It is one of the greatest mysteries in modern astrophysics.[47]

There is immense power at work in the universe, and nobody seems to know where it comes from. Hmm. Are scientists really so clueless that they have no idea where this energy comes from? It is the design of God, and it is pouring forth speech.

But hold on to your electromagnets. We're about to introduce you to something far stranger than the Higgs Field or Dark Energy. It's called the Quantum Enigma.

Quantum Mechanics was developed in the early 20th century when it was discovered that the energy of an object can change only by a discrete quantity, called a "quantum". It explains how atoms behave based on these quantum.

Quantum Mechanics is the most tested and proven theory of all time. It is the basis for over one third of our economy. Cellphones, tablets, modern medical equipment, and much more depend on Quantum Mechanics.

But along with tablets and smart-phones came some very strange baggage. Early on, experiments in Quantum Mechanics showed sub-atomic particles behaving in impossible ways. The now-famous two-slit experiment demonstrated that a photon or even an atom could be in two places at the same time.

Even stranger, if you observe an object, you change its behavior and position. This enigma is explained in detail in *Quantum Enigma: Physics Encounters Consciousness*, Oxford University Press, 2011. Here's a summary: The Quantum Enigma has two parts: Consciousness and Connectedness.

Consciousness.

Experiments demonstrate that a beam of electrons is affected by the act of being observed. The greater the amount of "watching", the greater the influence on what actually takes place. Consciousness somehow affects physical things. One physicist explains:

The doctrine that the world is made up of objects whose existence is independent of human consciousness turns out to be in conflict with quantum mechanics and with facts established by experiment.[48]

This borders on metaphysics. But it's *scientific fact*, "established by experiment". Human consciousness affects the material world. It's almost *spiritual*.

Connectedness.

Any things that have ever interacted are forever connected, or "entangled", even if they are later separated by great distances. Experiments have demonstrated that once two atoms have interacted, what happens to one instantly influences what happens to the other, even if they are later far removed from each other. Einstein was deeply troubled by such influences, calling them "spooky actions".[49]

These "spooky actions" are real. They've been proven over and over again. Human consciousness affects material objects. All things are "entangled" in mysterious ways. Listen to how physicist and cosmologist Sir James Jeans describes the Quantum Enigma:

> *Today there is a wide measure of agreement, which on the physical side of science approaches almost to unanimity, that the stream of knowledge is heading towards a non-mechanical reality;* **the universe begins to look more like a great thought than like a great machine.**[50]

This ought to be earth-shattering news! There is wide agreement in the scientific community — *approaching unanimity* — that the universe begins to look like *"a great thought"*. *Who's* thought? We hold that science has discovered evidence of *God!*

So let's review where this leaves us:

1. Matter doesn't really exist, it's just lots and lots of energy "wearing a wide variety of costumes".
2. An immensely powerful Force holds atoms together when they should fly apart at the speed of light.
3. Some mysterious force field fills the entire universe and hands out mass like lollipops.
4. 68.3% of all the energy in the universe is some mysterious Dark Energy which is not already busy masquerading as atoms or holding them together.
5. 84.5% of all the mass in the universe is made of some mysterious Dark Matter which nobody can see or detect, and which is not already bound up in atoms, or floating around waiting to be handed out like a lollipop..
6. Matter is somehow affected by consciousness, and the universe may really be just a "great thought".
7. Any things that have ever interacted are forever entangled like a warm cosmic hug, and what happens to one instantly affects the other, even if separated by trillions of miles.

God's design is wonderfully strange and utterly amazing!

We have spent this much ink on physics and the Quantum Enigma, not to confuse you with meaningless scientific data, but to show you God's glory. Science has uncovered the glory of God, and not even known it.

Things which are deep mysteries to science...the vast amount of energy bound up in atoms, the strange little Higgs Boson, a universal force field imparting mass, Dark Matter and Dark Energy, the connectedness and Great Thought of the Quantum Enigma...these amazing facts are pointing *directly* to God!

You may not fully understand all of this, but it is screaming the glory of God! Please step back and recognize that, while God's design may be mysterious, *it is declaring His glory*. These are undeniable facts for which science has absolutely no explanation. *This is how God designed the universe*. The Bible tells us that this Design daily "pours forth speech", declaring the Glory of God.[51]

This is "speech" which every human being needs to hear!

The Bible makes it very clear that God did not wind up the universe like a clock, putting the laws of quantum physics in motion and then sit back to watch it tick. God is intimately involved. *He* is supplying the vast amounts of energy behind these profound mysteries. *He* is the one who designed Quantum Mechanics. This leads us to a very important question:

Could it be that the spiritual is more real than the physical?

The universe is "fearfully and wonderfully made".[52] God spoke everything into being, and He's still breathing. If God were to withdraw His breath, everything would collapse. This is repeated throughout the scriptures. Here are two examples:

Job 34:14-15
*If he should set his heart to it and **gather to himself his spirit and his breath**, all flesh would perish together, and man would return to dust.*

Hebrews 1:3a
*He [Jesus] is the radiance of the glory of God and the exact imprint of his nature, and **he upholds the universe by the word of his power.***

What does one say about all of this? How can you respond to such truths? *Awesome* comes to mind. But like "love", "awesome" means almost nothing in current American culture. A skateboard has "awesome" trucks. An Xbox has "awesome" motion sensors. (We know these things only because our grandchildren have told us so.)

Leave it to Americans to trivialize the transcendent. There was a time when "awesome" was rarely used to describe any but Almighty God, or His creation. Our culture has left us with few ways to express the truly profound. Here's what "awesome" *really* means: *causing strong feelings of respect, fear, and wonder.*[53]

So what is your response? To paraphrase one of the founders of Quantum Theory, "Have you understood yet?"

Anyone not shocked by quantum mechanics has not yet understood it.[54] ~ Niels Bohr

If the facts we have presented in this section do not drive you to your knees before the transcendent, AWESOME, Creator God, then either you have "not yet understood it", or there is some external force causing blindness.[55] If the former, please re-read this section. If the latter, you will see that external force exposed in the next section.

If you're on your knees...you're in good company. Thomas had a similar response when he came face to face with the resurrected Jesus.

John 20:28
Thomas answered him, "My Lord and my God!"

---

[1] Isaiah 66:22, Hebrews 12:26-27, 2 Peter 3:10-13.

[2] Acts 3:21. See Section Seven for a closer look at the idea that the New Heavens and New Earth will be a restoration of the universe, not something completely unfamiliar.

[3] Genesis 3:17.

[4] Romans 8:19-24.

[5] 1 Corinthians 15:51-53.

[6] Isaiah 61:4, Revelation 21:10-22:5.

[7] Isaiah 60:21.

[8] Matthew 26:26-29.

[9] Matthew 25:23.

[10] 1 Corinthians 3:11-14.

[11] Psalm 19:1-3.

[12] *Signature in the Cell: DNA and the Evidence for Intelligent Design*, Stephen C. Meyer, PhD; Harper Collins 2009, pp. 211-213.

[13] *K12 Reader*: "A predicate nominative is a subject complement, a word or group of words that follows a linking verb or verb phrase such as is, are, was, has been, and can be. It renames, identifies, or defines the subject or subjects."

[14] *The New World Translation of the Holy Scriptures* (NWT) is a translation of the Bible published by the Jehovah's Witnesses. The NWT translates John 1:1b as "and the Word was a god". Other mis-translations in the NWT portray Jesus as an inferior god. As we will see in Section Three, if Jesus was not THE God, then it completely negates redemptive salvation on the Cross. We highly discourage use of the NWT for these reasons.

[15] See the *Vine's Complete Expository Dictionary* in reference to the Greek word *monogenes* (only-begotten), which in part states: "We can only rightly understand the term 'the only begotten' when used of the Son, in the sense of un-originated relationship. The begetting is not an event of time, however remote, but a fact irrespective of time. The Christ did not become, but necessarily and eternally *is* the Son."

[16] 1 Corinthians 8:6, Colossians 1:16, Hebrews 1:2.

[17] *A Hebrew and English Lexicon of the Old Testament*; by Francis Brown, Samuel Rolles Driver and Charles Augustus Briggs; first published in 1906.

[18] Genesis 1:4; 10; 12; 18; 21; 25.

[19] Genesis1:31.

[20] *Macmillan English Dictionary for Advanced Learners*, Macmillan Education, 2002.

[21] For those who may think this smacks of sexism, you need only read the very next verse to see that man and woman are treated equally here: (Genesis 1:27) *So God created man in his own image, in the image of God he created him; male and female he created them.*

[22] *Vine's Complete Expository Dictionary* gives an example from 1 Kings 11:18 to show that the word *tselem* refers to a statue in a temple.

[23] *Stephen Hawking. A Brief History of Time*, Bantam Books, 1988, p. 125. To be fair, while Hawking and most other scientists recognize the massive fine-tuning of the universe, he and many others do not accept this as evidence of a designing intellect. They attempt to get around a Designer with theories such as the "Multiverse", which we will look at in Section Three.

[24] *Cosmos, Bios, and Theos;* Margenau, H and R.A. Varghese, ed. 1992. La Salle, IL, Open Court, p. 83.

[25] *Big Bang Refined by Fire* by Dr. Hugh Ross, 1998. Reasons To Believe, Pasadena, CA.

[26] See *The Goldilocks Enigma: Why Is the Universe Just Right for Life?*; Dr. Paul Davies, Mariner Books, 2008.

[27] *The Universe: Past and Present Reflections*; Hoyle, F. 1982; *Annual Review of Astronomy and Astrophysics*: 20:16.

[28] Macmillan Dictionary.

[29] *Raum und Zeit* (1907; "Space and Time"); Minkowski, H.. Albert Einstein initially dismissed Minkowski's four-dimensional interpretation as "superfluous learnedness" (Abraham Pais, *Subtle is the Lord*, 1982). To his credit, Einstein changed his mind quickly.

[30] Hawking, S. W.; Ellis, G. F. R. (1973). *The Large-Scale Structure of Space-Time.* Cambridge University Press.

[31] *EarthSky Science Wire*, Feb. 16, 2015 edition.

[32] *Speed of Light May Not Be Constant, Physicists Say*; Jesse Emspak, *Live Science*; April 27, 2013 issue.

[33] There are two basic ideas on this Horizon Problem among Christian thinkers. One sees God taking billions of years to unfold the tapestry of creation (see www.reasons.org). The other sees the Biblical record placing all of God's creation at a point just several thousand years ago (see www.answersingenesis.org). The latter idea is based on the meaning of the Hebrew word *yom* (day) in context with "evening" and "morning" (repeated six times in Genesis 1), the genealogies in Genesis 4, 5 & 11 (which account for about 2,000 years form Adam to Abraham, who lived around 2.000 B.C.), and the fact that death did not enter creation until *after* Adam and Eve rebelled (Romans 5:12-21).

[34] Vine's Complete Expository Dictionary.

[35] Job 9:8, Psalm 104:2, Isaiah 40:22, Isaiah 42:5, Isaiah 45:12, Isaiah 48:13, Isaiah 51:13, Jeremiah 10:12, Jeremiah 51:15, Zechariah 12:1.

[36] This is a tip-of-the-hat to the award-winning children's novel *A Wrinkle in Time*, by Madeleine L'Engle; first published by Farrar, Straus & Giroux in 1963.

[37] *Relativity: The Special and General Theory*, Einstein A.; (Translation 1920), New York: H. Holt and Company.

[38] *Philosophiœ Naturalis Principia Mathematica*, Sir Isaac Newton, 1687.

[39] *Relativity: The Special and General Theory*, Einstein A.; (Translation 1920), New York: H. Holt and Company.

[40] Quoted in *Paul Adrien Maurice Dirac*, Behram Kursunoglu and Eugene Paul Wigner, (1990), Preface, xv. This should not be taken to mean that Dirac necessarily believed in God, any more than Einstein, who famously quipped, "God doesn't play dice with the world" (*Einstein and the Poet*, William Hermanns and Albert Einstein; Branden Press). Both men were expressing their awe at the orderliness and beauty of the universe. Dirac was an avowed atheist in his younger days, but after his death his wife is quoted as saying "he believed in Jesus Christ" (*The Voice Of Genius: Conversations*

With Nobel Scientists And Other Luminaries; Denis Brian, ed. ; Basic Books, 2001; pp. 28–29). Some question her veracity, dismissing it as wishful thinking. We'll find out when we get to heaven.

[41] Paul A. M. Dirac; *Proceedings of the Royal Society of Edinburgh* (1939), 59 122.

[42] The Large Hadron Collider (LHC) is the world's largest and most powerful particle accelerator. The LHC is located at the CERN accelerator complex near Geneva, Switzerland.

[43] *EarthSky Science Wire*, Sept. 27, 2014 issue: "On September 27, 1905, Albert Einstein published *Does the Inertia of a Body Depend Upon Its Energy Content?* in the journal *Annalen der Physik*. In it, he described the interchangeable nature of mass and energy, or $E=mc^2$."

[44] From *Quantum Diaries* Blog (www.quantumdiaries.org); *But what are quarks made of?*; Jim Hirshauer, CERN Large Hadron Collider; posted 11/18/2010.

[45] *Why the Higgs boson discovery changed everything: A special report from the Large Hadron Collider in Switzerland*; Kate Lunau and Katie Engelhart; July 17, 2012.

[46] Peebles, P. J. E. and Ratra, Bharat (2003). "The cosmological constant and dark energy". Reviews of Modern Physics 75 (2): 559–606.

[47] *Planck captures portrait of the young Universe, revealing earliest light*; University of Cambridge. 21 March 2013.

[48] As quoted in *Quantum Enigma: Physics Encounters Consciousness* by Bruce Rosenblum and Fred Kuttner, Oxford University Press, 2011.

[49] From *Speakable and Unspeakable in Quantum Mechanics*; Bell, J. S. (1987); CERN.

[50] *The Mysterious Universe*, Sir James Jeans, 1937; Cambridge University Press; p. 137.

[51] Psalm 19:1-4.

[52] Psalm 139:14.

[53] Merriam-Webster Dictionary.

[54] As quoted in Meeting the Universe Halfway (2007) by Karen Michelle Barad, p. 254, with a footnote citing The Philosophical Writings of Niels Bohr (1998).

[55] This statement does not preclude, from your perspective, a rational choice to reject the claims we make here. However, since we have already stated that we hold the Bible to be "God breathed", please understand that when we say your rejection of these claims is due to some external force of blindness, we only speak what the Bible itself reveals.

Section Three | Deception

In their case the god of this world has blinded the minds of the unbelievers, to keep them from seeing the light of the gospel of the glory of Christ, who is the image of God.
2 Corinthians 4:4

Quid Est Veritas?

P ontius Pilate once asked Jesus a very interesting question. What is truth?[1] Perhaps Pilate wasn't being sarcastic, but it rather sounds that way. As if there is no real answer. How can anyone know what is truth?

In this section we are going to look at deception. As any bank teller knows, the best way to spot a counterfeit is to know the genuine article. So before we can look at the lie we must first understand what is truth.

Here is the primary definition of "truth" (as a noun) from three respected dictionaries, Merriam-Webster, Oxford English, and Cambridge:

Truth: the quality or state of being true

That certainly helped. All three have the same definition. All three use truth to define itself. We're going in circles here. Truth is the state of being true, which is truth, which is the state of being true...round and round for eternity.

Merriam-Webster gives us a little more help with their secondary definition:

a statement or idea that is true or accepted as true

Truth is something that is *accepted* as true. So if you can get enough people to accept something, then it magically becomes truth. But how many people does it take to make something true?

Let's look at an example. In 1933 the National Socialist German Workers' Party began to convince an entire nation that people of Jewish ancestry were subhuman and evil.[2] Millions of people "accepted as true" the official anti-Semitic propaganda of the Nazi party. Did that make it truth?

If an entire nation accepting something as truth doesn't make it so, then how can you ever possibly know what is truth? What should you base your judgments upon? Whatever it is, you had better be extremely careful or you may end up with another Holocaust.

This is not just some intellectual exercise. How societies determine truth can have deadly consequences. Holocausts are not a thing of the past. The idea that public consensus can give birth to truth has produced a genocide which continues to this day.

There are human beings who are not terminally ill, have full brainwave activity, and every prospect of living a long life, yet they are killed simply because they are not wanted. They are not killed by removing them from life-support or administering a euthanasia drug. In many cases they are hacked to pieces limb by limb.

Hitler's genocide took the lives of over six million. This present atrocity has claimed the lives of over 56 million innocent human beings since it began in 1973.[3] You've probably already guessed that we are speaking of abortion.

The consensus "truth" of the Supreme Court of the United States in 1857 was that Negroes were not "persons".[4] Did that really make it truth? The consensus "truth" of the German Nuremberg Decrees in 1935 was that Jews were not "persons".[5] Did that really make it truth? The consensus "truth" of the Supreme Court of the United States in 1973 was that children in their mother's womb were not "persons".[6] Did that really make it truth?

This now becomes a very personal question. We're asking *you*.

What is truth?

If the answer to that question is up to each and every one of the 8,000,000,000 human beings who inhabit this planet, then there is no answer. How could there be? If truth depends upon the agreement of eight billion people, then there is no truth at all...only chaos. That is where Scientific Naturalism leaves you.

Would you like to hear our answer? It's a five-letter word:

JESUS

Since you already know that we hold the Bible to be "God breathed", it won't surprise you to learn that our answer, and the authority upon which we base it, comes from Scripture. Here are four short versus which lay out the reasons for our answer.

John 14:6a
Jesus said to him, "I am the way, and the truth, and the life.

Jesus is the First Cause and personification of truth. Since He created the entire universe, all truth necessarily traces back to Him and comes from Him. Jesus is the source of all truth.

Ephesians 4:21b
...the truth is in Jesus.

Jesus is the repository of truth. We asked a question in the previous section. Could it be that the spiritual is more real than the physical? That spiritual reality, being more real than what you can feel or touch or see, is the truth which is stored up in Jesus. He is the inexhaustible well of truth.

John 1:14b
...the only Son from the Father, full of grace and truth.

Truth is most fully realized, most complete, most perfect, in Jesus. He is *full* of truth. The Greek word for "full" here is *pleres*. It means completely full, as in a basket which can hold no more.[7] All truth that ever was, is, or will be, is found in Jesus. He is *full* of truth.

John 1:17b
...grace and truth came through Jesus Christ.

Jesus is the channel through which truth comes to the human race. He spoke, and the entire universe was created out of nothing. He then spoke through the Holy Spirit over a period of about 1,600 years, inspiring human authors who set down truth in the Bible. And He continues to speak truth as we go to him in prayer...and listen.

Truth by committee? Truth by acquiescence? Truth by national poll? Personal truth? Situational truth? Truth from the traditions of our forefathers? Truth as ruled by the Supreme Court? Truth by scientific or political or bureaucratic consensus? Truth, to paraphrase Mao Zedong, out of the barrel of a gun?

No!

Quid est veritas? Verum est Iesu .

What is truth? Truth is Jesus. Period.

Son Of The Morning

W e have seen the origin of truth. Now it is time to look at the origin of lies. This is that external force of blindness which we promised to expose. And just as truth resides in one person, so lies reside in a person. He is called the Father of Lies. We see this in John 8:44, where Jesus is speaking to religious traditionalists. First He equates their legalism with Satan. Then Jesus nails down the source of every lie ever told:

John 8:44b
When he [Satan] lies, he speaks out of his own character, for he is a liar and the father of lies.

But this Father of Lies did not start out as a liar. He actually started out rather well. When God created him, he was called Lucifer, which means "shining one", "light bearer", "Son of the Morning". He was "full of wisdom" and "perfect in beauty" (Ezekiel 28:12-13). He was called the "guardian cherub", the highest rank among the created angels (Ezekiel 28:14).

Everything was going fine until something tragic and unexplained happened. His great beauty was the seed of pride, and that got him cast out of heaven (Ezekiel 28:17). But Satan's problem wasn't just your garden variety pride. He felt he deserved a serious upgrade. He wanted a promotion to King of the Universe:

Isaiah 14:12a; 13-14 (NLT)
*How you are fallen from heaven, O shining star, son of the morning!...For you said to yourself, "I will ascend to heaven and set my throne above God's stars. I will preside on the mountain of the gods far away in the north. I will climb to the highest heavens and **be like the Most High**."*

The title Isaiah gives to Satan, "shining star, son of the morning", is the same title Jesus gives Himself at the very end of the Bible:

Revelation 22:16b
...I am the root and the descendant of David, the bright morning star.

It's as if Satan were a counterfeit Jesus, trying to masquerade as an angel of light in a cheap suit of half-truths.

This fallen Son of the Morning, this Father of Lies, started off his lying career with a bang. With his very first lie he overturned God's perfect creation, and set mankind on a path of destruction from which we are still reeling.

Genesis 3:4-5
*But the serpent said to the woman, "You will not surely die. For God knows that when you eat of it your eyes will be opened, **and you will be like God**, knowing good and evil."*

Notice that the "hook" in Satan's lie was the same hook which snagged him. To be like the Most High. Adam and Eve took the bait. They fell from grace, and we've been falling ever since.

The root purpose of all lies can be traced back to the original lie. One way or another, we all want to be our own little god, with personal sovereignty and independence.

How ironic, then, that what Lucifer aspired to, what he tempted Adam and Eve with, what he's tempting you with, is the very thing which God freely gives us in Jesus Christ:

1 John 3:2
*Beloved, we are God's children now, and what we will be has not yet appeared; but we know that **when he appears we shall be like him**, because we shall see him as he is.*

The lies and deception which we will look at in this section all have this one thing in common. Satan, as the Father of Lies, desperately wants to prevent the promise of 1 John 3:2 from being fulfilled. He is insane with jealousy at the thought that we puny humans may some day gain what he sacrificed everything for and lost...to be like God.[8]

Just as all truth traces back to Jesus, one way or another all lies are lies about the truth emanating from Jesus. Because the Father of Lies knows full well that Jesus is the means by which God the Father extends the promise to mankind.

Without Jesus on the Cross, and Jesus risen from the dead, the promise is emptied of its power. That is what Satan desperately desires, and that is what drives every single one of his lies.

Satan is the "external force causing blindness" which we hinted at in the previous section.

We can never see into another person's heart. But this much we know for a certainty, on the authority of the word of God...His very breath: If you cannot see the truth of Jesus, then at some level Satan is blinding you.

2 Corinthians 4:4
In their case **the god of this world has blinded the minds of the unbelievers**, *to keep them from seeing the light of the gospel of the glory of Christ, who is the image of God.*

The Kingdom of Me

W e now turn to some specific lies. This is by no means an exhaustive examination (that would take centuries). So we will narrow our field of view down to a manageable size. All lies are of the devil, but some are more damaging than others. We will focus on those lies which can keep you from heaven, or keep you from growing on the journey there.

There are three kinds of lies: lies, damned lies, and statistics.[9]

Reworking that into our own list, we will look at varying types of serious lies which distract, confuse, and lead many astray.

The Kingdom of Me.
The basic lie of self delusion is that we are OK. We are not OK. We are not partially OK. We are not even remotely OK. A quick look at the history of mankind reveals a landscape littered with corpses.

And lest we think that these horrors are of another time and place, look again. Just turn on the news for thirty minutes and you will see man's inhumanity to man writ large.

Muslims killing Muslims by the hundreds of thousands. One billion people facing starvation.[10] 17% of the world's population consuming 80% of the world's resources.[11] Over a billion people (mostly women, ethnic minorities, and Christians[12]) oppressed and persecuted. Over 20 million children sold into sexual slavery.[13] 51 million underage girls married off in exchange for property or livestock.[14] We could go on, but you get the picture.

Please do not fall for the deception that none of this touches you. If you have a human heart you have the capacity for evil. There's an old platitude that says, "There but for the grace of God go I". We think Jeremiah put it a little more succinctly:

Jeremiah 17:9
The heart is deceitful above all things, and desperately sick; who can understand it?

Someone once told us, "People of all faiths and non faiths do good on a daily basis...when I do a good deed, I just do it because it's the right thing."

Sounds reasonable enough, right? Here's the problem: The history of the human race is littered with the rubble left from those who thought they were doing the "right thing", who thought they were acting in righteousness.

3,000 years ago, little children were burned alive on the alters of the god Molech because without it, the crops would fail. It was the "right thing" to do.

1,000 years, ago those who cloaked themselves in the robes of Christianity, yet lacked the power of the New Birth, slaughtered and tortured in the Crusades and Inquisition because it was the "right thing" to do.

Today we have the Islamic State doing the "right thing", in their own eyes.

What determines what is "right"? Who decides what is "good"? While many of us might agree that helping the helpless is a good thing, in some cultures you would be interfering with the cosmic balance. What seems good to you would be an evil thing to them.

So who's to decide? Who will be the arbiter of Good?

That's where Jesus comes in. The same immense power which raised Jesus from the dead can give us that "new heart" and "new spirit" which God promised in Ezekiel 36:26. Isaiah said that, "When we display our righteous deeds, they are nothing but filthy rags." (Isaiah 64:6)

The term "filthy rags" is quite strong. It's a translation of the Hebrew phrase *iddah begged*, which literally means, a rag which holds the bodily fluids from a woman's menstrual cycle. On our own, our "righteousness" is simply self-righteousness.

If what is good and right is ultimately just the subjective judgment of all 8 billion people inhabiting this planet, then this is what we are left with:

A mountain of filthy rags!

The fundamental question is, are we trusting in our own righteousness or the righteousness imputed from Jesus Christ, and the new spirit birthed in us.

If you are basically OK, but just need a little tweaking here or there, then you don't really need a God. All you need is a few self-help books and a sermon on the gospel of health, wealth, and the power of positive thinking. That's a lie from the Kingdom of Me.

Placed against this backdrop it is preposterous to think that our good outweighs our bad and somehow this is enough to recommend us to God. The phrase "lipstick on a pig" comes to mind. Or as Jesus put it, "white-washed tombs" (Matthew 23:27).

But modern civilization pushes on, trying to reform corpses and build a worldwide utopia. If we are all basically OK, but just need a little tweaking here or there, then all we need is a better form of government to do the tweaking. Someday we can create a utopia here on earth.

That was the basic idea behind the *Communist Manifesto*, written in 1848 by Karl Marx and Friedrich Engels. The noble proletariat and the misguided bourgeoisie all thrown into a blender and everything equalized into Utopian bliss.

The results were a deadly nightmare. That is because human beings are far from "OK". Those communist utopias tried to right the sins of Adam with massive bureaucracies, and by enforcing their brand of righteousness from the barrel of a gun. What resulted was unimaginable brutality. Combined, the People's Republic of China and the Union of Soviet Socialist Republics slaughtered over 137,000,000 of their own people in the name of Utopian purity.[15] Almost every other communist regime has murdered millions as well.

So what is the answer? If we can't reform ourselves, and utopias always degenerate into living hell, then what are we to do?

Quoting the bumper sticker from 2012, "How's that hope & change working for you?"[16]

At this point it might be helpful to relate a personal story. On January 14, 1969, I (Stan) was a U.S. Navy photographer assigned to the flight deck of the aircraft carrier USS Enterprise.[17] At 8:18 AM the flight deck erupted in explosions and fire, which burned for four grueling hours. 15 aircraft destroyed. 28 sailors dead. 314 injured.

I was 21 years old at the time, and a hardened atheist; disdainful of Christians in the extreme. But as I watched men being literally blown to bits, for some reason I instinctively whispered a prayer: "God, whose name I do not know. If I survive this, I will seek you." I was just giving God the benefit of the doubt; confronting my own mortality. No atheists in foxholes and all.

But at that very instant...God answered. I heard an audible voice above the explosions saying three words: "I am here."

Over the next five years I kept my promise. I knew for certain that God was not to be found in Christianity. I had read Genesis and Exodus, and deemed it a bloody and authoritarian cult.

So I began my quest with Hinduism. But that didn't last long. I wasn't very good at that karma stuff. I new myself better than to think I could rack up brownie points with the cosmos.

Next stop was Buddhism. But I ran into the same wall there. Why did these monks think I could earn my way to Nirvana? It seemed so phony. Didn't they know who I really was? No amount of karma or chanting mantras or religious exercise was going to be enough.

Over the next few years there were others. But they all had the same thing in common. Building your own stairway to heaven (queue Led Zeppelin).

Then one day I met a young man who had just kicked heroin cold turkey, and he wouldn't shut up about Jesus. After weeks of harassment, I finally relented and prayed with him. I didn't mean a word of it, but I thought it would get him off my back.

To my surprise, two weeks later I had an uncontrollable urge to pick up a Bible. But this time, instead of Genesis or Exodus, for some reason I opened to the book of Romans. By the time I got halfway through chapter six, I was on my knees.

What I had discovered in those five years of spiritual wandering was that all religious systems, including humanism, depend to one degree or another upon human performance for salvation. All but one that is.

✳ Let's be clear. If you can in any way effect your own salvation, then you are setting yourself up as a god. And that's the original lie.

That's what got us into this mess in the first place.

Damned Lies

*You shall not take the name of the Lord your God in vain, for the
Lord will not hold him guiltless who takes his name in vain.*
Exodus 20:7

We should start by defining a Damned Lie. There is only
one of the Ten Commandments, quoted above, which
states that God will not forgive a person who violates it.
Does that mean if you say, "Oh my God!", you are going straight to
hell?

Let's take a look at some of the key Hebrew words and their
meaning. "Take" (*nacah*) means to lift up, or carry. "Vain" (*shav*)
means deception, malice, falsehood; to bear false witness. "Guiltless"
(*naqa*) means to forgive, make clean, or acquit. So a closer look at
the original Hebrew would render this commandment:

*You shall not carry the name of the Lord your God falsely, for
the Lord will not acquit or forgive him who represents his
name deceitfully.*

A Damned Lie, then, is a lie about who God is. And since we have
already demonstrated that Jesus is God, then a lie about who Jesus is
would also be a Damned Lie.

If Jesus was not at the same time both fully God and fully human,
then all bets are off, and you are back to being a dead man walking.

In ancient times a person's name was very important. It was who
you were. Your name was a representation of your character. You
didn't mess with someone's name. Far less, God's name.

God is very jealous for His "name". It's a big deal. More than
eighty times in the Bible, God says that His purpose is that human
beings "shall know that I am the Lord". Here's one example:

Exodus 7:5
The Egyptians shall know that I am the LORD, when I stretch out my hand against Egypt and bring out the people of Israel from among them.

God knows that we are most satisfied when He is most glorified.[18] The best thing that can happen for any human being is to come to the full and complete realization that Jesus is Lord, and God.

The truth that Jesus is God is absolutely crucial because of four inescapable facts. Fact One: Sin results in death. Fact Two: God's required payment for sin is the death of a perfect person. Fact Three: The only one who meets God's criteria is God Himself. Fact Four: God sent Himself as Jesus to die that death.

If Jesus is not God, then His death was useless, and we are all still damned.

Anything which undercuts the truth of Jesus as God come down to earth, anything which waters down the full power of the Cross and the Resurrection...these damned lies leave us at sea in an ocean of chaos and hopelessness and destruction.

In the first chapter of Colossians in the Bible, Paul lays out some key truths about Jesus. Not only did He create the entire universe, Jesus created "thrones" and "dominions" and "rulers" and "authorities". That means He created all of the angels, including Lucifer and Michael.

Jesus holds all things together. The physical realm of the universe, and the spirit realm of angels, are all created and held together "in Him".

Colossians 1:16-17
For by him [Jesus] *all things were created, in heaven and on earth, visible and invisible, whether thrones or dominions or rulers or authorities—all things were created through him and for him. And he is before all things, and in him all things hold together.*

Scientific Naturalism

I magine that you are a police detective called to the scene of a suspicious death. The body of a very elderly man lies on a bed. The bedroom door was locked, and an empty bottle of sleeping pills is on the nightstand. Having keen powers of observation, you notice an open window, and muddy footprints leading from the window to the bed, and back to the window.

As you scribble these details in your notebook, the police commissioner barges into the room. He walks to the window and slams it shut, then takes a towel and erases the footprints. Turning to you, he rips the page from your notebook and declares, "No evidence from outside this room will be permitted", and walks out.

You are stunned. But being the obedient public servant you are, you continue your investigation. There are four ways to die, and only one of them requires an intruder. Suicides, accidental, and natural deaths can occur without any evidence from outside the room. So you look at the empty bottle of sleeping pills. This could have been a suicide. Then you consider the advanced age of the deceased. This could have been a natural death due to old age.

But that open window and those muddy footprints keep tugging at your mind. What if... But you have been given a "closed system". There cannot be anything or anyone from outside that system which acts upon it. Your hands are tied. And so you reluctantly jot in your notebook, "*Death by naturalistic causes*".[19]

Scientific Naturalism *assumes* that the universe is a closed system, similar to that closed bedroom, where all events occur for naturalistic reasons and that there cannot be anything or anyone from outside that system which acts upon it.

We do not mean to say that all scientific inquiry is in doubt. At most levels it works quite well. We can examine the world around us, develop hypotheses, test them, and arrive at conclusions. That's fine for studying insects or atoms or weather patterns.

But Scientific Naturalism runs into trouble when it comes up against such things as first causes. There are simply no logical answers to how life can come from non-life, or how the universe could create itself out of nothing. The closed system will admit no open windows or muddy footprints. What you get is an entrenched bureaucratic scientific establishment.

Galileo Galilei faced a similar entrenched establishment in 1616, when he proposed a heliocentric structure of the solar system.[20]

The scientific establishment of the day would not permit any ideas contrary to the "settled science" that the sun revolved around the earth. Heliocentric books were banned and Galileo was ordered to refrain from holding, teaching or defending heliocentric ideas. In 1633 he was sentenced to indefinite imprisonment.

Similar intolerance is at work today. The bureaucratic scientific establishment will not allow any evidence which might point to an influence from "outside the room". Woe betide the scientist who dares examine anything which might expose chinks in the naturalistic party line. The "closed system" has resulted in closed minds.[21]

The truth is, Scientific Naturalism is facing five serious dilemmas: first causes, fine-tuning, evolutionary transitions, naturalistic information, and the laws of probability. We've already covered fine-tuning in the Design section. Let's dare to look "outside the room", and consider the other four dilemmas here.

First Causes.

How could life come from non-life? How could the entire universe be created out of nothing? We'll start with abiogenesis, which is the notion that life arises naturally from non-living matter.

In 1969, the book *Biochemical Predestination* laid out a convincing case for abiogenesis.[22] It was hailed as the "smoking gun" of abiogenesis, and was used as a textbook in many universities.

Then in 1976, one of the authors, Dean H. Kenyon, began to have serious doubts about his own research. Kenyon was confronted by one of his students with the challenge of how abiogenesis worked in the absence of DNA.

Kenyon concluded upon deep consideration that it couldn't work. Without the DNA instructions, just having the basic elements available could not produce the end product of life. You need to explain where the instructions came from.[23]

One attempt to get around this enigma, called "RNA World", posits that RNA, which only translates DNA code, somehow stored genetic information in primitive cells. Only later did DNA take over.[24] But if RNA stored genetic information, then you still have to explain where that information came from.[25]

Evolutionary Transitions.

Why is there almost nothing in the fossil record representing transitions from one species to a higher one? Why did the vast majority of major animal phyla suddenly pop into existence in a geologic instant, with no earlier forms before them?

Charles Darwin addressed both of these questions.

The several difficulties here discussed, namely our **not** *finding in the successive formations infinitely numerous transitional links between the many species which now exist or have existed; the* **sudden manner in which whole groups of species appear** *in our European formations; the* **almost entire absence,** *as at present known, of fossiliferous formations beneath the Silurian strata, are all undoubtedly of the gravest nature.*[26]

Darwin felt that these "difficulties" would be overcome as more fossils were discovered. It has been over 150 years since Charles Darwin wrote those words, and yet "infinitely numerous transitional links" have yet to be found, "the sudden manner in which whole groups of species appear" is even more stark, and the "entire absence" of earlier fossils persists.

That "sudden manner" is called the "Cambrian Explosion". At the beginning of the Cambrian epoch almost every known species suddenly appeared in what amounts to a geological instant.[27] In order for evolution to work, it needs gradual changes over billions of years, not everything popping into existence all at once.

We're talking about macro-evolution here: transitions from one species to another, which, as we have shown above, has serious problems. *Micro*-evolution, on the other hand, is well established. Natural selection works fine *within* a species. Darwin's famous Galapagos finches are an example. Their beaks adapted to changing weather patterns to enable them to get at food sources.

One big problem with macro-evolution has to do with Newton's second law of thermodynamics. For an organism to evolve from one species to a higher, more complex one, would seem to violate entropy. Things tend to disorder. They don't become more orderly. That's an established universal law.

Another problem deals with the macro-evolution of *homo sapiens* in particular. It all seems to hang on a handful of fragmentary fossils. The "family trees" we see reproduced *ad infinitum* in textbooks are founded more on conjecture and guesswork than on hard data.

Richard Leakey revealed that the reconstruction of the famous "Lucy" skull was so incomplete that most of it was "imagination, made of plaster of paris".[28]

An article in Science Digest points out the lack of evidence:

The fossils that decorate our family tree are so scarce that there are still more scientists than specimens. The remarkable fact is that all the physical evidence we have for human evolution can still be placed with room to spare inside a single coffin.[29]

Evolutionary biologist Stephen J. Gould, in the journal *Natural History*, points out that this lack of fossil evidence leads to inference:

*The **extreme rarity of transitional forms in the fossil record** persists as the **trade secret of paleontology**. The evolutionary trees that adorn our textbooks have data only at the tips and nodes of their branches; the rest is inference, however reasonable, **not the evidence of fossils**.*[30]

Lack of hard evidence? Guesswork and inference? Doesn't the scientific method demand more? Sounds a bit like blind faith to us.

Our position is that the ability of creatures to adapt to their environment — natural selection — is a *design* feature, which we see in action every day. The idea that this could somehow pierce the boundaries between species is a flight of fancy which defies the facts. It seems to us that clinging to a theory with such a stark lack of hard evidence is wishful thinking born of a predetermined conclusion that there can not be, there *must* not be, a designer.

If you disagree, would you please do the following: Produce the "infinitely numerous transitional links" which Darwin could not find. Explain how the Cambrian Explosion fits into macro-evolutionary theory.[31] And discover Darwin's missing earlier fossils. Thank you.

Naturalistic Information.

Why does complex specified information (DNA) occur in natural systems? We'll delve into the workings of DNA when we get to the Laws of Probability. Right now, let's look at the "Junk DNA" controversy. Junk DNA is defined as DNA sequences that do not encode protein sequences.[32]

As late as 2012 over 98% of the human genome was thought to be "junk". This supported evolutionary theory. If an organism evolves from lower forms over millions of years, you would expect the trial and error of natural selection to leave a large amount of DNA from all those previous "trials" in its wake. Most of this old DNA would no longer have any function in the higher-level organism.

But in 2012 came a bombshell. The ENCODE Project Consortium published research in the journal *Nature* which revealed that at least 80% of human DNA actually *does* serve biochemical functions.[33] Many of these were regulatory functions, and sophisticated error-correction programming.

Here's how one prominent evolutionary biologist reacted:

*If the human genome is indeed devoid of junk DNA as implied by the ENCODE project, then a long, undirected evolutionary process cannot explain the human genome. If, on the other hand, organisms are designed, then all DNA, or as much as possible, is expected to exhibit function. **If ENCODE is right, then Evolution is wrong.**[34]*

Laws of Probability.

How can naturalistic information have self-organized, given the overwhelming probabilities against it?

If you have a six-sided die, and you're looking to roll a three, then your probability is one in six, which is expressed as a ratio of 1:6. You're looking for a single target among six possible outcomes. But it becomes much more complex as you ratchet up the number of targets, and the possible outcomes. When you start calculating the probabilities of the simplest single-cell organism arising by pure chance, the ratios become utterly astounding.

Starting in the 1990's, scientists began to do "minimal complexity" experiments, reducing cellular function to its simplest form. Biologists have been able to make increasingly informed estimates of these statistical probabilities.

A tiny bacteria called *mycoplasma genitalium* is the simplest known cell. It requires 482 proteins in order to function, and 562,000 nucleotide bases of DNA to assemble those proteins. Each base is constructed from four possible "letters", adenine, cytosine, guanine, or thymine.

To calculate the probability of all this generating itself by pure chance, scientists first calculate the probability of a single functional protein of average length arising by chance alone. Then they multiply that probability by the probability of each of the other necessary proteins arising by chance. The product of these probabilities determines the chances that all the proteins necessary for the simplest living cell would come together by chance.

At each position on the gene, any one of a possible 20 amino acids could occur with equal probability. These amino acids must form what's called a *peptide bond* or else they won't fold into a functional protein. But amino acids form peptide and non-peptide bonds with equal frequency. So the probability of forming *only* peptide bonds is about 1 in 10^{45}. That's about half as many sub-atomic particles as there are in the whole universe.

But it gets even more complex. Amino acids each have a mirror image of themselves (called *isomers*). There is a left-handed version and a right-handed version. For a protein to function, it can only use left-handed versions, called *L-form isomers*. So the probability of attaining only L-form isomers in a biologically viable chain of amino acids is approximately 1 in 10^{45}. When we add this to the peptide bond probabilities, we get a chance of 1 in 10^{90}. We're now way over the total number of sub-atomic particles in the entire universe.

But there's even more. Amino acids, like words and letters in a sentence, must be in a very specific sequential arrangement, or all you get is gibberish. Because there are 20 biologically occurring amino acids, the chance of getting any one of them at a specific site is 1 in 10^{74}.

When we combine the above probabilities it yields a chance of 1 in $10^{40,000}$ that all of this could happen by accident.[35]

But building a functional cell requires much more than just a vast amount of DNA information, peptide bonds, L-form isomers, and meaningful, specified sequencing. It needs a *transcription system* to take all of that and use it to actually build a living, self-replicating organism. That transcription system is made up of an array of proteins and RNA molecules, which form things like polymerases, tRNAs, ribosomal RNAs, mRNAs, and much more. And it all must be in place *before* the process of gene expression can even begin.

Each additional component would add orders of magnitude to the statistical improbability. We found estimates as high as $1:10^{400,000}$. But when you're dealing with so many interacting dependencies, there seems to be an element of guesswork involved. We'll leave guesswork to the paleontologists, since they're so dependent upon it. All we can say with confidence is that the statistical improbability of the first living cells having created themselves out of mud lies somewhere between $1:10^{40,000}$ and $1:10^{400,000}$, and leave it at that.

It's hard to get a mental picture of such an enormous number. It is virtually infinite. But let's stretch our brains a little.

In all the known universe, there are about 10^{80} subatomic particles.[36] Each of these particles can change position no more than 10^{45} times per second (known as an "event"). The total number of seconds since the supposed Big Bang is about 10^{16}. So the total number of events which could ever have possibly occurred in the history of the universe is 10^{139}.

Now all these events aren't trying to produce an organism. They're just the total *possible* events. So even if you're *extremely* generous, the universe has only had 10^{139} chances to "roll the dice". But the laws of probability say that it would take *at least* $10^{40,000}$ rolls of the naturalistic dice before the simplest living cell could even have a remote chance of being produced by purely unguided means. Francis Crick, co-discover of DNA, is often quoted as saying this:

Biologists must constantly keep in mind that what they see was not designed, but rather evolved.

This has been taken by some to mean that Crick was stubbornly turning a blind eye to design, no matter what the evidence might show. But taken in context, he's saying there's just an *appearance* of design. It's really evolution pulling the levers behind the curtain.[37]

In researching all of this, we saw two different responses from the naturalistic community. The first involved squeezing your eyes shut tight, jamming your fingers into your ears, and chanting the naturalist mantra 'till your critical thinking skills go numb: "It was *not* designed...It was *not* designed...It was *not* designed...".[38] The second response was to concoct utterly preposterous alternatives, which we will examine next.

Magic Seeds

The first concoction is called "panspermia". It's the theory that the seeds of life are somehow embedded into the fabric of the universe, just waiting for a suitable host planet. Confronted with the evidence, many turn to panspermia because they admit that life could not have originated on earth in the time available.[39]

An alternate form, called "directed panspermia", is advocated by Francis Crick. In 1982 he determined that the earth was not old enough for life to evolve on its own. So he invented an alien race on a much older planet who shot life into space on rockets, hoping to seed the universe.[40] How ironic that Crick thought naturalistic theories of terrestrial abiogenesis were so improbable that he turned to space aliens in a desperate attempt to preserve some kind of naturalistic mechanism. Is this science or science fiction?

But whether they think life came from aliens, or it magically appeared everywhere, panspermia advocates still have to explain the origin of all that DNA information. This is just kicking the can down the road. Naturalism will *never* answer first causes.

Multiverse Soup
The second concoction is called the "Multiverse". Here's how *Discover Magazine* describes it[41]:

*Call it a fluke, a mystery, a miracle. Or call it the biggest problem in physics. **Short of invoking a benevolent creator, many physicists see only one possible explanation:** Our universe may be but one of perhaps **infinitely many universes in an inconceivably** vast **multiverse.***

Faced with these astronomically huge improbabilities, scientists are turning to an equally improbable concept called the Multiverse. It's a theoretical realm outside our universe, from which an infinite number of universes are constantly popping into existence from a bubbly froth of quantum fluctuations. (No, we're not joking.)

This creates a tidy sidestep of those nasty DNA improbabilities and all that fine-tuning. *National Geographic* magazine explains:

*If ours was the only cosmos spawned by a Big Bang, **these life-friendly properties would seem impossibly unlikely.** But in a multiverse containing zillions of universes, a small number of life-friendly ones would arise by chance—and we could just happen to reside in one of them.*[42]

If you've got an infinite number of universes randomly popping into existence from the quantum Multiverse soup, then sooner or later we humans are bound to show up. Hand God his pink-slip.

Physicist Bernard J. Carr sees only two possibilities:

*"If there is only one universe," Carr says, "you might have to have a fine-tuner. **If you don't want God, you'd better have a multiverse.***"[43]

But the Multiverse theory brings with it a lot of improbable baggage. First, it creates an impossible paradox, similar to the time-travel paradox where you go back in time and accidentally kill your own father. Poof! No more you. Oops. The Multiverse Paradox goes something like this:

Infinite is a hard concept to wrap you brain around. With infinite universes, every logical possibility becomes an inevitability. All possible options are *continually and forever* tried, so every remotely possible state eventually occurs. For instance, it is logically possible for super-evolved beings to try manipulating the Multiverse, and accidentally blow it all up. Poof! No more Multiverse. Oops.

There's another problem. All this quantum fluxing and universe popping is going on beyond the boundary of *our* universe. So it's impossible to observe or test or prove. A theory which is impossible to observe or test or prove is not really a scientific theory, is it? It fails the definition, and is degraded to desperate conjecture. Oops.

And one final fly in the Multiverse soup. It presents two mutually exclusive ideas. The core dictum of Scientific Naturalism is that our universe is a closed system where nothing from outside that system can act upon it. But the core dictum of Multiverse theory is that quantum fluctuations from *outside* our universe created it. Oops.

If you admit one outside force to the table, then isn't it intellectual dishonesty to exclude other outside forces, such as an intelligent designer? If you've got a theory where every remotely possible state is inevitable, then how about this "remotely possible state": An infinitely loving, infinitely wise, infinitely powerful being spoke four words: *Let there be light!*

An Impossible Dilemma

Infinitely tiny probabilities of abiogenesis. Abundant fine-tuning of the universe. *Ex nihlo* creation (everything from nothing). The embarrassing disappearance of Junk DNA. The inconvenient truth of the Cambrian Explosion. The utter lack of transitional fossils. Guesswork and inference as the basis of paleontology. The absurd science fiction of panspermia. The improbable baggage of Multiverse theory. Scientific Naturalism is facing an impossible dilemma.

In an American court of law, a jury can only convict in a criminal trial if they are convinced of the defendant's guilt "beyond a reasonable doubt". You may not agree with everything we have said in this chapter. But we believe that the evidence we've presented creates a *reasonable doubt* about naturalism. We hope that is enough to convince you to read this book with an open mind.

Back in the Peoples Republic of Naturalism, the Thought-Police are slamming every window and erasing every muddy footprint. Independent thinking is forbidden, and students are force-fed party doctrine. None will ever hear of a design alternative.[44] Hundred foot murals of Dear Leader Richard Dawkins adorn every campus.

But the citizens are growing restless. In the dead of night, when there's nobody listening, they admit to a niggling suspicion that the Emperor is wearing no clothes.

Romans 1:21-22
For although they knew God, they did not honor him as God or give thanks to him, but they became futile in their thinking, and their foolish hearts were darkened. **Claiming to be wise, they became fools.**

113

[1] John 18:38.

[2] *Encyclopædia Britannica*; "Nazi Party".

[3] This number of abortions is calculated from reports by the Guttmacher Institute, a division of Planned Parenthood of America.

[4] United States Supreme Court; DRED SCOTT v. SANFORD; 1857.

[5] United States Holocaust Memorial Encyclopedia; "The Nuremberg Race Laws".

[6] United States Supreme Court; ROE v. WADE, No. 70-18 Argued: December 13, 1971; Decided: January 22, 1973.

[7] Stong's Hebrew and Greek Dictionary.

[8] These motives of Satan are not spelled out explicitly in the Bible, but may be inferred from the actions of Satan which Scripture describes, just as we may infer the presence of the wind by its affect on the branches of a tree.

[9] *Mark Twain's Own Autobiography: The Chapters from the North American Review*, 1906. Twain credits this quote to Benjamin Disraeli, but historians can find no reference to this in Disraeli's writings. We will leave the quote with Samuel Clemens, who obviously read it somewhere and couldn't remember where.

[10] Per United Nations World Food Programme.

[11] Per World Resources Institute.

[12] Per Reuters News Service (January 8, 2013) about 100 million Christians are persecuted around the world.

[13] Per Amnesty International.

[14] Per Amnesty International.

[15] *Death by Government*, R.J. Rummel; Transaction Publishers, 1997. Data on the killings by communist regimes is hard to come by, but this seemed to be the best average from several sources.

[16] We do not mean to imply that working for social justice and helping the poor is useless. The Bible clearly teaches us to do these.

[17] This is one of your authors speaking: Stan Osterbauer.

[18] This is a reworking of a quote from John Piper: "God is most glorified in us when we are most satisfied in him." From a sermon given on Nov. 8, 2008.

[19] Stephen C. Meyer related a similar allegory in his book, *Signature In The Cell*; Harper Collins, 2009.

[20] Galileo's book Starry Messenger (1610) promoted the heliocentric theory of Nicolaus Copernicus (1543).

[21] We could cite numerous examples, but we did not want to clutter our text. See the documentary *Expelled: No Intelligence Allowed*, staring Ben Stein (Premise Media Corporation).

[22] *Biochemical Predestination*, Gary Steinman and Dean H. Kenyon; McGraw-Hill (1969).

[23] See *Of Pandas and People:*; Percival Davis and Dean H. Kenyon; Haughton Pub Co; (1993). Also see *Darwin's Black Box: The Biochemical Challenge to Evolution* by Michael J. Behe.

[24] *Molecular Biology of the Cell*; Alberts B, Johnson A, Lewis J, et al.; New York: Garland Science; 2002.

[25] Professor Hubert Yockey suggests that the RNA World hypothesis floats improbably in mid-air like the roof of a house built before the foundation and walls. (H.P. Yockey, "Information in bits and bytes: reply to Lifson's Review of Information Theory and Molecular Biology," *BioEssays* 17 (1995): 85-88; p. 87.)

[26] Charles Darwin, *On The Origin Of Species* (1859) , Chapter 9. ON THE IMPERFECTION OF THE GEOLOGICAL RECORD.

[27] WGBH Educational Foundation Evolution Library; *The Cambrian Explosion*. See *Darwin's Doubt* by Stephen C. Meyer

[28] Richard Leakey, Director of National Museums of Kenya, Africa, *The Weekend Australian*, May 7-8, 1983, p. 3.

[29] Dr. Lyall Watson, "The Water People", *Science Digest*, May 1982.

[30] Stephen J. Gould - "Evolution's Erratic Pace," *Natural History*, vol. 86 (May 1987), p. 14.

[31] Theories like *punctuated equilibrium* and *quantum evolution* attempt to deal with the Cambrian Explosion by compressing macro-evolution into a few bursts of a few hundred thousand years each. For natural selection to have created whole new species in such tiny ticks of the geological clock defies all known mechanisms. It contorts evolutionary theory into unrecognizable shapes in an attempt to fit the fossil record. Even "Dear Leader" Richard Dawkins doesn't buy

this poppycock (Dawkins, Richard, *The Blind Watchmaker*, 1996). If this was your answer to our challenge, nice try, but no cigar.

[32] Elgar G, Vavouri T; Vavouri (July 2008). "Tuning in to the signals. Trends Genet. 24 (7): 344–52.

[33] The ENCODE Project Consortium, *Nature*, 2012. ENCODE stands for "Encyclopedia of DNA Elements".

[34] From a speech given at the 2013 meeting of the Society for Molecular Biology and Evolution by Dan Graur, PhD. This does not mean that Dr. Graur has stepped away from evolution. He remains, in fact, a staunch evolutionist.

[35] Sir Fred Hoyle and Chandra Wickramasinghe, *Evolution from Space* (New York: Simon and Schuster, 1981). See also, *Signature in the Cell: DNA and the Evidence for Intelligent Design*, Stephen C. Meyer, PhD; Harper Collins 2009.

[36] From *The Physics of the Universe: The Universe by Numbers*.

[37] Francis Crick, *What Mad Pursuit* (1988). We had to clarify this quote because it has so often been taken out of context. We chose not to use another quote, which is also often taken out of context: "An honest man, armed with all the knowledge available to us now, could only state that in some sense, the origin of life appears at the moment to be almost a miracle, so many are the conditions which would have had to have been satisfied to get it going." The context makes it clear that Crick is arguing *against* any kind of "miracle".

[38] With their critical thinking skills thus numbed, these mantra-chanters often end up invoking what's called the *weak anthropic principle*. It goes like this: "Of course the universe is fine-tuned for human life. If it wasn't, you wouldn't be here to ask stupid questions. Case closed." This is so intellectually bankrupt that it's stunning. At least proponents of panspermia and multiverse theories have the honesty to admit the seriousness of the dilemmas they face.

[39] See Crick, F. H. C. and Orgel, L. E., 1973, *Icarus*, 19, 341.

[40] *Life Itself*, Francis Crick, 1982.

[41] "Science's Alternative to an Intelligent Creator: the Multiverse Theory" by Tim Folger; *Discover Magazine*, November 10, 2008.

[42] "Big Bang Discovery Opens Doors to the 'Multiverse'", by Dan Vergano; *National Geographic,* March 19, 2014.

[43] Bernard J. Carr, professor of mathematics and astronomy at Queen Mary University of London, as quoted in "Science's Alternative to an Intelligent Creator: the Multiverse Theory" by Tim Folger; *Discover Magazine*, November 10, 2008.

[44] In *Tammy Kitzmiller, et al. v. Dover Area School District, et al.* (October, 2004), the United States federal court held that students could not even hear of the existence of a design alternative, let alone learn anything about it.

Section Four | Dominion

*And Jesus came and said to them, "All authority in heaven
and on earth has been given to me."*
Matthew 28:18

Where Was God?

We have looked at our skewed perceptions and discovered the promise of a new body and the wedding garments we can weave. We've looked at the design of the universe, as a precursor of what will come. And we have seen the deception which blinds so many, and how the first two humans threw away the dominion they had been given.

Now it is time to look at how God stepped into space-time to redeem what Satan had stolen...how dominion was taken back. But before we do that, we need to see the effects of that lost dominion.

What follows are four true stories. Each provokes the same question, which millions have asked over the centuries. Finding no answer, many have rejected God. It is a fundamental misunderstanding of the nature of this present world, and becomes an easy pretext for unbelief. We maintain that there *is* an answer.

This may be difficult for you to read, but we need to look at it square on. Please do not turn a blind eye.

True story number one.

The year was 1952. The place was Seoul, South Korea. War had ravaged the country, propelling millions into abject poverty. The Korean people were broken and uprooted.

A young American walked the streets daily, praying. One morning, with the cold air stinging his face, he saw a truck rumbling through the streets. City workers collected piles of rags from the doorways and alleys. The men kicked each pile, presumably to ensure they were free from rats, before throwing them onto the truck.

As he walked closer, the young American saw a small arm extending from one of the bundles. These were not rags. These were the bodies of street children who had died in the freezing conditions overnight. Orphans of war were considered vermin, and could never escape their cultural disgrace.[1]

121

According to UNESCO, today there are as many as 150 million orphaned or abandoned children living on the streets, primarily in Latin America, Africa, and Asia. Millions die each year. Question: Where is God? If there really is an all-powerful loving God, how could He possibly allow the world's youngest and most vulnerable to suffer so cruelly, and die alone and despised?

True story number two.

The year was 2004. The place was Banda Aceh, Indonesia. 34 year old Armansiah Nyong was serving as a lifegurad at a popular local beach. The day was sunny, and the beach was packed with people. Nyong took a short break to check on his pregnant wife at their home just 200 meters away, leaving his two small children in the care of a friend.

At that moment a powerful earthquake struck the city, knocking Nyong to the ground. He rushed back to the beach, but was unable to find his children. Then something very strange happened. The ocean water began to recede. Soon the water was almost a mile away.

People ran into the dry ocean bed to collect the fish. Nyong didn't go. It looked weird to him...as if something ominous was about to happen. He was right.

Soon he spotted a gigantic body of white foam on the horizon, traveling at over 400 miles per hour. He heard several deafening booms, and started to run. But it was too late. Before he could reach higher ground, a wave almost 90 feet high knocked him down.

Nyong tumbled over and over, but somehow managed to fight his way to the surface of the surging water. Two more massive waves crashed into him. On the verge of drowning, he managed to grab a large piece of wood. He rode on it for what seemed like hours.

When the water finally started receding he ended up two miles inland, surrounded by thousands of bodies, and the debris which was all that was left of an entire city. Nyong lost his entire family that day. It was the largest natural disaster in history. 280,000 people died and 1.6 million were left homeless.[2]

Question: Where was God? Why could Jesus, who calmed the wind and waves with one rebuke[3], not prevent this colossal disaster?

122

True story number three.

The fourteen year old boy's name was Janda Weiss. As he stepped off the train with thousands of others, the first thing he noticed was smokestacks belching smoke and flames. He and the others were told to throw away all their luggage. The elderly were loaded onto dump trucks and driven to long trenches. Here they were dumped into the trenches, doused with naphtha, and set on fire. Burned alive.

The year was 1944. The place was Auschwitz-Birkenau, Poland.

Of the 2,000 people left by the train with Janda, he and 29 others were selected for work parties. The rest were led to dressing rooms outside what they were told were the showers. On the wall was a sign: "Put shoes into the cubbyholes and tie them together so you will not lose them. After the showers you will receive hot coffee."

Here the new arrivals undressed and went into the showers. When the room was full, the large steel doors were closed and locked. Guards grabbed infants by their little legs and swung them overhead, smashing their skulls against the wall.

Poison gas was let into the showers, and a loud clamoring could be heard. After about three minutes, the victims lungs slowly burst. Then the room was opened, and those who still showed signs of life were beaten to death.

Prisoner work details then pulled the corpses out, took their rings off, and cut their hair, which was gathered up and put in sacks. The corpses were counted, and taken to the ovens.

These scenes are repeated day after day. Each day a new train. Each day more fuel for the ovens. Soon the pace accelerates. Transport trains begin arriving with around 7,000 people daily.

Some time later the guards discovered that an Italian woman was a dancer. The roll call officer stripped her naked and ordered her to dance. She took advantage of a favorable moment, came near him, grabbed his pistol, and shot him dead. In the exchange of gunfire that followed, the SS won of course. What they did to her body is too gruesome to be described here.[4]

Question: Where was God? Weren't the Jews supposed to be God's chosen people? How could a just and righteous God allow the brutal genocide of His own people?

123

True story number four.

The year was 1996. The place was the rural district of Koh Thom in Cambodia. Five year old Sreypov Chan is a happy little girl. Her family owns a rice field, which gives them a little more than most. Little Sreypov's father tells her she will soon go to school, a happy prospect not many in this rural village enjoy.

But Sreypov's father dies. After that, her mother changes. All the love drains out of their lives. They are forced to move to a shack. When Sreypov is seven her mother sells her, telling her she will be a housekeeper.

When little Sreypov sees her first client, she repeatedly refuses and starts to cry. Furious, the pimp crushes up a handful of hot chili peppers and stuffs them into her vagina. He then takes a hot metal rod and jams it inside her as well. The pain is unbearable. Soon after, the client rapes her.

Virgins fetch an extremely high price, so the pimp stitches her up, so she'll scream in pain the next time, tricking the clients.

After Sreypov's initiation into sex slavery, she spends her days imprisoned in her room, with a guard stationed at the door. If she doesn't meet her quota of twenty men for the day, she is shocked with a loose wire from a socket in the wall.

This continues for three dark years. Life is reduced to a living hell. All hope has disappeared. Joy is a memory now faded into nothing.

But Sreypov is among the lucky few. At age ten she manages to escape the brothels and start a new life. Tens of millions are not so fortunate. As we write this, over twenty million children are enduring the same hell Sreypov once suffered.[5]

If you follow the end notes, you will find resources for how you can help the lost street children, and the victims of child sex trafficking.

But money and programs are not enough. For every child like Sreypov there are as many as 20 men per day willing to buy their services. The pimps are part of a vast mafia like network, which controls the police and government officials. Corruption often reaches the highest levels.

For every child who is rescued from sex slavery, dozens more are sold every day. It seems the demand for young children to rape is unceasing. There must be as many as 100 million degenerate men waiting to slake their sick appetites with these little children, using them like dishrags to mop up their lust.

Question: Where is God? Where is the Jesus who said, "Let the little children come to me and do not hinder them, for to such belongs the kingdom of heaven"?[6] If God lacks either the will or the power to rescue these little ones, how can He be worthy of being called God?

What is the answer? Where is God? What has become of this world, which seems to have descended into abject madness?

Dominion of the Damned

Where is God when disaster and evil prevail? The pat answer many give is "free will". While God is all-powerful, He is also all-loving. If God truly loves His children, it would be inconsistent to create us without free will. That would make us robots, not children who are free to respond to their Father's unconditional love.

Here's the rub. Free will opens the potential for evil. We just have to accept that. Too bad so sad. Get used to it.

But that's not a completely satisfying answer is it? In our gut we sense there's more. "Free will" is part of the answer, but it doesn't go nearly far enough. Let's set up an allegory to explain:

Your father is a local judge. He has built a dream house. It is absolutely stunning. It's perfect in every way. A comfortable, natural looking place to call home. There's a place for every activity, and the layout flows from one room to the next with exquisite design.

As soon as this wonderful house is complete, your father signs over the title deed to you. His only request is that you take care of his masterpiece and fill it with lots of beautiful grandchildren. You gladly agree, and take possession.

But along comes the con-man. He's a fast-talker who could sell refrigerators to polar bears. He's the world's most accomplished liar. Within minutes he has you questioning your father's motives. Before you know what's happened, you have signed over the title deed to the con-man, and given him possession of the house.

Your father, being a judge, calls the con-man into his courtroom. But it's too late. You've signed over the title deed. The papers have been filed with the county auditor. There's no legal recourse.

Cackling with glee, the con-man takes control of the beautiful home. Within days it is filled with drug dealers and prostitutes. Drunken partiers completely trash the once perfect masterpiece.

Do you see where we're going with this?

It's all about dominion.

Let's follow the trail of dominion.

The first to have dominion over the earth was God. God created the heavens and earth, and as creator He had the right of ownership and dominion (Genesis 1:1).

Then God gave dominion over all the earth and its creatures to mankind (Genesis 1:26). They had sovereign rule over the entire planet and all its creatures. But this wasn't to be done in isolation from God.

Before their rebellion, Adam and Eve enjoyed intimate connection with their Heavenly Father. They had access to infinite wisdom. Incredible resources were at their disposal as they carried out their task of dominion.

After Satan deceived Eve and she and Adam rebelled, God cursed the ground, and with it all the earth and the creatures on it. Clearly dominion was at that point taken from mankind.

No longer did they have access to God. Instead of infinite wisdom, they now had selfishness and pride and sin clouding their thinking. Murder was lurking in the wings.

Where previously mankind ruled over the earth, now the earth produced thorns and thistles. Instead of dominion, mankind was left with dust, and must return to dust at his end (Genesis 3:17-19). Nature itself turned against the human race.

So what happened to the dominion mankind once had? Without humans to rule, was the planet left to spin out of control? Was random chaos to replace dominion? Was everything left to a purposeless naturalism? Or was dominion given to another?

Let's listen in as Satan tempts Jesus:

Luke 4:5-6

*And the devil took him [Jesus] up and showed him all the kingdoms of the world in a moment of time, and said to him, "To you I will give all this authority and their glory, **for it has been delivered to me**, and I give it to whom I will."*

Clearly, Satan now has the dominion once possessed by mankind. He is described as the "god of this world" (2 Corinthians 4:4), the "ruler of this world" (John 12:31), and the "prince of the power of the air" (Ephesians 2:2).

Being now under the dominion of Satan, chaos and evil prevail in both nature and in human beings. But it is not the un-directed random chaos of naturalism. There is a very clear agenda.

Burn these words of Satan into your mind:

All this authority has been delivered to me!

Until you fully grasp this inescapable fact, you will never understand that what seems like random chaos and evil is in fact a well planned attack on the image-bearers of the Most High God.

Millions of street children are not dying because God is uncaring. Satan has dominion, and he hates them.

Massive natural disasters don't happen because God is impotent. Satan has dominion, and he hates God's creation.

Genocides and mass killing don't go on and on because God does not see. Satan has dominion, and he hates the human race.

Little children aren't trapped in the hell of sexual slavery because God lacks either the will or the power to rescue them. Satan has dominion, and he hates the most precious and vulnerable among us.

Evil and chaos are rampant because we human beings gave our dominion and our power over to the con-man.

This is the answer to the age-old question, which millions have asked over the centuries. This is that fundamental misunderstanding of the nature of this present world.

Satan now has tremendous power because WE gave it to him!

The evil kingdom which produces homeless children and sex slavery and genocides will never be overcome by throwing more money at the problems, or legislating more bureaucratic programs, or creating a utopia. The kingdom of Satan can only be overcome by transformed hearts. And hearts can only be transformed by the Kingdom of God progressively being established on earth.

The Cosmic Powers of This Present Darkness

For we do not wrestle against flesh and blood,
but against the rulers, against the authorities,
against the cosmic powers over this present darkness,
against the spiritual forces of evil in the heavenly places.
Ephesians 6:12

We have seen that Satan now has dominion over the earth. In Matthew 12:26, Jesus calls this dominion Satan's kingdom. The Greek word for "kingdom" in this verse is *basileia*, which is an abstract noun, denoting "sovereignty, royal power, dominion".[7] Just as it's not wise to give terrorists too much of the publicity they seek, we won't dwell on the kingdom of this present darkness long. But it is wise to know your enemy.

So here goes.

We saw earlier that the spiritual is actually more real than the physical. The spiritual world is populated by a variety of spirit-beings, divided into two kingdoms, with angels on the one hand, and demons on the other. According to Revelation 12:4, the ratio is one third demons to two thirds angels. The Bible tells us that there are "myriads" of angels, perhaps billions[8].

The first thing to notice is that Satan has a kingdom of "sovereignty" and "royal power". That sovereign royal power gives Satan and his demons the right and authority to control what happens on the earth. But as we will see in a couple of pages, Satan's dominion does not go completely unchallenged. The kingdom of Satan has its limits, but it is still a realm of pervasive evil.

There's a fascinating account of an encounter between angels and demons, and a hapless servant. It is recorded in 2 Kings 6:8-23.

The king of Syria has been trying to ambush the king of Israel, but someone always tips off the Israeli King, and he escapes. The Syrian king suspects a spy in his midst, but one of his servants tells him that "Elisha, the prophet who is in Israel, tells the king of Israel the words that you speak in your bedroom".

Enraged, the king of Syria sends a huge army, with cavalry and chariots. At night they surround the village where Elisha is staying. When Elisha's servant rises early next morning, he goes out and sees the massive army. Scared out of his wits, he runs to get Elisha.

Now focus your imagination and try to picture this. There stand Elisha and his servant, who's knees are undoubtedly knocking together. Two against thousands. With trembling voice, the servant says to Elisha, "Alas, my master! What shall we do?" Elisha's reply must have stunned and confused him:

"Do not be afraid, for those who are with us are more than those who are with them."

Imagine the servant's incredulity. "Master is off his rocker this morning! I've heard him say some strange things, but this takes the cake!"

Elisha just rolls his eyes, and prays:

"O Lord, please open his eyes that he may see."

So the Lord opens the eyes of the young man. When the servant looks up, on the surrounding mountains he sees horses and chariots of fire. An army of angels from the kingdom of God, come to do battle with the army of demons from the kingdom of Satan.

We'll let you read the rest of the story for yourself. The point is, the kingdom of this present darkness is very real.

It wasn't just back in Elisha's time that we see encounters between humans and the forces of evil. In the time of Jesus we read of people being possessed and harassed by demons. Even today, humans may encounter these evil powers.

The Prince of Persia

But the kingdom of Satan does not just concern itself with vulnerable individuals. As any kingdom does, Satan's kingdom has control over whole governments. The prophet Daniel got a glimpse of this when an angel named Gabriel came calling. Gabriel had been sent to bring a message to Daniel concerning the coming Messiah. But he had a little trouble getting through. Demonic forces, which Gabriel refers to as the prince and kings of Persia, prevented his passing through their territory:

Daniel 10:13
The prince of the kingdom of Persia withstood me twenty-one days, but Michael, one of the chief princes, came to help me, for I was left there with the kings of Persia.

Can you think of some current governments, and "non-state actors", which may be unknowingly operating under the influence of these satanic princes? How many unseen battles are taking place above our heads, and we never see them?

Billions of people are slaves in the kingdom of darkness, and don't even know it. They are victims, or perpetrators, or (more likely) both. Billions have never even heard of an alternate kingdom.

Mitigating Rays

This all may seem very depressing, but there are three mitigating rays of hope.

First, while Satan has a kingdom and dominion, he's on a leash. We see this in Job 1:12, when Satan must get God's permission before he messes with Job. His sovereign power can only extend as far as his kingdom. The Kingdom of God is present wherever the ambassadors of that kingdom take it. That's *you*, if you are a disciple of Jesus Christ. That's anyone anywhere, when they "call upon the name of the Lord" (Romans 10:13). It's like carrying a "bubble" of the Kingdom around with you wherever you go.

Second, God often takes evil and weaves it into good. We are told in Romans 8:28b that "for those who love God all things work together for good, for those who are called according to His purpose". Joseph learned this when his brothers sold him into slavery in Egypt. Years later he is raised to be Pharaoh's second in command, and becomes the means of saving millions from famine, including his jealous brothers. They "meant evil", but "God meant it for good".[9]

Third, there is a restraining power holding back the full impact of Satan's evil kingdom. This is revealed by the apostle Paul:

2 Thessalonians 2:7
For the mystery of lawlessness is already at work. Only he who now restrains it will do so until he is out of the way.

We learn three things from this: lawlessness is at work; some Person now restrains it; that Person will at some point be taken out of the way.

Who this "Restrainer" might be has been debated for centuries, but it really isn't pertinent to our current discussion.[10] The essential truth is that some Person is now restraining the full power of Satan's dark kingdom, and when the Restrainer is taken "out of the way", all hell will break loose. Quite literally.

Coram Domino
However, the Kingdom of God has not always been present on earth as it is now. Until about 2,000 years ago, the "ambassadors" of the King were rare. They were called prophets.

The original plan which God revealed to Abraham 4,000 years ago was for Israel to be a magnet, drawing the "nations" to God. This theme is all over the Old Testament. In Abraham and his descendants, the Jews, "all the families of the earth shall be blessed" (Genesis 12:3) . It's repeated again in Genesis 22:18, where God tells Abraham, "in your offspring shall all the nations of the earth be blessed".

When King Solomon dedicates the magnificent temple in Jerusalem, he makes it clear that "foreigners" will hear of this great God, and "pray toward this house", and he lays out the plan once more:

1 Kings 8:43b
...in order that all the peoples of the earth may know your name and fear you, as do your people Israel, and that they may know that this house that I have built is called by your name.

And the prophet Isaiah repeats it yet again. Israel is to be a "light for the nations":

Isaiah 49:6b
I will make you as a light for the nations, that my salvation may reach to the end of the earth.

But that didn't quite work out the way Abraham and Solomon might have thought. Instead of being a light to the nations, the Jews isolated themselves, and became extremely racist in their attitudes toward foreigners. Instead of drawing the nations to God, Israel adopted the idols of the nations, and trampled God's name in the mud.

In the 2,000 years between Abraham and Jesus there were very few ambassadors of the kingdom of God invading the kingdom of Satan.

Anno Domini

This was the state of the world when Almighty God stepped into history in the form of a baby, born to humble parents in a backwater village at the edge of the civilized world.

What happened over the next 33 years would turn Satan's kingdom on its head, inaugurate the Kingdom of God, and begin the recapture of dominion lost.

Bruised Head, Bruised Heel

*I will put enmity between you and the woman, and
between your offspring and her offspring; he shall bruise
your head, and you shall bruise his heel.*
Genesis 3:15

This is the very first "Messianic" prophecy in the Bible. It comes immediately after Adam and Eve have rebelled. God is laying out the consequences of that rebellion. But in the midst of the litany of "curses", God drops this hint as to how it will all eventually be resolved.

Satan, as the serpent, is being addressed here. He's going to get his head bruised (some translations have "wounded"). But first, Satan is going to bruise or "wound" the heel of the offspring of the woman. Note that Jesus had a human mother (Mary), but no human father. The "seed" of Mary (Jesus) can be traced directly back to the "seed" of Eve.

When the Roman nail was driven through the heel of Jesus to fasten Him on the cross, the prophecy quoted above was partially fulfilled. Satan "wounded" the heel of the seed of the woman. But while he may have thought this was a victory, he seems to have overlooked the rest of the prophesy:

he shall bruise your head

That's a potentially fatal wound. It will eventually take its fatal toll, but it's coming in slow-motion. This head-bruising did not start at the Cross. Jesus was confronting demons and invading Satan's kingdom long before that.

137

As the very first act of His public ministry, in a synagogue in His hometown of Nazareth, Jesus was asked to read from the scroll of Isaiah. Here's what He read:

Isaiah 61:1b
The LORD has anointed me to bring good news to the poor; he has sent me to bind up the brokenhearted, to proclaim liberty to the captives...

This was a prophesy of the *coming of the kingdom of God on earth*. For the Jews listening to Jesus, Isaiah was their most revered prophet. They were probably very familiar with this prophecy. They knew exactly what it was about. When He was finished, Jesus rolled up the scroll and sat down.

What He said next absolutely stunned the congregation.

Luke 4:21
Today this Scripture has been fulfilled in your hearing.

So according to Jesus, the kingdom of God was inaugurated that day. What Jesus and His disciples did from then until He hung on the cross, was the initial invasion of a long war. It was Inchon, it was Omaha Beach, it was the Rubicon, all rolled together.[11]

Satan's sovereign power and authority were directly challenged. Where Satan's kingdom brought sickness, Jesus healed. Where the kingdom of darkness caused blindness, Jesus opened eyes . Where demons possessed and oppressed, Jesus cast them into herds of swine. Even the dead were being raised to life.

But the most damaging blow was the "good news" being proclaimed to a people enslaved by the Kingdom of Satan; a people made captive to sin, and oppressed by the Curse.

Liberty! Freedom!

And best of all, *relationship* with our Heavenly Father! The Curse is cured! The slaves set free! We no longer have to be captive citizens in the dark kingdom, doing the bidding of its ugly king.

Wherever someone responded to the good news, a beachhead was established. Little bubbles of God's kingdom were popping up everywhere Jesus went.

But the best was yet to come. When Jesus died, Satan may have been dancing a jig around the cross, but what he didn't realize was that this was a major victory for the kingdom of God.

1 Corinthians 15:56
The sting of death is sin, and the power of sin is the law.

The power of sin is the law. The law required the death of a perfect person. Jesus, God in the flesh, paid that price. He paid the penalty of sin, and won the victory, and set the stage for the full-blown invasion of the kingdom of darkness.

On the cross, the death of Jesus met the *penalty* of sin. But what happened next broke the *power* of death. The Apostle Paul, quoting the prophet Hosea, was ecstatic in the victory.

1 Corinthians 15:55
O death, where is your victory? O death, where is your sting?

Here in the Pacific Northwest, some of us get very vocal when celebrating a hard-fought Seahawks win. How much more ought we celebrate the victory Jesus won over sin and death? It's $10^{400,000}$ more awesome than Super Bowl XLVIII!

Hallelujah! Hallelujah! Hallelujah!

An Empty Tomb Changes *Everything*

The power driving the dominion of Satan is the power of death. Death was the consequence of the rebellion of the first two humans. Death is the second most powerful force in the universe. It is stronger than the Strong Nuclear Force, which keeps atoms from flying apart at the speed of light. Death is stronger than the Higgs Field, which imparts mass to everything in the universe.

Death has the power to hold you in the grave in this age, and to hold you in hell in the next. And so the ultimate question is, what can conquer death? What has that much power?

Before we can answer that question, we must first know exactly what death is. Death is your ultimate enemy. You had better know what you're facing. The Greek word for death often used in the Bible is *thanatos*. Here's the best definition we've found. It's from *Vine's Complete Expository Dictionary*:

thanatos - the separation of the soul from the body, the latter ceasing to function and turning to dust, but the soul lives on.

However, there's more. Every human being who ever lived faces the possibility of *two* deaths. The first is *thanatos*. But the Bible describes a "second death".[12] Here's how Vines puts it:

Death is the opposite of life; it never denotes nonexistence. As spiritual life is conscious existence in communion with God, so spiritual death is conscious existence in separation from God.

At its essence, then, death is separation. It's like the inverted spiritual equivalent of the Strong Nuclear Force. Instead of binding things together which would normally fly apart, death rips things apart which were designed to be intimately bound. When God created human beings, He made their bodies and their spirits one, and He made them to be connected to Him. Death breaks both bonds.

At some point your soul will be separated from your body. Your body will turn to dust, but your soul will live on in one of two states. But what determines which state? Here's the critical piece of the puzzle. To avoid the second death, you must have what Charles Wesley called a *second life*.

> *Sudden expired the legal strife,*
> *'twas then I ceased to grieve;*
> *my second, real, living life*
> *I then began to live.*[13]

This, then, is the answer to the question of what can conquer death? What has that much power? According to the definition from Vines above, "death is the opposite of life". Death is the second most powerful force in the universe, but Life, it's polar opposite, has it beat.

But not just any life has that power. The most powerful force in the universe is the Life which was at work in the resurrection of Jesus Christ. This was a Life force which could withstand death on the Cross, and the weight of all the sins of all humanity.

The power which raised Jesus from the dead is the only power in the universe greater than the power of death. That's why the Apostle Paul said that if Jesus Christ was *not* raised from the dead, then we're all doomed.

1 Corinthians 15:17-19
And if Christ has not been raised, your faith is futile and you are still in your sins. Then those also who have fallen asleep in Christ have perished. If in Christ we have hope in this life only, we are of all people most to be pitied.

This is the central point of all history. The Resurrection of Jesus Christ. This is a non-negotiable tenant of Christianity. Without the Resurrection, all bets are off.

In the very next verse, Paul goes on to affirm that Jesus has *indeed* risen from the dead. But there's more. The resurrection of Jesus Christ is the "first-fruits" of more to come.

1 Corinthians 15:20-21
But in fact Christ has been raised from the dead, the first-fruits of those who have fallen asleep. For as by a man came death, by a man has come also the resurrection of the dead.

In the ancient Jewish culture, the first of a crop to be harvested was called the "first-fruits". If the first-fruits were good, it was a sign that the harvest to follow would go well. A portion of the first-fruits were to be offered to God in the Temple in Jerusalem.

Paul applies this terminology to the Resurrection of Jesus. It is the first-fruits of a great "harvest" of resurrection to come. Here's more from Vines:

[The first-fruits are] *the earnest or pledge, that the whole resurrection harvest will follow, so that our faith is not vain, nor our hope limited to this life.*

Many have compiled historical and logical analysis of the Resurrection.[14] Here are three main points.

Point One. There was a historical man named Jesus who lived between 4 BC and 28 or 30 AD, and was crucified by Pontius Pilate. For this we have the testimony of Roman historian Flavius Josephus, who was born just a few years after the Crucifixion:

Now there was about this time Jesus, a wise man. For he was a doer of startling deeds, a teacher of people...And when Pilate, because of an accusation made by the leading men among us, condemned him to the cross, those who had loved him previously did not cease to do so.[15]

Point Two. The burial of a *dead* Jesus. Some have claimed that Jesus wasn't really dead, or that he wasn't really buried in the tomb. The problem is, Joseph of Arimathea and Nicodemus, both prominent members of the ruling council, were involved in the burial preparations of Jesus. Modern scholars agree that the burial story is one of the best established facts. Joseph and Nicodemus were too well known for fictitious stories to be pulled off.

Point Three. The empty tomb. This is the biggie. Over 500 people claimed to be eyewitnesses.[16] They *saw* the risen Jesus. Nobody would be foolish enough to claim this when everyone knew where the tomb was, and could go look. If the body was still there, then all these witnesses would have been debunked long ago.

The Jewish priests bribed the soldiers who guarded the tomb to say that "His disciples came by night and stole him away while we were asleep".[17] There are several problems with this fabrication, besides the fact that they're admitting that the tomb was empty.

First, no 1st century soldier would ever fall asleep on duty. The penalty was death. They were paid to lie, but they never would have actually fallen asleep on duty in the first place. It was just too risky.

Second, a large boulder, big enough to cover the entrance to a tomb, was rolled in place, and sealed with wax, imprinted with the official government stamp.[18] Allowing this seal to be broken was an act of treason, even more serious than falling asleep. The soldiers would have done everything in their power to prevent that.

Third, assuming that *all* the soldiers were sound asleep, could the disciples have rolled a massive boulder away from the mouth of the tomb without waking them up? The soldiers had more than one problem with their lie. Not only did they fall asleep on duty and allow the official seal to be broken, but they were too zonked to notice a huge stone rumbling across the ground?

Fourth, if they had all remained asleep, then how did they know that it was the *disciples* who stole the body? It could have been grave robbers. If they somehow woke up and identified the thieves, then why couldn't these trained soldiers overpower a few fishermen?

Fifth, the empty tomb was discovered by *women*. In 1st century Jewish culture, the testimony of a woman was considered worthless.

The fact that lowly women were the chief witnesses to the fact of the empty tomb means it is highly unlikely that this was a story concocted by Jesus' followers, or even a legend which later developed. Nobody planning a hoax would cast women as their prime witnesses.

Here are the established facts, acknowledged by most historians[19]: Jesus was a real person. He was crucified by Pontius Pilate. He died. He was buried in a rock tomb which was covered by a huge boulder, bearing an official seal, and guarded by a squad of soldiers. After three days, the tomb was discovered to be empty.

The story concocted by the Jewish priests is riddled with impossible holes. Over 500 eyewitnesses saw Jesus after His resurrection. There is no valid explanation for the empty tomb other than the Resurrection. The evidence is conclusive far beyond a reasonable doubt.

The power which raised Jesus from the dead is the only power in the universe greater than the power of death. The power which raised Jesus from the dead is the same power which will "resurrect" the vast universe at the end of history. It's the same power which can give you that "second life" Charles Wesley spoke of.

Romans 8:11
*If the Spirit of him who raised Jesus from the dead dwells in you, **he who raised Christ Jesus from the dead will also give life to your mortal bodies** through his Spirit who dwells in you.*

On the cross, the death of Jesus met the *penalty* of sin. But the Resurrection of Jesus broke the *power* of death. It is on this basis, and this basis alone, that you can escape the kingdom of darkness and enter the kingdom of God.

Colossians 1:13
He has delivered us from the domain of darkness and transferred us to the kingdom of his beloved Son.

An empty tomb changes *everything*!

Kingdom Come...Now And Not Yet

J esus inaugurated the kingdom of God on earth. Satan's kingdom and dominion are being directly challenged. Victory over sin and death were won on the Cross and through the Resurrection. "Thy kingdom come", as we pray in the Lord's Prayer, is already here.

Jesus told the Pharisees that the kingdom of God was "in the midst of you". What did He mean by that?

Luke 17:21b
...for behold, the kingdom of God is in the midst of you.

Was Jesus telling the Pharisees that the kingdom of God was in their hearts? No! The kingdom of God was most definitely *not* in the hearts of the Pharisees. Jesus was telling them that it was within their *grasp*. That's the meaning of the Greek word translated "midst". The Kingdom is here, in our midst, within our *grasp*.

But the ultimate victory is yet to come, when the "kingdom of the world has become the kingdom of our Lord", as the angels shouted:

Revelation 11:15b
The kingdom of the world has become the kingdom of our Lord and of his Christ, and he shall reign forever and ever!

There's a war on. There are still enemies to defeat:

1 Corinthians 15:25
For he must reign until he has put all his enemies under his feet.

There are enemies yet to be crushed under the feet of King Jesus. The clash of kingdoms goes on. And we are a part of it. In fact, we humans are at the front lines:

147

Ephesians 6:12
For we do not wrestle against flesh and blood, but against the rulers, against the authorities, against the cosmic powers over this present darkness, against the spiritual forces of evil in the heavenly places.

Jesus is reigning. The King has come. The Kingdom is here and now. The King is crushing His enemies underfoot. But look who's feet He is using to do the enemy-stomping:

Romans 16:20
The God of peace will soon crush Satan under your feet. The grace of our Lord Jesus Christ be with you.

But let us not think that we have a commission to do battle with demonic forces in our own power. If any of Christ's enemies are to be crushed under our feet, it must be done the way He began it.

Think about it. How did Jesus defeat sin and Satan? How was His kingdom inaugurated? Before there could be His resurrection, there had to be the Cross. Jesus died. So must you. You must die to Self. We'll unpack this in the upcoming chapters.

The kingdom of God is present and active in this world, but there's a war on. In the next section we will look at how you can become a citizen of that kingdom, and join the fight.

Listen carefully to some of the last words Jesus spoke on earth:

Matthew 28:18-20
And Jesus came and said to them, "All authority in heaven and on earth has been given to me. Go therefore and make disciples of all nations, baptizing them in the name of the Father and of the Son and of the Holy Spirit, teaching them to observe all that I have commanded you. And behold, I am with you always, to the end of the age."

[1] The young American was Everett Swanson, who went on to found Compassion International. The story of their founding, and how you can help the world's street children, can be found on their website at www.compassion.com.

[2] This story was carried in *The National*, December 1, 2015 edition; by Matteo Fagotto.

[3] Matthew 8:23-27.

[4] From *The Buchenwald Report*, translated and edited by David A Hackett, (Westview Press, Boulder/San Francisco/Oxford, 1995); pages 349-350.

[5] Sreypov Chan's life story was told in *Marie Clair* magazine by Abigail Pesta, July 20, 2011 edition. See www.humantrafficking.org for ways to help the victims of sex trafficking.

[6] Matthew 19:14.

[7] Vine's Complete Expository Dictionary.

[8] Revelation 5:11.

[9] Genesis 37-50.

[10] Some think this Restrainer is the Holy Spirit, some think he is the archangel Michael, others think it is human governments. The problem with him being the Holy Spirit is that lots of people are going to be saved *after* the unleashing of Hell, and the Holy Spirit is the only means of new birth, so that can't happen if He has been taken "out of the way". The problem with him being Michael is that, no disrespect, he just seems to lack the juice to go head to head with Lucifer. Human governments are a non-starter for obvious reasons, since it's a "he" who restrains.

[11] The invasion at Inchon Bay was General Douglas MacArthur's brilliant end-run around invading North Korean forces in 1950. Omaha Beach was part of the 1945 D-Day invasion, the largest in history. In 49 BC, Julius Caesar crossed the Rubicon river with his legions, to launch the Roman Civil War.

[12] Jude 1:12, Revelation 2:11, Revelation 20:6, Revelation 20:14, Revelation 21:8.

---

[13] Charles Wesley (1707-1788), *O For A Thousand Tongues To Sing*. This stanza is one of many which are not included in the version of this hymn we sing today.

[14] See Josh McDowell. *Evidence That Demands a Verdict*; William Lane Craig's *Reasonable Faith*; J.P. Moreland's *Scaling the Secular City*; Gary Habermas' *The Case for the Resurrection of Jesus* and *Did Jesus Rise from the Dead?*, a debate with then-atheist Anthony Flew; Arthur Michael Ramsey, *God, Christ, and the World*.

[15] Book 18, Chapter 3, 3, *Jewish Antiquities*, Flavius Josephus (37 AD - 100 AD). The section we quote is often called the *Testimonium Flavianum*. See note 19.

[16] 1 Corinthians 15:3-8.

[17] Matthew 28.

[18] Matthew 27:66.

[19] A majority of secular (atheist, agnostic) historians, Jewish scholars, and Christian theologians, acknowledge these basic facts about the historicity of Jesus, His crucifixion, death and burial, and the empty tomb. Much of the evidence comes from Josephus, a Jew who grew up in Israel shortly after the events of the crucifixion, and who later defected to the Romans, became a Roman citizen, and one of their most respected historians. Most surviving copies of Josephus' *Jewish Antiquities* include detailed descriptions not only of the empty tomb, but of the Resurrection, and a clear declaration that Jesus was the Jewish Messiah, the Son of God. Arabic copies of *Jewish Antiquities* closely match surviving Latin copies, but omit these overtly Christian details. Most scholars reject these "Christianized" portions, and we have not used them in the evidence we've presented.

Section Five | Citizenship

Behold, I stand at the door and knock. If anyone hears my voice and opens the door, I will come in to him and eat with him, and he with me.
Revelation 3:20

Twisted, I Is

N otice anything wrong with the title of this chapter? The verb conjugation is just slightly off. The base verb is "to be". "Twisted, I Is" sounds a little off to a native English speaker. It probably should have been "Twisted, I Am". But since "I Am" is the name God gives Himself[1], we didn't want to sound presumptuous (insert smiley-face).

Here's the point we're trying to make. That title is a picture of you. You don't have to be "off " by much to be on the wrong side of God. You don't have to be an ISIS terrorist to be "bad". In God's economy, if you miss the mark, even by just a little, you have still missed the mark. The Greek word used in the Bible for "sin" is *hamartano*, which literally means "to miss the mark"[2].

Many people — perhaps a majority — hardly ever think about it. We're too busy just surviving from one day to the next. We all like to think of ourselves as basically decent human beings. We walk out the days of our lives in a blind self-justification. I'm OK. Or at least OK *enough*.

That's not the way God sees it. That's not the way the Bible describes the situation. We know this may sound harsh, but in its essence a sin — any sin — is eternally deadly. If it's by an inch or a mile, a miss is still a miss.

Think about that for a moment. A harmless bit of gossip, a slightly unkind word, carries in its essence the same poison as terrorists slaughtering thousands of people.

Don't think so? Listen to how Jesus describes it:

Matthew 5:22
But I say to you that everyone who is angry with his brother will be liable to judgment; whoever insults his brother will be liable to the council; **and whoever says, 'You fool!' will be liable to the hell of fire.**

That doesn't leave much wiggle room. Jesus is presenting a stark contrast between who we think we are, and who we really are. Are you ready to face the clear cold truth? It would be easy to read the list of horrors we've presented in previous sections and think, "Wow, I'm glad I'm not *that* bad".

Please don't try to insulate yourself from this. The Kingdom of Satan and the Kingdom of God are at war, and there's no middle ground. You are either in one kingdom or you are in the other.

Being a *mostly* good person will not buy you a passport into the kingdom of God. Satan would like nothing more than for you to be a "good" person. "Good" people are in no need of a savior. Healthy people don't think they need a doctor.

Luke 5:31-32
And Jesus answered them, "Those who are well have no need of a physician, but those who are sick. I have not come to call the righteous but sinners to repentance."

You can think you're healthy, but have a malignant cancer growing undetected inside. No matter how good and kind and loving you may be, if you are walking around in a human skin, then you carry a cancer inside far more deadly than bronchogenic carcinoma[3]. Sin.

What are you going to do about it?

Look, God's standard is perfection. That's how Adam and Eve started out. That's where we need to get back to. Are you there yet? Anything less, and we are left with future centuries of bloodshed and destruction, if we even last that long.

The problem started in Eden. Two humans believed the lie and it brought a curse of death. The link to God, the only source of life, was broken. The curse of death is on you. You are *dead*. That's a pretty serious disease.

Just about every belief system on earth (with the exception of Humanism) recognizes the poison. For Hindus, karma is the cure. For Buddhists it's the "Noble Eightfold Path". For utopian-minded political systems, repressive bureaucracies and redistribution are the answer.

When you examine their core doctrine, even some supposedly-Christian groups and legalistic churches rely on what is essentially *behavior modification* for the "cure". That's what they all have in common. They all involve lots and lots of human effort. They all have their long lists of do's and don'ts They all tell you that the poison must be transformed, the cancer must be reformed, the universities turned into Marxist reeducation camps. Behavior modification.

But stop and think for a moment. Can a poison be transformed? Can a cancer be reformed? Can sin be legislated away? As we said earlier, the phrase "lipstick on a pig" comes to mind.

You don't transform a poison, you counteract it with an antidote. You don't reform a cancer, you kill it. You don't reeducate sin, you crucify it.

The cure for the cancer was prescribed by Isaiah more than seven hundred years before Jesus was born:

Isaiah 53:5
But he was pierced for our transgressions; he was crushed for our iniquities; upon him was the chastisement that brought us peace, and with his wounds we are healed.

So the real question is, how can you lay your hands on that cure? You have a poison. You have a cancer. External band-aids are useless. You can't put a topical cream of human effort on the outside, and expect sin to magically go away. How do you get the antidote and the cure *inside* of you?

That's a question which Jesus addressed head-on, when an unlikely visitor came calling one night.

Jesus And The Night Visitor

I
t was late at night. No prying eyes. No listening ears. Little chance of discovery. The risk was great. He had a reputation to maintain. He was a Pharisee, and a prominent member of the Sanhedrin, the ruling council. He was probably one of the most respected men in Jerusalem. But the one he sought was known as a rebel. A troublemaker who defied the Establishment.

Nicodemus went searching in the night for the man he called "Rabbi", the teacher whom he somehow instinctively knew was sent from God. When he finally found Him, he acknowledged as much. "No one can do these signs that you do unless God is with him", he said.

The reply which Jesus gave stunned Nicodemus, and rocked his tidy Pharisaic worldview to its core.

John 3:3b
Truly, truly, I say to you, unless one is born again he cannot see the kingdom of God.

In order to understand where Nicodemus was coming from, let's look at the beliefs the Pharisees held in 26 AD[4].

Moses gave us the Ten Commandments. But in the years between then and the time of Nicodemus, 613 other commands, compiled in the *Mishneh*, had been added. To these, the Pharisee's had added thousands more in the form of oral laws and interpretations, which we know today as the *Midrash*.

The tithing of herbs, how to pray out loud, the exact distance which may be traveled on the Sabbath, were among the meticulous lists of religious rules and regulations.

Pharisees revered the oral law so highly that it was said to go back to Moses himself, paralleling the written law. Josephus records that the Pharisees were "experts in the interpretation of the Law".[5]

Nicodemus had apparently come with deep questions. Perhaps he sought clarification on which parts of the Mishneh and Midrash were most important. He had spent a lifetime building his stairway to heaven, and he wanted to make sure he had every rung in place.

He honored Jesus by calling Him "Rabbi". He acknowledged that He was "a teacher come from God". Jesus didn't even give him a split second to ask any questions of legality. "Unless one is born again he cannot see the kingdom of God", was all the information He was going to give. Huh?

Nicodemus was obviously confused. "How can a man be born when he is old? Can he enter a second time into his mother's womb and be born?" he asked. Jesus now takes an ax to the old man's stairway to heaven, and chops it into splinters.

John 3:5b-6
Unless one is born of water and the Spirit, he cannot enter the kingdom of God. That which is born of the flesh is flesh, and that which is born of the Spirit is spirit.

"That which is born of the flesh is flesh". It will always be flesh. Dear friend Nicodemus, your rules and regulations will never transform flesh into spirit. "That which is born of the Spirit is spirit."

The alternate meaning of the Greek phrase "born again" is "born from above". The Greek, being purposely ambiguous, can mean either "again" or "from above".[6] In this case, we suspect it means both. If you've only had a *human* birth, then you're going to need another, different kind of birth...one from above. Born of the Spirit.

Jesus is telling Nicodemus that he can't reform the flesh. The poison cannot be transformed. The cancer can't be reformed. Sin will never be legislated away. Old man, your rules and regulations are only smearing lipstick on a pig.

Romans 8:8
Those who are in the flesh cannot please God.

The flesh can never please God. Nicodemus, you need the Spirit of God, birthed inside. A new life. A spirit life.

As long as you walk this old earth, you'll still have the flesh to contend with. But something new and powerful and alive is here. Being born again, born from above, born of the Spirit, is not something you can learn. No amount of practice will ever get you born again.

Trying to debate faith is like trying to explain quantum mechanics to an amoeba. Faith is beyond intellectual comprehension. You can't study your way to the new birth. Nobody can debate you into it. Think about it. A human baby doesn't study to be born. She can't be debated into coming out of the womb. It's a natural process. Life comes from life. That's a universal law, and it applies here, to the spirit life being born in you. Spirit comes from Spirit.

So how does it work? That's the final question Nicodemus asked.

John 3:9
Nicodemus said to him, "How can these things be?"

How can Nicodemus be "born again"? As with everything, the process begins with God. He is calling. Are you listening? Jesus is knocking. Will you open the door?

Revelation 3:20
Behold, I stand at the door and knock. ***If anyone hears my voice and opens the door,*** *I will come in to him and eat with him, and he with me.*

Is that all there is to it? You respond? You open the door? Well, there's more to opening the door than you may think. There are consequences to letting Jesus in. God has very specific surrender terms, which we will look at in the next chapter.

As a side note, it appears from John 19:39 that old Nicodemus finally got it. By the time of Jesus' death, he is bold enough to publicly reveal what he now believes. He comes with Joseph of Arimethea, in the blazing light of day for all to see, to take the body of Jesus and prepare it for burial.

Battleship In Tokyo Bay

On July 26, 1945, the Allies called for the unconditional surrender of the Japanese armed forces. The alternative was "prompt and utter destruction". The Japanese response was to ignore the ultimatum.

Eleven days later, on August 6, the U.S. dropped an atomic bomb on Hiroshima, Japan. About 146,000 human beings died as a result. Some of them were instantly vaporized where they stood, leaving nothing but a shadow scorched on the ground.

President Truman called for Japan's surrender 16 hours later, warning them to "expect a rain of ruin from the air, the like of which has never been seen on this earth". There was no response.

Three days later the U.S. dropped a plutonium implosion bomb on the city of Nagasaki. 80,000 dead. Seven days later the Japanese finally agreed to the Allies' terms. Total unconditional surrender.

The battleship USS Missouri, with an armada of 150 Allied ships, steamed into Tokyo Bay on the morning of August 29. Four days later, at 8:05 AM, Fleet Admiral C.W. Nimitz boarded the Missouri. By 8:45 AM, General of the Army Douglas MacArthur arrived. The Japanese delegation arrived in a whale boat ten minutes later.

MacArthur read a very short prepared statement, then the "Instrument of Surrender" was signed. Nimitz signed for the United States, and representatives of Britain, France, Russia, and China signed. Finally, the Japanese signed. It all took less than 30 minutes. World War Two was officially over.

Total unconditional surrender.

Those are the surrender terms being offered in the clash of kingdoms we looked at in the previous section. The Kingdom of Satan and the Kingdom of God are at war. There is no middle ground. You are either in one kingdom or you are in the other.

Total unconditional surrender means there can be no half-measures. Simply praying a formulaic prayer, or filling out a card, or walking down an aisle, or raising your hand, are not enough if you have not met God's surrender terms. It's total unconditional surrender, or something infinitely more devastating than a plutonium implosion bomb.

This clash of kingdoms will one day end. You already know which kingdom will win. Where do you want to be standing when the dust settles? Ground Zero at Hiroshima, or the deck of the battleship Missouri?

Now, you may be thinking, "What about John 3:16? Didn't Jesus say all you have to do is believe in Him?" OK, let's take a look at it.

John 3:16

For God so loved the world, that he gave his only Son, that whoever believes in him should not perish but have eternal life.

Our answer would be to ask a question back at you. "Believe what, exactly?" That Jesus was a real person? That He died for your sins? That He is God? Well, according to James, that kind of belief won't get you very far.

James 2:19 (NLT)

You say you have faith, for you believe that there is one God. Good for you! **Even the demons believe this, and they tremble in terror.**

Demons know who God is, and they know who Jesus is. It is very likely that demons were present at the Crucifixion and Resurrection. They know the facts. They believe these things because they saw them in person. Believing the facts *about* Jesus won't help demons any more than it will help you.

The key phrase in John 3:16 is "believes in". The Greek word is *piteuo*. It means "to place confidence in", "to trust". It is reliance upon, not mere credence. To commit, to entrust oneself wholly.[6] Do you see the difference? Demons will never do that. Will you?

Some may answer us back by citing Romans 10:9:

Romans 10:9
Because, if you confess with your mouth that Jesus is Lord and believe in your heart that God raised him from the dead, you will be saved.

Does that mean that if you speak the words "Jesus is Lord", and acknowledge the fact that God raised Him from the dead, then you've got your passport to God's kingdom? Let's look a little closer. This Scripture doesn't say just *speak* the words. It says *confess*.

You're not just *saying* Jesus is Lord, you are *surrendering* to His lordship. And His lordship is based on the power of His resurrection. Do you see the difference? Jesus made it abundantly clear that just calling Him "Lord" won't cut it:

Matthew 7:21
Not everyone who says to me, "Lord, Lord," will enter the kingdom of heaven, but the one who does the will of my Father who is in heaven.

So, what is the "will of the Father"? Jesus answered that one:

John 6:40
For this is the will of my Father, that everyone who looks on the Son and believes in him should have eternal life, and I will raise him up on the last day.

The will of the Father is for people to "look" on Jesus (turn their attention from self to Him), believe, and receive eternal life. To see how that works, let's look at a *promise*, and a *presence*.

Ezekiel 36:26-27
*And I will give you a new heart, and a new spirit I will put within you. And I will remove the heart of stone from your flesh and give you a heart of flesh. **And I will put my Spirit within you, and cause you to walk in my statutes** and be careful to obey my rules.*

A "new heart". That's the *promise*. God's "Spirit within you", causing you to "walk in my statutes". That's how you do "the will of my Father who is in heaven".

The *presence* came on the Day of Pentecost in the year 29 AD, in an upper room in Jerusalem:

Acts 2:4
And they were all filled with the Holy Spirit and began to speak in other tongues as the Spirit gave them utterance.

That's the fulfillment of the promise given in Ezekiel 36. The presence of God in human hearts. The immediate result was "doing the will of the Father". Thousands "looked on Jesus", and believed.

See how the Father works His will. Those "other tongues" the disciples were speaking were not an unintelligible babble, or the "tongues of angels". They were the distinct human languages of every nationality gathered in Jerusalem for the Passover.

This drew a huge crowd, and they said to each other, "We hear them telling in our own tongues the mighty works of God". Peter's sermon pointed them to Jesus, and about 3,000 looked on the Son, surrendered, and received eternal life. The will of the Father.

Still think just believing in Jesus is enough? Then here's another question. Which Jesus do you believe in? The Jesus Who said this:

Matthew 16:24-25
*Then Jesus told his disciples, "If anyone would come after me, let him **deny himself** and **take up his cross and follow me**. For whoever would save his life will lose it, but whoever **loses his life** for my sake will find it."*

Look at the *verbs* in these verses. *Deny* yourself (that's surrender). *Take up* your cross (an instrument of surrender). *Follow* Him (surrender to His way). And then the final verb: *Lose* your life. That's the ultimate surrender.

Total unconditional surrender.

If you respond at all, we see three possibilities here. (1) You *say* you believe in Jesus and go on your merry way. (2) You *accept* Jesus as Lord, and try your best to live that out. (3) You *surrender* to His lordship, and learn to walk in a new spirit-life.

First possibility. You pray a "sinners prayer", get your fire insurance, and then skip through life as if nothing happened.

When I (Stan) first surrendered to Jesus, it was during the 1970's "Jesus" movement in Southern California. The group I hung out with would go up to Angeles Temple every week to get "slain in the spirit", just for the high. Then they'd go back home, shoot up, and sleep with their girlfriend. After a short time with these "Jesus Freaks", it was clear that I was changing, but they weren't.

I had surrendered to Jesus, and was learning what that meant. God had led me to Romans 6 when He first called me. I wanted to walk in that "newness of life", but I knew that it came by way of *total* surrender...being "baptized into His death".

Romans 6:3-4
Do you not know that all of us who have been baptized into Christ Jesus were **baptized into his death?** *We were buried therefore with him by baptism into death, in order that, just as Christ was raised from the dead by the glory of the Father, we too might* **walk in newness of life.**

Second possibility. You "accept" Jesus, and work very hard to do "good works". Nowhere in the Bible does anyone "accept" Jesus. He doesn't need your acceptance. If you haven't surrendered to Him "by baptism into death", then all your efforts are in the flesh. Nicodemus learned that lesson. Jesus had a few words for folks who try to perform "mighty works", but have never really surrendered:

Matthew 7:22-23
On that day many will say to me, 'Lord, Lord, did we not prophesy in your name, and cast out demons in your name, and do many mighty works in your name?' And then will I declare to them, 'I never knew you; depart from me, you workers of lawlessness.'

Third possibility. You surrender to Jesus. You now have two natures. The flesh and the spirit. You're walking around in a skin of flesh, but your *real* life is in the spirit. That's the life which will go on into eternity. The more you learn how to live that life now, the richer your life in eternity will be.But it comes by way of the Cross.

Galatians 2:20
I have been crucified with Christ. It is no longer I who live, but Christ who lives in me. And the life I now live in the flesh I live by faith in the Son of God, who loved me and gave himself for me.

Our analogy of the Japanese surrender is a picture of your surrender to God. The Japanese people were still there. They were not annihilated or deported. They surrendered. The Allies came in. And a new country was born from the ashes.[7]

It's the same with you and God. He loves you as a unique creation. When you surrender, God is not going to annihilate who you are. A new "you" will be born from the ashes, but you're still going to be uniquely *you*.

All this talk of total surrender and losing your life and being baptized into His death may sound rather scary. But it's not. It's the exact opposite. It's the ultimate expression of *LOVE*.

Look at how Jesus defined love:

John 15:13
Greater love has no one than this, that someone lay down his life for his friends.

God so loved the world that He *gave*. The Son of God loved me, and *gave* Himself for me. That's *your* best expression of love to Him. *Give* yourself.

It isn't complicated. This isn't rocket science. God is calling. Are you listening?

Turn to Him. Listen. *Surrender.*

A Tale of Two Selves

*To put off your old self, which belongs to your former
manner of life and is corrupt through deceitful desires,
and to be renewed in the spirit of your minds, and to put
on the new self, created after the likeness of God...*
Ephesians 4:22-24a

So what happens when you finally surrender to God? If all
your sins are forgiven, then does that mean you will never
sin again? Are you now perfect? Or if you do sin, does it
really matter? Jesus paid the price, so does that mean you can sin all
you want, and God is required to look the other way?

We see too many Christians today who are confused about who
they are in Christ. The apostle Paul, in the verse quoted above, refers
to the dual nature of the believer. We have an "old self", the flesh,
and we have a "new self", the spirit.

How do these two "selves" interact? How does the spirit affect the
flesh? It's in the renewal of your *mind*. That is always going to be the
battleground.

Your mind sits between your flesh-self and your spirit-self. The
flesh will always be flesh, and will never submit to God, and will
always pull your mind away from Him. The spirit will always submit
to God, and will always pull your mind to God.

God "began a good work in you" the moment you surrendered to
Him. God will continue that work. He will bring it to completion, as
your mind is progressively set on the things of the Spirit.

Philippians 1:6
*And I am sure of this, that he who began a good work in you
will bring it to completion at the day of Jesus Christ.*

Understanding that there's a battle going on for your mind is very very important. If you don't understand the pull your two "selves" are making, then the flesh will win by default. Guaranteed. You must start by recognizing your dual nature. There are some who do not. They claim that once you have been "saved", then you no longer have a sin-nature.

This is so dangerous that we must be very careful here. The lie of the "sinless" Christian has led to shipwrecked faith for many, when the house of cards comes crashing down, and the promised sinlessness never materializes.

The Bible makes it very clear. Everyone, even Christians, have that old sin nature we all inherited from Adam:

1 John 1:8; 10
If we say we have no sin, we deceive ourselves, and the truth is not in us...If we say we have not sinned, we make him a liar, and his word is not in us.

Do you see what the Holy Spirit is revealing through John? If we say we have no sin, we not only deceive ourselves, but we make God out to be a liar! John says God's word is not in such people. Please, do not listen to them!

The apostle Paul gives us a vivid picture of his own battle with the dual natures:

Romans 7:21-23
So I find it to be a law that when I want to do right, evil lies close at hand. For I delight in the law of God, in my inner being, but I see in my members another law waging war against the law of my mind and making me captive to the law of sin that dwells in my members.

We don't know about you, but we certainly don't claim to be better than the apostle Paul.

Some claim that Paul was speaking of his *past* condition. But every one of the verbs in these passages from Romans 7 is in the *present* tense.

Paul found a better way. So can you.

Ephesians 4:23-24a
And to be renewed in the spirit of your minds, and to put on the new self, created after the likeness of God...

Remember these truths the next time you choose what to watch on TV, or what music to listen to. The battle is in your *mind*.

Your act of surrender is not a one-time thing. The more you surrender to God daily, the more room He will have to work. He hasn't left you alone in this. He's right there, working in you.

Philippians 2:13
For it is God who works in you, both to will and to work for his good pleasure.

Those Big Words

Words ending with the suffix "ation" compress complex ideas or actions into a single word, frequently used in specialized branches of knowledge. An accountant deals with "amortization". A physicist may study "quantization".

In this chapter we'll take a look at five "ation" words used by theologians, but often misunderstood by us regular folk. First, let's look at "thumbnails" of each word. They are sequential in history, and we will take them in the order they occur.

Predestination.
A one-time occurrence, before the creation of the universe, and thus outside of time. God "predestined" those who would respond to His love. The Greek word means literally, "to limit in advance".[8]

Propitiation.
Also a one-time occurrence. It happened on the Cross, when the blood of Jesus "propitiated", or *satisfied*, God's wrath, so that His holiness was not compromised in forgiving sinners.[9]

Justification.
A one-time occurrence in the life of those who surrender. It is the judicial act of God, by which He pardons all their sins, and accounts, accepts, and treats them as righteous in the eyes of the law.[10]

Sanctification.
This is an ongoing process by which the Holy Spirit makes us more like Christ in all that we do, think, and desire.[11]

Glorification.
This is a one-time *future* event, when God transforms our mortal physical bodies to our eternal physical bodies.[12]

Now let's look all of them as a "progression unto perfection".[13]

Predestination is a very difficult concept for a human mind to grasp. That's because it occurs outside of our space-time universe. Try this thought experiment, and see how far you get: Imagine a place and time where there was no place and time.

We can't even construct the sentence accurately, because we can't really use the word "where". There was no space for "where" to exist. And we can't use the word "was", because that's past tense, and without the existence of time there can be no past.

Theologians sometimes refer to "eternity past", but that's really an oxymoron. Eternity past didn't exist in the past because it exists *outside* of time. It just *is*. We humans trying to imagine eternity past is like a bacteria trying to imagine quantum mechanics.

Invoking more than the four space-time dimensions to describe the realm of God's existence won't work. That would be limiting God to human physical concepts. He's infinitely bigger than that.

A twisted concept called Open Theism[14] claims that God is trapped in time, just like us, and thus He cannot know the free will choices of humans before they happen, let alone predestine them. But that's not the God of the Bible. That's not an omniscient God, is it? That's a different god entirely!

Finite human imagination will always diminish who God is. The oxymoron of "eternity past" may be the closest we can get to describing where God exists/existed.

But to say that God exists only outside of time is not entirely accurate either. God is intimately involved in His space-time creation, and thus operates in time. He could not "uphold the universe by the word of his power" (Heb. 1:3) if He were not. It seems that God is *simultaneously* outside of time and in time...an impossibility for us, but certainly not for an omnipresent God.

We cannot prove it, but the realm of God's existence may be *all* time, *all* dimensions, *all* love, *all* power...*everything* encompassed in one *Self-Existent Cause*...It may be *God Himself*.

And that's where/when Predestination happened/happens. Is your head spinning yet?

From the perspective of God, every second of your life, every decision, every breath you take, has been predestined. But from our perspective inside this space-time bubble, it all looks like random chaos and "free-will".

We think it was best expressed by one of the great philosophers of our time, Forrest Gump:

I don't know if Momma was right or if, if it's Lieutenant Dan. I don't know if we each have a destiny, or if we're all just floating around accidental-like on a breeze, but I, I think maybe it's both. Maybe both is happening at the same time.[15]

With Predestination, God set boundaries. The Greek word used in the Bible is *proorizo*. It means to *limit in advance*, determine before, ordain, predestinate.[16] It's like bowling with the "bumpers" up...the rails which a bowling alley puts up on either side for little kids.

If God has predestined you to be His child, then He has "limited in advance" the trajectory of your life. There's a limit to how far you can go to the left or right. Between the "bumpers", you have free will. You may not knock down many pins, but you will never go off into the gutters. God has got it rigged.

However. The closer you bowl to a strike, the richer your life in heaven will be. Each pin is a treasure worth far more than pure gold. Remember those wedding garments? Remember your "Magic Jacket"? Why flail around bouncing off the bumpers when you could be storing up exquisite treasures. With God's Spirit in you, you can knock down some pins!

Propitiation is a strange-sounding, unfamiliar word. But once you fully understand its meaning, you will see that it is the single most wonderful word ever devised in any human language.

God found a way, where there seemed (humanly speaking) to be no way. Of the attributes of God, His justice and holiness seem to be diametrically opposed to His mercy and forgiveness.

If your little child was brutally murdered, how would you feel about a judge who said, "I'm feeling generous today, so even though the jury has found the defendant guilty, I'm going to set him free"?

That's not justice, is it?

On the Cross, the blood of Jesus "propitiated", or *satisfied*, God's wrath, so that His holiness was not compromised in forgiving sinners. The penalty has been paid in full, and this renders it consistent for God to exercise His grace towards sinners.

Propitiation has two parts to it. First, the act of paying the price for the offense. The second is the act of being reconciled to God. Here's an illustration:

What if you were the defendant in a debt-collection case, and the judge was not only your father, but the one to whom you owed twenty billion dollars? If your father the judge decides to pay the debt himself, then you are not only free of the debt, but also reconciled to your father.

Because (and only because) God, to whom you owe the penalty for sin, paid the price Himself in Jesus, you are both free of the penalty, and reconciled to your Father the Judge.

All of the above is wrapped up in the word "propitiation". Now *that's* the most wonderful word there ever was!

Justification is a forensic judicial term. It could sound rather dry and uninteresting until you grasp its consequences. Then it becomes the most reassuring word imaginable.

Justification is the exact opposite of condemnation. The legal consequence of sin is condemnation, by which you are barred from the presence of God, and excluded from heaven. The legal consequence of justification, on the other hand, is entry into the presence of God, and a guarantee of admission into heaven.

Because, by Jesus' blood, the claims of the law have been satisfied on your behalf, you are now entitled to all the advantages and rewards of perfect obedience (Rom. 5:1-10).

It is a crediting to you, by God Himself, of perfect righteousness (Rom. 10:3-9). The sole condition on which this righteousness is credited to you is faith in, and surrender to, Jesus Christ. God now sees you through the sacrifice of Jesus. He "sees" you without sin.

Is that reassuring or what!? You have the *assurance* of being in the presence of God, and living with Him in heaven for eternity!

Once you have got past the surrender part, and you understand your dual nature, then *Sanctification* becomes the most beautiful word in the English language. Propitiation is wonderful, but Sanctification is beautiful.

When God starts working in your heart, beautiful things begin to happen. Your mind is progressively renewed. God The Spirit (our preferred title for "the Holy Spirit") makes you more like Christ in all that you do, think, and desire.

Fruit begins to show up. You *want* to become more like Jesus. His spirit joins your spirit. More fruit. You are becoming a "partaker of the divine nature" (2 Pet. 1:4). Even more fruit.

Self-control, the last of the fruits of the Spirit listed in Galatians 5:22-23, comes by the renewal of your *mind*. It often seems to be the first to show up. Love, Joy, Peace, and the rest will follow in time.

Sanctification is a lifelong process, with many ups and downs. You'll know it's working when you see the fruit. This is the topic of Section Six, so we won't go into more detail here.

Propitiation is wonderful, Justification is reassuring, Sanctification is beautiful, but *Glorification*, oh my! It is something on a higher level altogether. It is breathtaking, electrifying, overwhelming, and wondrous. The best word we could come up with is *thrilling*. But even that doesn't come close.

The Greek word used in the Bible for "glorify" is *doxazo*. It means "to magnify, extol, praise". When used of God, it means acknowledging His being, attributes and acts. The glory of God is the *revelation and manifestation of all that He is*.[18]

When applied to you as a believer, glorification is a one-time *future* event, when God transforms your mortal physical body into your eternal physical body. And since your new body will be exactly like Jesus in form and function, it too will be a *"revelation and manifestation of all that He is"*.

But not only that, glorification brings participation in the kingdom of God (1 Thess. 2:12). You will be *reigning* with Jesus Christ (2 Tim. 2:10-12). This is the inheritance awaiting you! We honestly cannot imagine anything more *thrilling* than that!

There is a sense in which our glorification is happening now, as well. You have the Holy Spirit as the guarantee, or "down-payment" of your future inheritance (2 Cor. 1:22). He is helping you, as you progressively become more like Jesus. You are preparing for your ultimate glorification, at "the end of the age".

This present space-time universe will one day collapse in on itself, and be drawn back from whence it came...to God. And then, God will breath out a new universe, a new earth, and a new you!

Reigning with Jesus Christ will be amazing! Your inheritance will be astounding! Your new body will be magnificent! We can hardly wait! No more aches and pains. No more fear. No more tears. No more death. And our personal favorite, no more sin!

It will all be utterly beyond *thrilling*! Are you ready?

In Section Seven, you will watch it unfold before your eyes!

Romans 8:29-30
For those whom he foreknew he also predestined to be conformed to the image of his Son, in order that he might be the firstborn among many brothers. And those whom he predestined he also called, and those whom he called he also justified, and those whom he justified he also glorified.

The Land Where Everything is Small

What folly to seek great things for ourselves here,
where everything is little, and nothing certain!
(JFB commentary in reference to Jeremiah 45:5)

T he Glory of God is the preeminent motivating force of the universe! *Everything* here in the Shadowlands is "little". Everything is uncertain. What folly indeed, to chase after littleness and vapor! What folly to settle for pies made of dung, when a banquet of God's Glory is before us!

Matthew 6:33
*But **seek first the kingdom of God** and his righteousness, and all these things will be added to you.*

This verse is often quoted in the context of God's provision. It's a contract. We seek first the kingdom, and God will provide all those "things"...the necessary things of life. But there is so much more!

God has designed us to be most satisfied, most fulfilled, most complete, *in Him!* When His Glory is our focus and guiding vision, "all these things will be added"!

And whatever doesn't get "added"...doesn't really matter. When the Glory of God is your vision, so much of what makes up the value systems of this world shrinks to the point where it becomes barely noticeable.

In our survey of negative opinions of heaven in Section One, we quoted someone as saying this:

If God is so great and goes on about free will, why is he bribing us in order to accumulate groupies?

Does God desire worship because He is egotistical? Does God want His name to be made great among all people because He's got a swelled head? Does God's passion for His glory seem out of place?

In the next section we are going to look at what it means to be so saturated with the glory of God that you wouldn't trade it for anything this world has to offer. King David said, "Oh, taste and see that the LORD is good!" (Psalm 34:8). The apostle Paul said, "In Him you have been made complete." (Colossians 2:10a).

David was so saturated with the glory of God that he could *taste* it! Paul knew God so intimately that he was made *complete*! What did these men know that we may be missing?

Everything you ever wanted. All your hopes. All your dreams. The fulfillment and purpose and *life* which the whole world wears itself out chasing...*this* is what God is offering us!

It's called His Glory. Do you remember that Greek word which is translated as "glorify" in the Bible?

doxazo: the revelation and manifestation of all that God is

The Glory of God is the unfolding revelation of Who He Is! And since God is *infinite*, it will take all of eternity to plumb the depths of His Glory.

The Glory of God is the fuel which can power your life here on earth, and launch it to unimaginable joy on the New Earth!

We are living in a land where everything is small. It's called "the Shadowlands" for a reason. Planet Earth is just a dim shadow.

This world settles for *small*. Your flesh will always default to the *small* things. The devil wants to make you *small*.

Please don't settle for *small* when *Glory* is being dumped in your lap. If you have God's Holy Spirit living within you, then you have His *Glory* within your grasp! Why settle for *small*?

There are treasures beyond imagining ahead. Please don't miss out.

Hang on! You're in for the journey of a lifetime!

[1] Exodus 3:13-14.

[2] Vine's Complete Expository Dictionary.

[3] Bronchogenic carcinoma (lung cancer) is the most deadly of cancers, killing over 1.6 million people every year.

[4] Our reckoning of dates is based on the best archaeological and historical evidence, which indicates that Jesus was born in 4 BC, and had His public ministry between 26 and 29 AD.

[5] *The Life of Flavius Josephus*; Josephus, 94 AD.

[6] From the ESV Bible footnotes.

[7] We do not wish to demean the Japanese people with this analogy. The Japanese culture and history are rich, and the Allies and Americans were far from God-like. As all analogies, it isn't perfect, but it is very instructive in its similarities to our topic of total unconditional surrender to God.

[8] Vine's Dictionary of the Bible.

[9] From the ESV Study Bible notes for Romans 3:25.

[10] Easton's Bible Dictionary.

[11] Easton's Bible Dictionary.

[12] Christian Apologetics and Research Ministry.

[13] A paraphrase from *The Search After Truth: A Book of Sermons and Addresses*, Charles William Pearson (1908).

[14] According to the *Christian Apologetics & Research Ministry*, "Open Theism is the teaching that God has granted to humanity free will and that in order for the free will to be truly free, the future free will choices of individuals cannot be known ahead of time by God." Open Theism claims that time did not begin at the creation of the universe. See *Beyond the Bounds: Open Theism and the Undermining of Biblical Christianity* (2003) by John Piper, Justin Taylor, and Paul Kjoss Helseth.

[15] *Forrest Gump*, Paramount Pictures, 1994; screenplay by Eric Roth, based on the novel by Winston Groom (1986).

[16] *Strong's Dictionary of the Bible*.

Section Six | The Non-Existent Now

So be careful how you live. Don't live like fools,
but like those who are wise. Make the most
of every opportunity in these evil days.
Ephesians 5:15-16 (NLT)

A Brief History of Non-Time

H ave you ever taken a moment to be quiet? Amid the semi-controlled chaos you call your daily life, have you ever really been still and quiet for a few brief minutes? Have you taken the time to be *present in the moment?*

Dwelling in the "present moment" is a concept often attributed to Gautama Buddha, who is quoted as saying:

Do not dwell in the past, do not dream of the future, concentrate the mind on the present moment. [1]

Modern psychologists have appropriated this idea in their counseling, and it has some merit. Often Buddhists and psychologists advocate meditation as a tool to live in the moment. That could be fine, as long as you are meditating on the right things. Remember, an empty mind is an invitation to the forces of this present darkness to set up shop.

The Bible speaks of being still, and waiting on the Lord.

Psalms 46:10a
Be still, and know that I am God.

Isaiah 40:31a
But they who wait for the LORD shall renew their strength;

Have you ever done that? Have you been still? Have you waited on the LORD? Have you ever sat back in the present and been still, and known in your soul that He is God? Have you ever rested in the "now" and waited, and felt your strength renewed?

This brings up an interesting question. What is the "present". When is "now"?

It might surprise you to learn that, when you take a closer look, "now" doesn't really exist. It is non-existent.

Quid est enim tempus?

"For what is time?" asked St. Augustine in *Confessions* (400 AD). Augustine's view of time was that it really doesn't exist at all. "The present must become past in order to be time (otherwise, it would be eternity)" he reasoned. Then he asked a very interesting question. "If time present comes into existence only because it passes into time past, how can we say that even this exists, since the cause of its being is that it will cease to be?"

Augustine then comes to this astonishing conclusion: "Thus, can we not truly say that time is only as it tends toward non-being?"

The future isn't here yet, and so it doesn't yet exist. The past is gone, and it too no longer exists. All we are left with is the *present*. But, as Augustine points out, the present only exists as it "tends toward non-being".

When is "Now"? How long is it? We recorded the word "now" into our computer, and looked at the waveform. From the start of the "n" to the trailing edge of the "w" took about 3 tenths of a second. Is that "Now"? By the time the "w" was pronounced, the "n" had flown into the past.

Time is an oddity. It can be slowed by extreme speed. Physicists consider it one of the four physical dimensions of the universe. It pushes us headlong into the future. But by the time we get there, the future has become the past, and the present never really materializes.

We cannot stop it, even to be able to say the word "now". We can't stop time long enough to even contemplate what the present really is. We are slaves, it seems. Trapped in the "arrow of time".[2]

Before it can become "now", the future flies into the past in an infinitely small spec of time.

The smallest value of time measurement is an *attosecond*, which is 10^{-18} of a second. One 10,000,000,000,000,000,000th of a second. One attosecond is the time it takes for light to travel the length of two hydrogen atoms. Twelve attoseconds is the record for the shortest time interval ever actually measured.

We could keep slicing Now smaller and smaller forever. Eventually we'd have to admit that it really isn't there. It's the non-existent Now.

So here's a question. If Now is a speck of time which is *infinitely* small, then could that be where eternity intersects our universe? In the non-existent Now? Is that where you meet God, if you can ever stand still long enough to grasp it?

This is a very important question. If you never turn your thoughts away from what is coming up next in your frenzied day, how can you ever know God. Not know *about* God. *Know* Him, as a real Person.

Knowing God is a love relationship.

We have talked about the truths of the Bible, about weaving wedding garments and storing up treasures. We have talked about design and deception and dominion and surrendering. But all of that is nothing without *relationship*. Christianity is not a religion, it is a relationship with your Eternal Father.

The non-existent Now is where you build that relationship. It's where you sit on your Father's lap, lean back against His chest, feel His love, and *be* with Him.

Have you ever heard the song which God is singing over you?

Zephaniah 3:17 (NLT)
*For the Lord your God is living among you. He is a mighty savior. He will take delight in you with gladness. With his love, he will calm all your fears. **He will rejoice over you with joyful songs.***

Has anyone ever taken delight in you? Has anyone's love ever calmed your fears? Has anyone ever rejoiced over you?

God, your Eternal Father, is at this very moment singing a joyful song over you. Can you hear it? Have you *ever* heard it? You never will, unless you meet Him in the non-existent Now.

Have you ever been in love? Can you remember when love was young? To look into the eyes of your beloved, and see the love come back, was enough. No words were needed. You could just sit in each others' presence, and it spoke volumes. You were "in the moment", together. As if all the wide universe existed in that one point in time.

That is where the One who loves you best is calling you. To be with Him in the moment. To shut out the clamoring world. To be still and know that He is God, and know that it is enough. That's all you need.

When you meet your Eternal Father in the non-existent Now, and hear the song which He is singing over you, His love will flood your being. No one who has thus met God has ever come away unchanged. It is impossible. When you have been in the *Presence*, you will never be the same.

When Moses came down from Mount Sinai with the stone tablets of the Ten Commandments, he was unaware that his face was shining. It shone so bright that it scared the people of Israel.[3] He had been in the Presence of God Almighty. He had seen His *Glory*.

When *you* have been in the Presence, your face may not be shining like Moses, but God's light will be shining in you so brightly that you will be changed. That's what absolute, pure love does. That's what God's *Glory* can do, in a land where everything is small.

This is something intimate and beautiful. This is not some wild spiritual ecstasy. This is not the drug-like high of being slain in the spirit, like my old Jesus Freak friends used to chase. This is a cherished oneness with He Who is all-in-all. The Great I Am.

In the Bible, Song of Songs portrays this beautiful, intimate, oneness. Over the centuries, many have seen this book as a sexual marriage manual, and in a way it is. But the Song of Songs is so much more. It is also a passionate, personal love story of you, and the One who loves you best.[4] In it, you will see a conversation between "he", the King, and "she", the "Shulammite" woman, his bride.

It is a picture of God the King, and the Church, His "bride". We think you can legitimately read it as a picture of the love relationship between God and *you*.

The King says to you, "Arise, my love, my beautiful one, and come away" (2:10). He brings you into His chambers (1:4), a place of quiet, solitude, and intimacy. He tells you that you are "altogether beautiful" (4:7). You are His, and His desire is for you (7:10).

We challenge you to read the Song of Songs, and put yourself in the place of the King's beloved.

During His earthly ministry, Jesus often went off by Himself to be with the Father.[5] It seems this was essential for Him. Think about it. If Jesus needed this, how much more do we?

We've invented a word to describe it. It's our word for intentional solitude with God. We call it being "solitudinal". It is not just about some warm fuzzy God-hug. More often than not, you may find yourself confessing sin to your Father. When you take the time to "be still and know that He is God", the light of His presence will reveal the hidden things of the heart.

This is essential to everything else in your Christian walk. How can you bear fruit, or do the will of the Father, if you do not know Him? If you have not spent time being with God, then most of your efforts may be in the flesh.

The main theme of this book is how you can store up treasures in heaven, how you can weave your "wedding garments", how your life now drastically affects your life in eternity.

This, then, is the key!

There has to be a relationship with the Everlasting Father. You can't have that relationship unless you have been in the *Presence.*

But this is not something which happens naturally. You can't just go off by yourself and stare at your navel and expect God to show up. Like any love relationship, your relationship with God is going to take some effort. That's upside-down from our instant-gratification culture. That's radically different from what we see for the most part in the American Church. In the whole spectrum, from spiritual emotionalism on one end, to cold legalism on the other, it seems we seldom hear anything of real spiritual discipline.

Pastor Wang Ming Dao knew a thing or two about getting alone in the presence of God. Wang was a Chinese house church pastor and noted Christian writer who was thrown into prison. He spent 23 years in solitary confinement. Denied his Bible, paper or pen, all he had was the Scripture he had memorized. Wang spoke of those solitary years as the sweetest, most intimate time with his Heavenly Father. He had this advice for American Christians:

I was pushed into a cell, but you will have to push yourself into one. Simplify your life, so you have time to know God.[6]

You don't have to spend 23 years in solitary confinement to get closer to God, but you will need to "simplify your life", and find your "cell". This is something we have been working on, and we admit we're not entirely there yet. We can find our "cell", and be in the Presence as we walk around the block, or along a wooded path. We can find it in our morning quiet time. There are sweet times to be had with the Father throughout the day, if we look for them.

But eventually there has to be more. We may have to leave the TV off some nights. We may have to surrender what we Americans often value most...our time. That doesn't come naturally. We're going to need some help. In our experience there are two tools which help get us there. God uses both, it seems, at various times.

The first one is the Spiritual Disciplines. There is a "cloud of witnesses" who have gone before. You are not the first to face this. In the next chapter we will look at some of the Spiritual Disciplines which the saints of old have learned.

The second tool God uses to get you into His presence is what we call "The Fellowship of the Wring". Can you guess what that is? You'll find out two chapters ahead.

The Spiritual Disciplines and the Fellowship of the Wring are time-tested tools for entering into the Presence, and walking out a succession of non-existent Now's throughout your life.

Before it can become "now", the future flies into the past in an infinitely small spec of time. *That's* where you meet God. *That's* where you live out the life which leads to eternity. *That's* where you learn the Spiritual Disciplines, and how to abide in Jesus.

The Spiritual Disciplines

*For those whom he foreknew he also predestined
to be conformed to the image of his Son.*
Romans 8:29

I n this present time where the future is constantly rushing by
that elusive Now into the expanding past, God is doing
something rather wonderful in our lives. In Romans 8, Paul
tells us that He is conforming us to the image of His Son. He is
renewing and transforming us.

His desire is that the family resemblance be increasingly growing.
Later, in Romans 12, he tells us that we are to let it happen. "Be
transformed by the renewing of your mind". Again, in I Timothy 4:7,
Paul tells Timothy to "discipline your self for the purpose of
godliness". We are to contribute to the process.

Spiritual disciplines are tools at our disposal to assist us in that
transformation. They are called disciplines because it takes continual
effort to use them consistently. They are called spiritual because they
are instrumental as the means by which we cooperate with God in
what He is already doing. Let us share a few of the disciplines.

The discipline of **Study** is the first that comes to mind. So often,
as believers, we have our pet phrases and verses on which we build
our understanding of God and life. But God has given us a volume
with 66 distinct books under one cover. That book, the Bible, gives
us the complete picture of God's heart and His ways.

We go through life with a distorted view of what God is doing in
the world, in the church and in the life of the individual when we do
not take the time to grow in our knowledge of the whole counsel of
God. It takes discipline to set aside time consistently to study, but
how can we be conformed to that which we do not know?

Inductive Bible study is one option available to us. In this kind of study, we choose a book of the Bible to scrutinize. We read it and ask questions of the text. Who is speaking and to whom? When is it taking place? What does it say, and so on?

We lay aside our own ideas of what it says and let the context of the whole book speak for itself. We find key words and themes. We do cross reference studies to correlate what is being taught in this book with other places in Scripture that speak of the same ideas. Our goal is to discover for ourselves what God was saying when He told the author to pen the words we are reading.

Another valuable option is character study. Read the life experiences of the individuals whose stories the Bible tells us and gain insight into the ways of God.

Look! God promised Abraham he would be the father of a multitude and have a posterity in history. And Abraham waited 25 years for a son.

Look! God intends to use Moses to lead his people. Then he takes him out of the country where His people are and leaves him in a dessert place for 40 years.

Look! God told Samuel to anoint David king of Israel. Years go by as David slays giants, lives in King Saul's household and hides from King Saul in the countryside with his life perpetually in danger.

Look! God promised Adam and Eve that He would send a redeemer for the sin that had destroyed their relationship with their creator. 4,000-ish years go by before the angel Gabriel appears with his pronouncement to Mary.

Could we conclude that one of God's ways is to builds years of preparation into His plans for us individually and for the world in general?

Study the nation of Israel in the promised land. It is an Old Testament foreshadowing of our life today in the kingdom of God. They lived in a time of "now and not yet", as do we. They were in the land, but there was still trouble. There were conflicts, sickness, wars, challenges from nature. It was not an easy life, not a perfect life.

But there was a promise of a Savior they were waiting for and there was victory so long as they continued to seek the face of God.

We live *after* the coming of the Savior they awaited and the establishing of His kingdom, but we also await the promise of His returning. What insight can we gain by observing their life, recognizing the source of their blessing and cursing. Are there parallels in our own? Remember this:

Romans 15:4
For whatever was written in former days was written for our instruction, that through endurance and through the encouragement of the Scriptures we might have hope.

And there are word studies. Take a concordance and trace words through the whole Bible. What does grace really mean when you have noted its use exhaustively? What about mercy, wrath, judgment? What about love? Ideas based on pet phrases and favorite verses are proved or disproved as we renew our minds with the complete understanding of what God means with the words He uses.

Even simply reading the Word of God in context is a monumental learning experience. Try reading from a study Bible with cross references. Trace a theme through the whole of the Word.

In addition to studying the word, we can study nature to see God's handiwork and understand His faithfulness more fully. When we study the political activity in the world in concert with a more thorough understanding of the whole Bible, we see God working in history to accomplish His purpose and establish His kingdom. Studying people we can see the consequences of individual decisions people make for good or evil and we can see the profound impact words and actions have on those around us.

Prayer is a discipline. We are instructed in I Thessalonians 5:17 to "pray without ceasing". This is the product of a disciplined heart and mind. Study the prayers of Paul, Abraham, Moses, David, Solomon, Daniel. You will discover that much of their prayer was praise. They acknowledged the sovereignty of God and asked Him to act in specific situations according to His character and for the glory of His name. Study the prayer that Jesus taught His disciples to pray and the one that He prayed before the crucifixion. Follow the pattern of prayer laid out in the scripture.

As we study the Word, we take what we see and turn it back to God in prayer. As we study the world around us, it becomes a catalyst for prayer. Praise God for His exceeding great and precious promises[7]. Pray for the mandates uttered by the Lord to be carried out by His people[8]. Pray for leaders who will foster a lifestyle of peace so that the gospel can spread[9]. Pray for the gospel to be carried to every people group on the planet[10].

Prayer fosters more study and study fosters more prayer.

But neither prayer nor study are natural to most of us and must be maintained through discipline.

Silence and **Solitude** are companion disciplines. We live in a noisy, chaotic world. God speaks in a still small voice.[11] It takes discipline to find a time and place to escape for a few minutes.

Solitude involves finding a few minutes in the day when you are truly alone with God. I (Margie) remember getting up at 5:00 am when my children were at home to have an hour before making breakfast, packing lunches and welcoming children who were arriving for day care.

Still today, I like to take my coffee and my Bible and spend an hour listening to what God has to say to me before I interact even with Stan. The time is sweet and often sets the course of the day. It requires determination to maintain this time, but for me, the discipline has become a habit that I would be loath to forego.

Silence means shutting out noise that competes with the voice of God. This can mean turning off the noises around us. Even Christian music can be a distraction.

For me, it more often means silencing the chaos that goes on in my own mind. The mind is often a loud place with various responsibilities competing for preeminence in my thoughts. Fretting instead of trusting. Nurturing hurt or angry feelings. God speaks quietly. All of these other things prod, shout, whine away in our subconscious and block the gentle voice of God.

The Spirit of God helps us to quiet these noisy distractions, but it is often a struggle. The reward for our effort is the sweetness of hearing God.

Meditation happens when I have come into solitude and silenced the outside and inside voices that vie for attention and then begin to let the Word of God that I have read or studied speak into my being.

This is not emptying my mind of everything, but it is allowing the truth of God to digest in my understanding and become a part of my thinking and decision making. It is in this time that the Spirit of God speaks to reveal how this truth applies to my day, my relationships, my life, the life of the church, etc.

Worship is that for which we were made. It is coming together with the people of God to express with our combined voices the truth of God. It is opening our hearts in anticipation to absorb what the Word of God will say to us as the message is delivered. It is remembering together the death and resurrection of the Lord Jesus in communion and observing the commitment of new believers as they express their obedience in the act of baptism.

And worship is more. Worship is doing "whatever we do in word or deed for the glory of God"[12] throughout the whole week. It is loving one another way Jesus loved us.[13] It laying down our life. It is having the mind of Jesus[14] in the way we conduct ourselves. As we realize this and seek God's help in doing it, we are taking on the family resemblance that our Lord desires. We are worshiping.

Celebration. This one is not a no-brainer for me. As a sequential, goal oriented person, celebrations interrupt the momentum of what I am getting done. In the Old Testament, God built into the year several times when He asked His people to lay aside their responsibilities and celebrate. He gave explicit directions for some and others they were told to save money and get whatever they wanted to celebrate before the Lord.[15]

We also have celebrations built into our year. They invite us to stop. Think about the savior that was born and died for our salvation. Think about the freedoms that we enjoy and the price that was paid for us to have them. And give thanks.

But maybe some mini celebrations are also in order. Celebrate the finished project. Celebrate the efforts of a friend or family member. Celebrate the sunny day or the first snowfall of the year. Celebrate the first ride without training wheels. Set a special table. Create a yummy desert. Dance in the wind as the leaves fall from the trees. Be still in awe of unexpected beauty. Find a reason and let joy reign...often and regularly!

The list of Disciplines could go on.[16]

Simplicity. Learn to say "No" to busyness so that you can say "Yes" to what really matters.

Service. Giving time to advance or nurture the Kingdom and it's people.

Guidance. Seek God's heart in decision making. Ask for input from others. Listen for checks in your heart, pursue a plan cautiously to see if God is indeed directing.

Fasting. Giving up something for a prescribed time — often food —to dedicate time to pursuing God.

You may say of many of these, "I already do that." It may be true! What we call disciplines, pursued consistently over time become habit and we no longer need to work at them.

If you find that to be true, take a few moments to think back over the years and recognize what God has accomplished in you through your faithfulness to them. Look at the way your life bears the family resemblance in more distinctive ways than it did a few years ago.

Praise the One who has been committed to conforming you. Worship Him! Celebrate!

Romans 12:2 (NLT)
*Don't copy the behavior and customs of this world, but let **God transform you into a new person by changing the way you think**. Then you will learn to know God's will for you, which is good and pleasing and perfect.*

The Fellowship of The Wring

*Wring: to twist and squeeze to remove water;
to get something out of someone with a lot of effort;
to twist so as to form into a different shape*
Merriam-Webster

Have you ever felt like you've been twisted and squeezed by life until you're wrung out. Have you ever felt drained? Have you ever been pushed and formed into a different shape? If so, what do you do? How do you react?

We can remember helping our grandmothers on wash day in the 1950's. They still had their old fashioned washtub and wringer. After the clothes had been washed and rinsed, grandma would let us put them through the wringer. It consisted of two heavy rollers and a crank. We'd feed the wet clothes in, turn the crank, and it would squeeze them between the rollers and *wring* most of the water out.

That's what God does with His children. He will allow life to put you through the wringer. It's His chosen process for squeezing out the junk in you. God disciplines His children. It's for our good. It's for our *best*. If we resist or avoid it, we're missing out big time.

Hebrews 12:8 & 10
*If you are left without discipline, in which all have participated, then you are **illegitimate children** and not sons...but he disciplines us for our good, **that we may share his holiness**.*

Did you catch those two astounding statements in Hebrews 12? (1) If you aren't being disciplined by God, *you are not a child of God*! (2) God's purpose in allowing suffering is to *share His holiness*!

We don't want to minimize suffering and troubles. It can be scary when it's winter and your electric bill is two months past due and you have no money to pay for it.

I (Stan) faced just such a situation several years ago: I was a single parent with two teenage boys. I was past due on my electric bill, and had no money. I had tried to take the easy way out, and ended up deeper in debt.

So I finally went to God. He didn't send an unexpected check, or inspire someone to pay the bills. Instead, He said, "Are you giving Me your full tithe?" I said, "Lord, that's $70 a month!".[17] Can you guess what He said?

Sometimes God is more interested in fixing your heart, than fixing your immediate problem.

God used those difficult days to build obedience and faith. The electric bills eventually got paid, and when He was ready God gave me a great job, and to top it off, He gave me a beautiful Godly wife. But best of all, I had a faith that was more precious than pure gold!

Margie and I had both made mistakes, and been through divorce. We had much to learn. God was taking the broken pieces and making something new. The wringer kept on turning.

A few years later I was laid up with pneumonia and a partially collapsed lung. I was out of work for over two months, about to be forced onto disability, and facing the remainder of my life as an invalid. Days before the deadline, God healed me. Like flipping a switch. Poof! I was well again.

I count those months struggling for every breath as the sweetest time I've ever had with God. I couldn't even walk to the bathroom without help, but my Heavenly Father was drawing me into deep times of prayer and solitude. I devoured the Word. Some of what's in this book was written during that time.

But God wasn't through yet. Another turn of the wringer crank, and a few years later my younger brother died unexpectedly at the age of 63. We were very close, and it hit me hard.

I didn't have time to catch my breath (literally) before the wringer crank turned again. An allergic reaction to dust caused severe asthma. For seven months I was often fighting for every breath again.

One of the medications I was given caused severe insomnia. Another turn of the crank. For nine nights straight I got only an hour of sleep each night. My Abba was drawing me even deeper. Much of what's in this chapter and the next was written during those long hours of solitude in the night watches.

I was learning what the apostle Paul learned long ago:

Philippians 4:12-13 (NLT)
I know how to live on almost nothing or with everything. I have learned the secret of living in every situation, whether it is with a full stomach or empty, with plenty or little. **For I can do everything through Christ, who gives me strength.**

That lesson never comes easy. In God's love, He appoints seasons of trial, and we go through the wringer. The Bible calls such times *The Fellowship of His Suffering*:

Philippians 3:10 (NASB)
*That I may know Him and the power of His resurrection and the **fellowship of His sufferings**, being conformed to His death.*

This isn't Frodo and Gandalf and Sam in the "Fellowship of the Ring". This is the Father and Son and Spirit and you in the *Fellowship of His Suffering*. This is the method God uses to "share His holiness".

This verse is not one people usually highlight in pink in their Bibles. We don't put yellow stars and little hearts around verses like this. Words like "sufferings" and "death" aren't what Pollyanna would call the "glad passages".[18]

We tend to hurry past such verses to get to the "good" stuff. But if all we ever focus on are the warm fuzzy love passages, then we're missing the real *power* of the Bible.

The power of His resurrection.

Take a closer look at Philippians 3:10. Do you want to *know* God? Do you want the *power* of His resurrection fueling your spiritual life?

These things come by way of suffering, and being conformed to His death. If you let Him, God will put you through the wringer of life. You'll come out on the other side knowing Him better, and tapped in to the power of His resurrection.

Remember the second most powerful force in the universe? Sin. It's so massive and so powerful that only the Resurrection of Jesus Christ, God in the flesh, has any power over it. Do you want the power of His resurrection? Here's how you get there.

The power of His resurrection is found in the *Fellowship of His Sufferings*. It's not power to perform flashy miracles or gain health and wealth. It's power to conquer sin and share His holiness.

In God's hands, trouble is a tool, and death just a doorway. Your Heavenly Father loves you with a perfect love. He is constantly working out His very best for you. Often His very best lies on the other side of a storm.

Suffer with Him and you will have His holiness, purified faith, and the power of His Resurrection!

This is not the message many congregations hear on Sunday morning. This is not what many worship choruses focus on. The word we seem to hear most is "I". We want God's love and forgiveness and power and purpose. We want all that good love stuff. Yes, God loves us with a fierce love. He has plans for our good, to give us a future and a hope (Jer. 29:11). But we often miss God's path to those things.

In the Bible, James lays out that path:

James 1:2-4
Count it all joy, my brothers, when you meet trials of various kinds, for you know that the testing of your faith produces steadfastness. And let steadfastness have its full effect, that you may be perfect and complete, lacking in nothing.

God wants you to be perfect, complete, lacking nothing. What's the opposite of nothing? *Everything!* In His fierce love, God will not relent until He has completed that in you. It comes by "trials of various kinds". It comes by the testing (refining) of your faith.

Count it all joy!

If you were to shout, "I lost my job. Hooray! Let's dance for joy!", people would think you're nuts. Our nature is to avoid pain. We don't like sorrow and difficulty. But God has a process here. He's producing something. "Steadfastness". As James says, "Let steadfastness have its full effect." It will "perfect" and "complete" you. The apostle Paul elaborates on this theme:

Romans 5:3-4
Not only that, but we rejoice in our sufferings, knowing that suffering produces endurance, and endurance produces character, and character produces hope.

Rejoice! Count it all joy! God is producing endurance and steadfastness and character and hope! Can you do that? Can you be joyful in adversity? What does that look like?

The Bible gives us a vivid picture of this in action. Paul and Silas were in Philippi. A riot erupted, and the crowd started attacking them. The town magistrates tore off their clothes and had their naked backs beaten with rods.

They were thrown into prison, with their feet fastened in stocks. Did they cry and complain? Were they angry or depressed? They must have been exhausted. Did they fall asleep? Let's peek in around midnight and see what was happening:

Acts 16:25
About midnight Paul and Silas were praying and singing hymns to God, and the prisoners were listening to them.

Paul and Silas knew who they were. They knew what God was up to. Somehow, with bruised and bloodied backs, with feet clamped into stocks, in the dark damp "inner prison", they found joy.

The most beautiful suffering comes as a consequence of your faith in Jesus. That's what Paul and Silas were suffering for. You may never be beaten with rods. But as you follow hard after God, there will be times when He asks you to let go of something which has been very precious to you. Guaranteed. It will happen (see Gen. 22). This too is the Fellowship Of His Sufferings.

Real physical suffering for Christ is not just a thing of bygone centuries. Right now, in the 21st century, there is immense suffering by Christians around the world. Perhaps the starkest example is in North Korea. There is indisputable evidence that the North Korean regime is perpetrating the *genocide* of Christians "through executions and state-sanctioned murders, the systematic use of torture, state-induced mass starvation, forcible abortions and infanticide, and the forcible transfer and enslavement of children."[19] Reverend Eric Foley, CEO of *Seoul USA* says he was surprised when he asked members of the North Korean underground church how Americans could pray for them.[20] Here's what he said:

"They answered, 'You pray for us? We pray for you!' When I asked why, they responded, 'Because Western Christians often put so much faith in their prosperity and political freedoms that they don't know what it's like to have to depend completely on God. And because of that, they often do not get to know him in all the ways he invites us to.' They pray for us because they feel we are persecuted by our prosperity and it distances us from God."

Let that sink in. Our prosperity and political freedoms may actually be keeping us from God's highest and best. These dear North Korean brothers and sisters pray for us because they feel we are persecuted by our prosperity and it distances us from God.

What a humbling prayer. They have *nothing*, and yet they know God in ways we never will. They have to depend completely on God, and that brings an intimacy and faith which we can only dream of.

But it doesn't have to be this way. The next time God lets life put you through the wringer, don't try to go around it. Go *through* it with Him, knowing that "the testing of your faith produces steadfastness. And let steadfastness have its full effect, that you may be perfect and complete, lacking in nothing."

Enter into the Fellowship of His Sufferings, and He will draw you into a deep intimacy that defies anything this world has to offer. You will be progressively transformed. The end result will be fruit produced in you, and glory going up to God.

That's what your Heavenly Father is about. That, as always, is the goal. Producing fruit in you, and glorifying His Name.

We see this at work in the life of a man who was born blind. We meet him in the ninth chapter of the Gospel of John. Jesus' disciples asked him, "who sinned, this man or his parents, that he was born blind?" The conventional wisdom of the day held that all suffering is the result of sin. So if this man was blind, *someone's* sin must be the cause. Look at Jesus' reply:

John 9:3
Jesus answered, "It was not that this man sinned, or his parents, but that the works of God might be displayed in him.

This man suffered with blindness his whole life, not because of sin, or disease or accident. The purpose of his suffering was "that the works of God might be displayed in him". Jesus healed him, and he gave glory to God.

Do you remember Pastor Wang Ming Dao? We met him in the first chapter of this section. He spent 23 years in solitary confinement in a Chinese prison, and spoke of those solitary years as the sweetest, most intimate time with God. He said he was pushed into a cell, but you will have to push yourself into one.

In our experience it is far better to "push yourself into your cell" through the Spiritual Disciplines, than to wait for God to "crank the wringer". You will never completely avoid suffering, but you can learn your lessons well, and "let steadfastness have its full effect". If you keep trying to avoid it, your Abba Father will just have to keep cranking.

In God's hands, trouble is a tool, and death just a doorway.

The Fellowship Of The Wring

When peace, like a river, attendeth my way,
When sorrows like sea billows roll;
Whatever my lot, Thou hast taught me to say,
It is well, it is well with my soul.[21]

Abiding Love

Whoever abides in me and I in him, he it is that bears much fruit, for apart from me you can do nothing.
John 15:5b

J ohn 15:5 is one of the most important verses in the Bible. Why? Because Jesus tells us here that we can do nothing. Nothing is a huge word. It's absolute zero. It's a bottomless black hole of utter emptiness, and it creates a huge locked door in our path. Let's call it "The Nothing Door".

When Jesus says we must abide in Him, He's talking about something much more than just staying put, or making yourself at home. This kind of abiding is what we talked about in the first chapter of this section. This is an intimate personal relationship with Jesus in the non-existent Now.

We've seen that the Spiritual Disciplines and the Fellowship of the Wring are two tools to help you get to a place of intimate relationship. But that's not an end in itself. The goal Jesus lays out here isn't just a cozy relationship with Him. We're sorry to have to break this news to you, but it's not all about you. You are not the center of the universe.

Remember: anyone who has been in the *Presence* of God will be forever changed. That change is what Jesus is talking about when He says "abide". Jesus lays out a two-way proposition. We abide in Him, and He abides in us. Us abiding in Jesus is only half. The other half is Jesus abiding in us, and we need to see how that works.

We must resist the temptation to gloss over this and move on. When Jesus says we can do nothing, He's talking about anything with lasting value; anything which will survive the trial by fire which the apostle Paul spoke of:

1 Corinthians 3:14-15
If the work that anyone has built on the foundation [of Jesus]
survives, he will receive a reward. If anyone's work is burned
up, he will suffer loss, though he himself will be saved, but
only as through fire.

Do you remember back in the first section of this book, we talked
about the wedding garments you are weaving? Jesus is giving us the
key to how to weave those wedding garments. If we aren't doing it
the way Jesus prescribes here, then you're wasting your time. You're
wearing yourself out for *nothing*.

So if "abiding" is the key, we need to know exactly what that is,
and how to do it. Let's start by asking how and what questions. First
"what". Jesus says we can do nothing unless we abide in Him, so let's
ask our first "what" question:

What is "abide"?

The Greek word used here for "abide" is *meno̅*. It's a primary
verb meaning to stay in a given place, state, or relation.[22] Back in the
very first chapter of this book we saw the Greek word *moné*, which
is the noun form of this verb. It's what the King James Version
translates as "mansions". *Moné* is where you live. *Meno* is what you
do there.

But knowing what "abide" means and *doing* it are two completely
different things. So let's ask:

How can I abide?

Well, we could search the whole Bible, doing a word study on
"abide", and spend many months in the process. Letting the whole
Bible speak is always good, and we leave ourselves open to
deception if we don't know the "whole counsel of God" (Acts 20:27).
But we have found that we can often look right in the surrounding
verses for the answer. When we force Scripture to answer how and
what questions, the answers are often right there in the context.

Is the Holy Spirit cool or what?

So if we look just five verses down, we find the answer:

John 15:10a
If you keep my commandments, you will abide in my love...

So that's the answer. If we keep His commandments, we'll abide in Jesus. But what commandments? We could do a search of the Bible and compile a comprehensive list of commandments. But how about sticking with the context. It has gotten us this far.

Let's let the context answer the next "what" question:

What are His commandments?

If we look just two verses down, we find the answer:

John 15:12a
This is my commandment, that you love one another...

Now we're getting somewhere. Love is the commandment which gets you "abiding". Love is the key. Be kind to strangers and cats. Hug a friend. Hug a tree. Let's all sit around a bonfire and sing *cumbayá* and toast s'mores. Who would have guessed. The Beatles were right all along:

All You Need Is Love
And in the end, the love you take
is equal to the love you make.[23]

OK, let's turn the sarcasm off, and look a little closer. A popular bumper sticker from the 1960's said, "Make love not war". That may have been referring to sex, but let's broaden the context and ask an important question: Can love be manufactured? Is it a commodity to be packaged and sold? Our popular culture seems to think so.

But that is not the kind of love Jesus is talking about here. We need to know more about love than pop-culture songs and slogans. Jesus is talking about more than just an emotional response, or sociological ethics or kindness.

So here's our next "what" question:

What kind of love is Jesus talking about?

We won't tease you by pretending that the answer is anywhere but right here in the context. In fact, it's right there in the very same verse. We purposely quoted the verse out of context. Here's what we left out:

John 15:12
*This is my commandment, that you love one another **as I have loved you**.*

Sorry for tricking you, but we're trying to make a point, and we want it to stick. Now obviously this isn't just some group hug here. This isn't warm touchy-feely lovey-dovey. Jesus tacked those crucial five words on the end: "as I have loved you".

So now we have our final "how" question:

How has Jesus loved?

And you guessed it, the answer is in the very next verse:

John 15:13
*Greater love has no one than this, that someone **lay down his life** for his friends.*

The definition which Jesus gives for love is "lay down your life". This is way beyond what the Beatles sang about. This is far above our pop culture ideas of love. The Greek word used in this verse for "lay down" is *tithēmi*. The Strong's Dictionary defines it as "to place in a passive or horizontal posture; to kneel".

Tithēmi is similar to two other Greek words. One is *histēmi*, which means to stand upright. The other is *keimai*, which is utterly prostrate, flat on your face. Do you see the difference? Jesus is telling you to kneel before others, and don't *stand* defiantly for your own way, but don't fall down and be a *doormat* either.

206

Jesus didn't just define love, He lived it. He demonstrated *tithēmi* in action. He loved us, and gave Himself up for us.

Galatians 2:20b (NASB)
And the life which I now live in the flesh I live by faith in the Son of God, who loved me and gave himself up for me.

Jesus is giving us an equation here, and it's far more powerful than Einstein's $E = MC^2$. This equation is the key to eternity:

LOVE = LAYING DOWN YOUR LIFE

Let's connect the dots here. Jesus says that laying down your life is how you love, and that kind of love is his commandment, and if you keep that commandment you will abide. So we can legitimately restate our equation thus:

ABIDE = LAYING DOWN YOUR LIFE

Now the Nothing Door swings open! Now you've got the other half of Jesus' "abide" proposition. The Spiritual Disciplines and the Fellowship of the Wring help you get to the first half, which is you abiding in Jesus. *Tithēmi*, laying down your life, gets you to the other half, Jesus abiding in you.

There can only be one Lord of our life. Whether we recognize it or not, if we have not reached the point of *tithēmi*, then *we* are lord, not Jesus. As we progressively learn to lay down our life, Jesus has room to come in, abide in us, and be Lord of our life.

By faith, lay down your life, first to God, and and then to others. That's how you make room for Jesus to abide in you. That's how you open the Nothing Door.

We've created an acronym to help us remember this key. We call it LDYL. Remember those WWJD bracelets kids used to wear a few years ago? Maybe someone should make LDYL bracelets. If you've mastered LDYL, you don't need to ask "What Would Jesus Do?" You're already doing it!

As with all things, LDYL starts with God. The only reason we can love is because Jesus loved us first.

1 John 4:19 (NLT)
We love each other because he [Jesus] *loved us first.*

What's the opposite of nothing? *Everything.* As we enter into the abiding love of Jesus, it opens up *everything.* God is passionate that we "bear much fruit". That fruit glorifies Him. But it also benefits us. That "fruit" is our wedding garments. It explodes the richness of our life in heaven exponentially.

Laying down your life is how you start your walk with Jesus. It's your passport into the Kingdom of God. Remember His terms of total unconditional surrender? That's not a one-time event. Surrender is a lifetime act. LDYL every day.

An Eternal Perspective.

In a land where everything is small, we can get so caught up in the details of daily life that we can't see the bigger picture. Let's back up, and get an eternal perspective.

| --- |

Imagine this line represents about 700 billion years. That's more than one hundred million times the supposed age of the universe.

Your entire lifespan might be 70 or 80 years. Can you pick out 80 years on that 700-billion-year-long line? It wouldn't even be the width of an atom on that line. Not even the width of a quark.

Now imagine a line with no ends at all. It goes on forever. That's eternity. That 700 billion years wouldn't even be a non-blip of time on the line of eternity.

Does it really matter that somewhere in that non-blip of time which you call your lifespan, someone hurt your feelings or treated you unfairly? Does it really matter that you didn't always get your own way?

From an eternal perspective, does it really even matter if you get cancer and die? It's time to ask yourself what you really believe.

If a young person dies, we're often sad for how much of life they missed. They never had a chance to fall in love, or realize their full potential. *Really?* This non-blip of time isn't your whole life! It's just a tiny dot at the beginning of an infinite line.[24] For a disciple of Jesus Christ, "to die is gain" (Philippians 1:21). Do you really believe that? Do you *live* like you believe that? Or are you just playing church?

The closer we get to God, the more we see how little it matters what happens to us in this short life, except for how it moves us toward Him, and produces fruit. We said it before, and we'll say it again:

In God's hands, trouble is a tool, and death just a doorway.

Jesus says this is non-negotiable.

It's Lay Down Your Life or nothing!

We need to stop right now and make it very clear that Jesus is *not* talking about salvation here. He begins His teaching by saying this:

John 15:3
Already you are clean because of the word that I have spoken to you.

You are "already clean" if you have surrendered to Jesus. What He wants now is *fruit*. Let's revisit the verse which started this chapter:

John 15:5b
*Whoever abides in me and I in him, **he it is that bears much fruit**, for apart from me you can do nothing.*

The goal of abiding is fruit. And that fruit will glorify God the Father. In the same passage, Jesus says this:

John 15:8
*By this my Father is glorified, that you **bear much fruit** and so prove to be my disciples.*

You'll know you've mastered abiding when you see the fruit. So what does that fruit look like? The most common answer is to look at Galatians 5:22:

Galatians 5:22-23a
But the fruit of the Spirit is love, joy, peace, patience, kindness, goodness, faithfulness, gentleness, self-control...

That's a good list. But we'd like to see that in action. Jesus gives us a picture in Matthew. He's describing the Final Judgment, and He lists what the righteous have done. He's describing their fruit:

Matthew 25:35-36
For I was hungry and you gave me food, I was thirsty and you gave me drink, I was a stranger and you welcomed me, I was naked and you clothed me, I was sick and you visited me, I was in prison and you came to me.

The righteous answer, asking when did they ever do those things for Him. Jesus answers this way:

Matthew 25:40b
Truly, I say to you, as you did it to one of the least of these my brothers, you did it to me.

Laying down your life to God is going to lead you to laying down your life to others. Laying down your life to others is going to produce the fruit God is looking for, which Jesus describes here.

You won't even be aware of it, but as you bear the fruit which glorifies God, you'll be weaving your wedding garment. You'll be making your life in eternity unimaginably richer. And it all starts with Abiding Love. That's what God's *Glory* can do, in a land where everything is small.

We call that a win-win proposition!

L * D * Y * L

The Weapons of Our Warfare

*For the weapons of our warfare are not of the flesh but have
divine power to destroy strongholds. We destroy arguments
and every lofty opinion raised against the knowledge of God,
and take every thought captive to obey Christ.*
2 Corinthians 10:4-5

I t's all-out war.

When you first surrendered to Jesus, you entered into an epic
battle. It will only intensify as you progress. Your enemy hates
you with a vengeance. He hates you every time you "go into your
cell" and learn to be solitudinal with God. He hates you even more as
you learn the Spiritual Disciplines.

And as you begin to abide in Jesus, lay down your life, and bear
the fruit which glorifies God, your enemy will throw everything he's
got at you.

What will that look like? Will Satan hit you with a debilitating
disease? Will he wipe out your finances? Will he strike at your loved
ones? Will you loose your job?

We don't think so. It has been our experience that the attacks of
Satan are targeted primarily on the *mind*. He sows discouragement
and doubt and fear. He knows you all too well, and he pricks at your
weakest spot, be it lust or anger or pride or fill-in-the-blank.
Whatever Satan sees as your greatest weakness, that's where you can
expect a full-blown frontal assault.

The battle, as always, is in the mind.

That was the battleground of Satan's first attack on humankind.
Remember the lie which he hissed at Eve?

211

Genesis 3:4-5
*But the serpent said to the woman, "You will not surely die.
For God knows that when you eat of it your eyes will be
opened, and you will be like God, knowing good and evil."*

Satan, that old serpent, launched his first-wave attack at the point
of Eve's trust in God. He messed with her *thinking*. He sowed the
seeds of *doubt*. The battle was in the mind.

Centuries later Satan was at it again. He attacked Job at the point
of his faith in God. Satan accused Job of loving God only because
God had "put a hedge around him and his house and all that he has".
Satan said to God:

Job 1:11
But stretch out your hand and touch all that he [Job] *has,
and he will curse you to your face.*

So God gave Satan permission to take all that "stuff" away from
Job. But pay close attention to the nature of Satan's attack. On the
surface it might appear like the attack was against Job's possessions
and family. But it was *not*. Satan's attack was against Job's *faith* and
devotion to God. The stated purpose of Satan's attack was to cause
Job to "curse you [God] to your face". The battle was in the mind.

Flip the calendar ahead two thousand years, and we find Satan at
it again. Only this time he's playing mind-games with God Himself, in
the flesh: Jesus. Twice Satan challenges the deity of Jesus, taunting
Him with the sarcastic: "*If* you are the Son of God".

And then Satan tries to buy Jesus' worship by offering Him "all
the kingdoms of the world":

Matthew 4:9
*And he said to him, "All these I will give you, if you will fall
down and worship me."*

Worship is an act of the will. It's a decision of the mind. By getting
Jesus to worship him, Satan would have won a victory over His mind.
The battle was in the mind.

Let's look again at the two verses which started off this chapter:

2 Corinthians 10:4-5
For the weapons of our warfare are not of the flesh but have divine power to destroy strongholds. We destroy arguments and every lofty opinion raised against the knowledge of God, and take every thought captive to obey Christ.

We see six attributes of the weapons of our warfare. They are:
1. Not of the flesh.
2. Have divine power.
3. Destroy strongholds.
4. Destroy arguments.
5. Destroy lofty opinions raised against the knowledge of God.
6. Take every thought captive to obey Christ.

The weapons you have are all of the mind, and they have divine power. Let's look now at the apostle Paul's classic inventory of the "Armor of God" in Ephesians chapter six.

First, Paul tells us to "put on the whole armor of God" (v11). We are not to leave any of it off, or we will be dreadfully vulnerable.

Next, we are reminded that we do not "wrestle against flesh and blood" (v12). Our enemy is not other human beings, or the circumstances swirling around us. Our enemy is "the cosmic powers over this present darkness".

Paul then goes on to specify the seven components of this "armor". The first three are foundational, the next two are defensive, and the last two are massively powerful offensive weapons.[25]

1. belt of truth (v14)
2. breastplate of righteousness (v14)
3. shoes of the gospel of peace (v15)
4. shield of faith (v16)
5. helmet of salvation (v17)
6. sword of the Spirit, which is the word of God (v17)
7. spear of prayer (v18)

Prayer and the Word of God are the thermonuclear missiles in your spiritual arsenal. Every time you pray, you fire nuclear-tipped missiles at Satan. That's because of what prayer does for the state of your *mind*. Prayer aligns your mind with the mind of God. Prayer banishes anxiety, gives you peace, and "will guard your heart and your mind".

Philippians 4:6-7
*Do not be anxious about anything, but in everything by prayer and supplication with thanksgiving let your requests be made known to God. And the peace of God, which surpasses all understanding, will **guard your hearts and your minds** in Christ Jesus.*

In order to wield the Sword of the Word you need to *know* the Word...the Bible. It is a razor-sharp "two-edged sword" in your hand. But notice that this sword does not chop off demon heads, or slice out demon guts. It pierces the "thoughts and intentions of the heart". The battle is in the mind. *Your mind!*

Hebrews 4:12
*For the word of God is living and active, sharper than any two-edged sword, piercing to the division of soul and of spirit, of joints and of marrow, and **discerning the thoughts and intentions of the heart**.*

You can read how Jesus used the Sword of the Word against Satan in Matthew 4:1-11. Notice that Jesus didn't say to Satan, "Please wait while I consult my concordance and look up an appropriate verse. He had hidden God's Word in His heart (Psalm 119:11).

Satan is a billion times more powerful than you, and he wants to kill you. How can you possibly expect to go up against him without a sword in your belt? You can't carry a bible around with you everywhere. You're going to have to memorize some key Scripture! We're old, and sometimes feel like we barely have two brain cells to rub together, but when we bring God into it, even we can memorize Scripture.

If we can do it, so can you!

Ask God to lead you to verses to memorize. If you are facing a particular trial, God is faithful. He will show you Scripture to memorize. Often God will give you what some call a "life verse". Something which will carry you through a particular season of life. God gave Margie just such a verse many years ago. Here is her story:

I have been told that there are 365 times in the Bible that God tells us to "fear not". God knows that when those created in His image chose sin over obedience, a by-product would be fear. And He gave us a "fear not" for every day of the year!

Fear can be present in many forms. Mine has always been God's provision. He says He will meet all of our needs, but will there really be enough left at the end of the month to buy that last gallon of milk needed to make it to payday? Do we buy apples and salad ingredients or new shoes for the kids? And what if the car breaks down or we need to buy a new washing machine?

God desires trust from us and He longs to infuse us with His peace. But in many situations, we choose fretting over resting.

One of the proven remedies of a loving heavenly Father is to put us in exactly the situation that fosters the greatest fear and demonstrate to us His willingness and ability to provide just what the circumstance requires. And that is exactly what He did with my fear.

When my two oldest daughters were somewhere between six and ten years of age, I began to sense that we were entering a time of serious financial stress. Everything I picked up to read spoke of God's provision in difficult times.

One morning, in my quiet time, God especially impressed my heart with a verse in Matthew:

Matthew 6:33
But seek first the kingdom of God and his righteousness, and all these things [necessary food and clothing] *will be added to you.*

I remember praying, "OK, Lord. If that's where we're going, I trust You."

The income did indeed shrink and the expenses didn't. I remembered the promise and I trusted, but in fear almost every day of what this was going to mean. One day as I sat at my kitchen table trying to make the money stretch for all of the bills I was paying, I looked up at the digital clock on my stove. 6:33! God reminded me of His promise in Matthew 6:33. He would keep His promise.

As the days and weeks went by, God continued to use that number to remind me of His faithfulness. Standing in a check-out line fretting about the total that would soon be calculated, I glanced at the check I was writing. #633. Driving my girls to their piano lessons and wondering if we could really afford to continue, we came to a stop light. The license plate number of the car in front of us is — you guessed it — 633!

I cannot remember the details of how God met our needs in those two years before our situation turned around. I remember simply that the number 633 turned up everywhere. And I know that everything we really needed was provided.

The most dramatic time God used it to communicate His commitment to me came many years later. My daughters were grown and my oldest was living southeast of Portland. I had been there for a few days and was headed home. My head and my heart were full of fretting. I drove through the countryside without seeing its beauty as I fretted about whatever it was that time.

I was just a few miles south of the Columbia River when I looked down at my odometer. 633. "OK, Lord. I get it," I said, and went right back to my fretting. I drove across the bridge and continued on for several miles, still fretting and stewing. As I glanced down at the odometer again, I was shocked to see that it still said 633!

Persistently and miraculously God was saying "Fear Not! I will take care of everything that concerns you!" When He had used that little miracle to jolt me out of my sinful fretting, the odometer began to move forward again.

That number has been a gentle reminder to me over and over again that I belong to a loving heavenly Father who knows my needs before I do and is committed to providing everything that I need to carry me through my days.

Margie's story is a reminder of God's faithfulness. He will give you Scripture to hide in your heart for every season of your life.

We have found that our Scripture memorization needs to be more than mere snippets. John 3:16 and Psalm 23:1 will only get you so far. The really powerful weapons come when you memorize whole passages. Don't let that intimidate you. If we can do it, so can you.

If you don't know where to start, how about Psalm 1? It's only six verses, and is easily doable. You will become acquainted with a man who meditates on the law of the Lord day and night. He's "like a tree planted by streams of water". As you memorize, you'll find yourself becoming like him. Meditate on Psalm 1, and repeat it back to God.

God is the One who is ultimately fighting for us. He has given us all the tools we need. He's given us the Armor of God. He's given us the Weapons of our Warfare. He's given us Abiding Love. He's given us the Fellowship of the Wring. He's given us the Spiritual Disciplines. He has given us relationship with Him in the Non-Existent Now.

The apostle Peter says God has given us "all things that pertain to life and godliness". He has given us the knowledge of Himself. He has even allowed us to become "partakers of the divine nature"! Let that one sink in for a minute! *You* can have the very nature of God!

Read these two verses very carefully, and *memorize* them. There is incredible power packed into such a small space:

2 Peter 1:3-4
His divine power has granted to us all things that pertain to life and godliness, through the knowledge of him who called us to his own glory and excellence, by which he has granted to us his precious and very great promises, so that through them you may become partakers of the divine nature, having escaped from the corruption that is in the world because of sinful desire.

"Sinful desire" is overcome in the *mind*. Your Heavenly Father has given you everything you need to escape.

The battle, as always, is in the mind.

The Last Enemy

For he [Jesus] must reign until he has put all his enemies under his feet. The last enemy to be destroyed is death.
1 Corinthians 15:25-26

T he Resurrection from the dead of Jesus the Messiah crushed the head of Satan, and inaugurated the reign of King Jesus, ushering in the Kingdom of God, bringing His will to Earth as it is in Heaven.

But something is terribly wrong. It sure doesn't *look* like Heaven on Earth when little girls by the millions are sold into sexual slavery, and the Western world chokes on the gluttony of crass materialism and rampant sexual immorality.

So what are we to think? Is Jesus really reigning or not? Has His Kingdom really come? The answer lies in verse 25: "For he must reign until he has put all his enemies under his feet." His victory will not be complete until the last enemy has been put under His feet.

Satan is wounded, but he is still the "god of this world" (2 Cor. 4:4). He is still the "prince of the power of the air" (Eph. 2:2). "We do not yet see everything in subjection" to King Jesus (Hebrews 2:8).

We are still in a war. That war has one goal: that all enemies of King Jesus be put under His feet.

The obvious question now is, "Who or what are His enemies?" For an answer, let's look at the fruit we talked about in the Abiding Love chapter. Remember Jesus' list in Matthew 25?

The assault is against Injustice, Poverty, Sickness, Bigotry, Idolatry, Materialism, Lust, Greed, Ignorance of the Gospel...and much more. And the last enemy to be destroyed is Death! Praise God!

So here are 7 questions, 7 challenges, and 7 prayers, regarding this ongoing war:

1. What are His enemies?

If putting all His enemies under His feet is the focus of the reign of King Jesus, and I am to join Him as a co-worker in His kingdom, then it's pretty important that I recognize those enemies, and not waste my time on lesser things. LORD, open my eyes and give me discernment, that I may see Your enemies...and not with the eyes of my flesh, but with spiritual eyes, from Your perspective!

2. Which enemies are in me?

If putting all His enemies under His feet is the focus of His reign, and there be any of those enemies residing in me, then putting those enemies under *my* feet ought to be my focus. "Woe is me! For I am lost; for I am a man of unclean lips, and I dwell in the midst of a people of unclean lips..." (Isaiah 6:5). LORD, create in me a clean heart, O God, and renew a right spirit within me! (Psalm 51:10)

3. Which enemies affect those for whom He has given me a burden?

If putting all His enemies under His feet is the focus of His reign, then I cannot sit idly by while that which is His enemy consumes those I love, and those for whom God has given me a burden. LORD, give me eyes to see, as You gave Elisha's servant eyes to see. LORD, may You grant me to see the true battle, and the specific enemies who are attacking, and show me how You want me to join the battle, in deed and in prayer!

4. Which enemies has He called me to attack with my resources?

If putting all His enemies under His feet is the focus of His reign, then I need to surrender my time, my talents, and my treasures to that purpose. LORD, loosen my grip on that which You have blessed me with; my abilities, my time, my money, and my very self. Take my focus off of myself and my dreams and my goals, and turn it like a laser onto those enemies You are trampling under Your feet!

5. Which enemies has He called me to attack with prayer?

If putting all His enemies under His feet is the focus of His reign, then that ought to be the focus of my prayer life. How can I continue to pray for my petty comforts and all the ups and downs of life in the Shadowlands[25], when there are image-bearers of the Living God being trampled by the very enemies which ought to be crushed to dust under the feet of King Jesus! LORD, may the Holy Spirit help me in my weakness, for I do not know what to pray for as I ought...may the Spirit himself intercede "with groanings too deep for words", according to the will of God! (Romans 8:26-27)

6. What is His plan for putting His enemies under His feet?

If putting all His enemies under His feet is the focus of His reign, then I have no hope of doing that on my own. This is His war, and it must be fought His way! He calls me to join Him as a co-laborer and soldier, but He is the One doing the fighting. It is His feet these enemies are being crushed under. It is His power at work. Woe to those who attempt in their own feeble power to "claim" and "declare" and "command" the spiritual powers of this present darkness! LORD, I surrender to Your will and Your way. Fill me with Your Spirit. And by the Spirit, first in me and then in the world, do some enemy-stomping!

7. What is His priority?

If the last enemy to be destroyed is death, then there is a sequence to which enemy is to be attacked and when. I can wear myself out struggling against enemies before their time. It is not my responsibility to go stomping on every enemy I see. I need to be careful not to take on a God-sized burden. I need to let God choose the timing. He has a plan and a process. If I rush in where God is already at work and try to "help" Him, I may mess it up. LORD, I know You are at work in me, and in those around me, and in the world. Help me not to rush ahead. Help me to trust Your perfect timing and Your amazing process. I am eager for all Your enemies to be put under Your feet!

A Melting Universe

We are in the midst of an epic battle between good and evil. It's all-out war. We all know how this war will end. King Jesus is going to return *in person* to destroy the last enemy:

Revelation 20:14a (NLT)
Then Death and the grave were thrown into the lake of fire.

Once Jesus has put *all* His enemies under His feet, some drastic changes are coming.

2 Peter 3:10b (NLT)
Then the heavens will pass away with a terrible noise, and the very elements themselves will disappear in fire...

The elements — atoms, quarks, energy — are all going to disappear in fire. Across the wide universe, all the elements are going to melt!

The apostle Peter asks a very pointed question:

2 Peter 3:11-12a
*Since all these things are thus to be dissolved, what sort of people ought you to be in lives of holiness and godliness, waiting for and **hastening the coming of the day of God...***

The universe you know will one day melt with intense heat. In light of that absolute truth, what sort of person ought you to be? Did you know that you can actually *hasten* the coming day of the Lord? As you live out a life of holiness and godliness, you can bring Jesus back that much sooner!

Did you know that Jesus told His followers *exactly* when He would return? Take a close look at this verse:

Matthew 24:14
*And this gospel of the kingdom will be proclaimed through-out the whole world as a testimony to all nations, **and then the end will come.***

When will the end come? When "all nations" have heard the gospel of the kingdom. When Jesus says "nations" here, He's not talking about France or Italy or India. The Greek word used here for "nations" is *ethnos*. It literally means specific ethnic groups, language groups, or tribes.[26]

For instance, Nigeria is a single political "nation". But Nigeria is a collection of over 530 distinct ethnic groups, many with differing languages or dialects.

There are about 16,300 "people groups" in the world. Of those, about 6,550 (32% of the world's population) have never had a chance to hear the "gospel of the kingdom". Many have never even heard of someone called Jesus Christ.[27]

You can be part of bringing the "day of God" closer. Massive efforts are going on right now to proclaim the gospel of the kingdom to those last ethnic groups. But you don't have to go to Papua New Guinea or Yemen as a missionary. There are six ways you can be involved, and only one of them entails "going". You can learn, pray, go, send, welcome, or mobilize. See the end-notes for more.[28]

As you progressively develop your relationship with your Abba Father, learn the Spiritual Disciplines, surrender to God's discipline, practice Abiding Love, take hold of the Weapons of Warfare, and find your place in proclaiming this gospel of the kingdom, you will be "hastening the coming of the day of God"!

Frankly, we can hardly wait! We are utterly sick of this world of sin. We hate the evil we see spreading around the globe. We hate the evil which still lingers in us. Sometimes it almost makes us sick to our stomach. Soul-sick.

We long to see Jesus face to face, and be like Him! Everything in us groans...yearning for that day.

Remember LDYL (Laying Down Your Life)? That was the definition Jesus gave for love. Imagine a world where *everyone* has mastered LDYL! A world where hate has been replaced by compassion, anger turned into understanding, fear turned into courage, lust transformed into the purest love.

We're sorry to tell you that it ain't gonna happen this side of the Second Coming of Jesus Christ. It's only going to get worse.

2 Thessalonians 2:3b (NLT)
For that day will not come until there is a great rebellion against God and the man of lawlessness is revealed —the one who brings destruction.

The destruction which the "man of lawlessness" brings will be beyond anything the world has ever seen.

I (Stan) remember witnessing a hydrogen bomb test when I was ten years old. My father got us up around 3:30 AM. We went out and sat on the front porch. It was pitch black. The stars were shining brightly overhead. It was still three hours until sunrise.

Then an intensely bright light flashed from the East. It lit up our little neighborhood as if it was sunrise. To this day I can still see the house across the street in my mind. It was painted barn-red, and in the eerie light from the thermonuclear detonation, the house looked like it was on fire.

As I watched in awe, my father described what was happening 200 miles to the East. The sand beneath the blast was being fused into glass. Lizards nearby turned to vapor, and disappeared in a puff of steam. Cactus standing a mile away were blasted into a thousand pieces, and hurled outward faster than the speed of sound.

I have recently discovered that what I witnessed that day in 1957 was the test code-named "Hood". It was the only hydrogen bomb test ever conducted in the continental United States, and it was almost four times as large as the bomb which destroyed Hiroshima.[29]

My young mind couldn't take it all in at that time, but I knew I was in the presence of something truly awful and terrifying. It was a visceral impression which has stayed with me ever since.

I believe that one day such destruction will be witnessed world-wide. Instead of lizards and cactus being vaporized, whole cities will disappear beneath the mushroom clouds. That time is coming, and nothing mankind can do will stop it. The clock is ticking.

When God promised Abraham that his descendants would inherit the land of Canaan, He said it wouldn't happen yet, "for the iniquity of the Amorites is not yet complete" (Gen. 15:16). Daniel's prophecy of the end of the world reveals that the end will not come until "the transgressors have reached their limit" (Daniel 8:23).

There is a limit God has set to the transgressions He will bear before He acts in judgment. The Hebrew word used for "complete" in the Genesis passage above literally means "perfected".[30] So it seems that the Amorites had *perfected* iniquity. It appears that "transgressors" will do the same in the "end times". The "man of lawlessness", the one who brings destruction, will one day be revealed...and all Hell will break loose!

But we must not despair. Jesus WILL come back! It is all going to be turned around. We are very much like the disciples on the Friday Jesus was crucified. All hope seemed lost. But there was something wonderful they didn't know..."Sunday is a comin'!"[31]

2 Peter 3:13
But according to his promise we are waiting for new heavens and a new earth in which righteousness dwells.

Even so, come Lord Jesus!
Revelation 22:20b (KJV)

[1] From *The Teaching of Buddha: The Buddhist bible*: A Compendium of Many Scriptures Translated from the Japanese, published in 1934 by The Federation of All Young Buddhist Associations of Japan.

[2] In 1927, British astronomer Arthur Eddington developed the concept of "The Arrow of Time", involving the one-way direction or "asymmetry" of time. Time moves in only one direction: forward. We are trapped in that forward movement, and can never escape. Though the future, the present, and the past may appear to us to not really exist, we can still measure time. The velocity of time drastically changes at speeds approaching the speed of light. And time and space can be "warped" by massive objects.

[3] Exodus 34:29-30.

[4] See *The Song of Songs*, by Watchman Nee, and *Union And Communion*, by James Hudson Taylor.

[5] Luke 5:16 (NLT).

[6] From an article by Alex Buchan; *Voice of the Martyrs*, Jan. 2000, Vol. 15, Issue 1.

[7] 2 Peter 1:4.

[8] Matthew 28:19-20.

[9] 1 Tim. 2:1-2.

[10] Matthew 24:14.

[11] 1 Kings 19:12.

[12] Colossians 3:17.

[13] John 15:13.

[14] 1 Corinthians 2:16.

[15] Deuteronomy 14:26.

[16] See *The Spirit of the Disciplines* by Dallas Willard, and *Celebration of Discipline* by Richard Foster.

[17] Some of you doing the math will figure out that I was living on $700 a month, my "full tithe" being $70. My electric bill in the dead of winter in those days averaged $120 per month. You can see what God was asking of me. It was a turning point. Obedience, or self-reliance.

[18] In *Pollyanna*, by Eleanor H. Porter (1913), young orphan Pollyanna Whittier urges the Reverend to preach on the "happy texts", or "glad passages", as she calls them.

[19] As reported in the *Christian Newswire*, Oct. 29, 2013 edition.

[20] *World Policy Journal*, February 6, 2012 issue.

[21] *It Is Well With My Soul*, by Horatio Spaffort (1876). This hymn was written after traumatic events in Spafford's life. While crossing the Atlantic, the ship carrying his wife and daughters sank, and all four of his daughters died. His wife survived and sent him the now famous telegram, "Saved alone …". Shortly afterwards, as Spafford traveled to meet his grieving wife, he was inspired to write these words as his ship passed near where his daughters had died. - McCann, Forrest M. (1997). *Hymns and History: An Annotated Survey of Sources*.

[22] Strong's Dictionary.

[23] *All You Need Is Love*, by John Lennon (1967), and *The End*, by Paul McCartney (1969).

[24] Author Randy Alcorn frequently uses the metaphor of the dot and the line. The dot represents your lifespan, and the line represents eternity.

[25] From the JFB commentary.

[26] In *the Last Battle*, part of *The Chronicles of Narnia* by C. S. Lewis, Aslan the lion refers to life on earth as "the Shadowlands".

[27] Strong's Dictionary.

[28] Per the U.S. Center for World Missions.

[29] See https://class.perspectives.org/psp/sixways.html.

[30] According to *Wikipedia* and *The Nuclear Weapon Archive*, "Hood" was the only fusion (thermonuclear) "H-bomb" test conducted in the continental United States (the rest were in the Pacific). It was the largest detonation to take place at the Nevada test site.

[31] Strong's Dictionary.

[32] From Pastor S. M. Lockridge's famous sermon, *It's Friday...but Sunday's Coming!* See the inspiring video at https://www.youtube.com/watch?v=Tn94B3GHcjY

Section Seven | Eternity

Then I saw a new heaven and a new earth, for the first heaven and the first earth had passed away...
Revelation 21:1a

A Singularity of Love

I t starts with a total collapse of the Higgs Field. You may remember the Higgs Field from our discussion in the Design section. It's a field which stretches across the whole universe, and imparts mass to all constituents of matter.

In about 10^{-43} seconds, a fraction of a time so small it can barely be measured, the Higgs Field reverses its effect. Instead of imparting mass, it now *rips* mass out of everything.

The Strong Nuclear Force releases its grip. Every atom in the universe melts into the pure energy they are made of. Being the "breath of God", all the energy of the universe now returns to Him.

At 10^{-33} seconds, the Higgs Field has gathered all the mass of the universe to itself, and has collapsed. Gravity now joins the other fundamental forces in a unified quantum-gravitational force.

This draws the free-floating energy released from atoms. Dark Energy and Dark Matter follow. The fabric of space is compressed into a singularity...an incomprehensibly tiny spec.

Time, one of the four dimensions of the universe, is now crushed violently into this singularity. All of Time in a single point. Eternity.

The word, which God spoke at the creation of the universe, has accomplished its purpose. It has returned to Him, and is not empty.

Isaiah 55:11
So shall my word be that goes out from my mouth; it shall not return to me empty, but it shall accomplish that which I purpose, and shall succeed in the thing for which I sent it.

In Genesis, God spoke, and the universe exploded into being. God now withdraws His breath, and it all returns to Him. But God will not remain silent. He will yet speak once more:

Let there be love.

This end-of-the-universe scenario is pure imagination, of course. We don't know exactly how it will happen. But we do know that out of those melted elements, God will create a new universe; a New Heavens and a New Earth. And we know for certain that at the start of that process "the elements will melt with intense heat".

2 Peter 3:12b (NASB)
...the heavens will be destroyed by burning, and the elements will melt with intense heat!

The Old Creation will wear out like a garment, and God "will change it like a robe" (Psalm 102:26). It will all be transformed into something wonderful and amazing.

Isaiah 65:17a (NLT)
Look! I am creating new heavens and a new earth...

We believe that the foundation of the New Creation will be *Love*. Let us explain why. The very first thing which God created in the Old Creation was light (Gen. 1:3). Light burst forth from nothing when God spoke. The foundation of our present universe is light.

The foundation of the New Creation will be *love*. Think about it. The very nature of God is love (1 John 4:8). Love had no beginning, and love will have no end.

1 Corinthians 13:8a
Love never ends.

Love never changes. Love never ends. Love is transcendent. Even citizens of the Peoples Republic of Naturalism[1] recognize the transcendent nature of love. Look at this dialog from the movie *Interstellar*, which some have called an "Ode to Humanism"[2]:

So listen to me when I tell you that love isn't something we invented — it's observable, powerful...Love is the one thing we're capable of perceiving that transcends dimensions of time and space.[3]

232

What do you think of that? Even secular humanists will admit that love is not an artifact of evolution. Even *they* recognize the powerful, transcendent nature of love. If they can admit as much, how much more should those who know the source and true nature of love stand in awe?

We *know* where love comes from, and it's not evolution. We *know* the nature of love, and it's light years above pop-culture's trite ideas. We *know* the definition Jesus put on love.

John 15:13
Greater love has no one than this, that someone lay down his life for his friends.

Do you remember LDYL?[4] The New Creation will be founded on that principle. *Everything* and *everyone* will be in perfect synchronization. Universal LDYL.

In the last chapter we asked you to imagine a world where *everyone* has mastered LDYL. A world where hate has been replaced by compassion, anger turned into understanding, fear turned into courage, lust transformed into the purest love.

We have now reached a point in our narrative where that hope, that imagined world, has become real. A world without sin. Wow!

The power which raised Jesus from the dead is the same power which will "resurrect" the vast universe at the end of history. It's the power of love. The greatest power in the universe. The greatest power in eternity.

A "singularity" is a point at which something takes on an infinite value. The Big Bang started with a singularity of space-time when everything which now makes up our universe was crushed into an infinitely dense point.

Imagine all of the attributes of Love compressed into an infinitely small point, waiting to erupt. A New Big Bang. A New Creation. We can almost feel the incredible power of love about to explode. Use your imagination. Can you picture it? Something wondrous is about to come. Even plants and animals and stars and galaxies know what's coming. And they're "groaning as in the pains of childbirth"!

Romans 8:21-22 (NLT)
*The creation looks forward to the day when it will join God's children in glorious freedom from death and decay. For we know that **all creation has been groaning as in the pains of childbirth** right up to the present time.*

A Singularity of Love is coming!

Resurrection!

We are going to take a detour around what's called the Tribulation, and the Millennium. There are too many different ideas bouncing around out there. People we respect have so many differing opinions, and they all seem to back them up with the same Scripture, and they all seem so certain.[5]

We tend to fall on the "Pre-Trib" side of things, but there just is not enough evidence in the Bible to be dogmatic. We're not even going to go there, so you can put away your End-Times charts. What we're focusing on here is the New Heavens and the New Earth and the New Jerusalem and *Eternity*.

What we know for sure is this:

1 Thessalonians 4:16-17
For the Lord himself will descend from heaven with a cry of command, with the voice of an archangel, and with the sound of the trumpet of God. And the dead in Christ will rise first. Then we who are alive, who are left, will be caught up together with them in the clouds to meet the Lord in the air, and so we will always be with the Lord.

Let's unpack what's going to happen. First, the Lord—that's Jesus—will descend from heaven. We get some detail on this in the book of Acts. The disciples have just witnessed Jesus being taken up, when two men in white robes stand by them and say this:

Acts 1:11
*Men of Galilee, why do you stand looking into heaven? This Jesus, who was taken up from you into heaven, **will come in the same way as you saw him go into heaven**.*

So Jesus is going to come back *visibly*, and in the air.

The next thing we notice is that His coming is going to be very noisy. A cry of command. Archangels shouting. A trumpet blaring. What a racket! It will be enough to wake the dead. In fact, that's *exactly* what's going to happen next: "The dead in Christ will rise".

Notice the progression here. Resurrected first will be believers who have died. Their spirits will at last be reunited with their bodies. Next, "we who are alive, who are left". Now there's a thought...some of us will never die! We'll go straight from this corruptible body to a transformed heavenly body! Paul gives us a glimpse of this:

1 Corinthians 15:51-52
Behold! I tell you a mystery. We shall not all sleep, but we shall all be changed, in a moment, in the twinkling of an eye, at the last trumpet. For the trumpet will sound, and the dead will be raised imperishable, and we shall be changed.

Finally, notice *where* the reunion with Jesus will take place: "in the air". Ever had a dream about flying when you were a child? I can remember dreams where I rose out of our bed, and floated above the heads of our amazed friends and family. What fun!

Guess what? It's *going* to happen! You will fly up into the air to meet Jesus when He returns! And the best part is, "we will *always* be with the Lord"!

Resurrection is *transformation*. "We shall be changed"!

Philippians 3:21 (NLT)
He [Jesus] will take our weak mortal bodies and change them into glorious bodies like his own, using the same power with which he will bring everything under his control.

The JFB Commentary gives some insight into this:

As Christ's glorified body was essentially identical with His body of humiliation; so our resurrection bodies as believers, since they shall be like His, shall be identical essentially with our present bodies, and yet "spiritual bodies".

Your Resurrection Body will be very much like the one you're walking around in right now. Your friends and family will have no trouble recognizing you, just like Jesus' disciples recognized Him after He rose from the tomb (John 20:19-20).

Now pay close attention to this next bit, because it's the best! At the Resurrection, we will not just be like Jesus in the form and function of our bodies. We will be like Him in character and holiness!

Romans 8:29
For those whom he foreknew he also predestined to be **conformed to the image of his Son**, *in order that he might be the firstborn among many brothers.*

The Greek word used here for "image" means to be conformed to a preexisting pattern. In this context, it means that we will be conformed to the pattern, or "image" of Jesus in our nature, in holiness.[6]

In the very next verse, we are introduced to a wonderful word which is essential to understand as we talk about the Resurrection: *glorified*.

Romans 8:30
And those whom he predestined he also called, and those whom he called he also justified, and those whom he justified he also glorified.

The Greek word used in the Bible for "glorify" is *doxazo*. It means "to magnify, extol, praise". When used of God, it means acknowledging His being, attributes and acts. The glory of God is the revelation and manifestation of all that He is.[7]

When applied to you as a believer, glorification means that when God transforms you at the Resurrection, you too will be a "*revelation and manifestation of all that He is*".

2 Thessalonians 1:10
When he comes on that day to be glorified in his saints, and to be marveled at among all who have believed, because our testimony to you was believed.

Holiness is glory in the bud; glory is holiness manifested.[8]

When Jesus is glorified in you on that day, you will be reflecting His glory. That glory will be His holiness reflected in you.

The revelation of God's glory is like pealing back successive layers of an onion, one layer of glory after another after another for all eternity. The depths of the glory of God are so enormous that it really will take every minute of all of eternity for the revelation and manifestation of all that He is. God is *infinite*, and so is His glory!

Reflecting God's glory reminds us of one moonlit winter night a few years ago. We don't get very much snow here, but this winter we had almost two feet of the white stuff. Late one night we looked out from our back porch across a field covered with new-fallen snow. The trees looked as if they were covered in bright silver lace.

A full moon stood over the mountains to the South, reflecting light down on this snowy scene. It looked like a fairyland. The fields and trees and mountains were glowing in the moonlight. It was magical. It was *glorious*.

Now, the snowy field had no light of its own. It had no "glory". The trees and mountains had no personal glory. Even the moon had no glory. They were all reflecting the glory of the light from the sun.

That's what *you* will be doing at the Resurrection! Reflecting the glory of God! But it gets even better. Each new layer of God's glory reflected in you will transform you "into the same image from one degree of glory to another".

2 Corinthians 3:18
And we all, with unveiled face, beholding the glory of the *Lord, **are being transformed into the same image from** **one degree of glory to another.***

Remember the "Magic Jacket" we spoke of in our Introduction? That's your wedding garments, and we are now at the point where they come into play. You've been "weaving" your wedding garments ever since you surrendered to King Jesus. Those wedding garments are your "righteous deeds" (Rev. 19:7-8).

Your righteous deeds will not *save* you, of course. It is "by grace you have been saved through faith" (Eph. 2:8). But authentic faith will always *produce* righteous deeds. And those deeds, as we have seen, are your "wedding garments".

If this is a little unfamiliar, you may want to review the "Fashion Police On Steroids" chapter in Section One, and the "Abiding Love" chapter in Section Six.

Carrying our analogy of the moonlit snowy field a little farther, if there was no snow, and a pile of dung filled the field, how much glory do you think would be reflected? Here are words of wisdom to carve on a plaque and hang on your wall:

Dung does not reflect as much glory as snow.

Are you seeing the connection? Unless you have the wedding garments of righteous deeds, all you'll be wearing when you step into eternity is *dung*!

If it wasn't dressed up in a garment of snow, the field would not have reflected much glory. Unless you are wearing your wedding garments, neither will you. In fact, if you aren't wearing any wedding garments at all, you're going to get kicked out! Remember the poor guy in Jesus' parable of the wedding feast in Matthew 22?

So now it is finally time to put those garments on and see how much glory they reflect! You will *uniquely* reflect His glory in a way only you can. God doesn't want robots. Every reflection of His glory will be utterly unique!

The level of glory you reflect will affect *everything* you do on the New Earth. It will also affect your "treasures in heaven". There are varying levels of joy there, just as there are varying levels of torment in Hell (Luke 10:12). In many respects, your GRQ (Glory Reflecting Quotient) will *be* your treasure.

1 John 3:2
Beloved, we are God's children now, and what we will be has not yet appeared; but we know that when he appears we shall be like him, because we shall see him as he is.

Abandon All Hope, Ye Who Enter Here!

"Through me you pass into the city of woe:
Through me you pass into eternal pain:
Through me among the people lost for aye...
All hope abandon ye who enter here."
Such characters in colour dim I mark'd
Over a portal's lofty arch inscrib'd.[9]

Inscribed on the archway of the portal leading to Hell are the words quoted above. These words may only be a figment of the imagination of Dante Alighieri, but they are certainly no less chilling. We now come to the most difficult chapter we will write. Hell.

It is very real. But for many, that is hard to accept. It seems so over-the-top cruel. Excruciating pain and torment, on and on forever, with no hope of relief, seems to our limited understanding to be harsh in the extreme.

Hell does not fit our concept of a loving, forgiving, long suffering God of grace. There must be some way around it. Surely, those passages in the Bible which describe Hell have been mis-translated or misunderstood. Let's take a look.

A common claim of those who doubt the existence of Hell is that it is not mentioned in the Old Testament. The problem is with the Hebrew word *she'ol*, which means "place of the dead". It is used 65 times in the Old Testament, and was thought of as an underground cavern to which all the dead go. *She'ol* is often incorrectly translated "hell" in the King James.[10]

Those who deny Hell say *she'ol* was merely a "waiting room", and that the Old Testament never speaks of the punishment of the wicked after death. Let's look at three witnesses who contradict this lie.

First up is Isaiah, who tells us of "prisoners in a pit", who are "shut up in a prison", and "will be punished".

Isaiah 24:21-22
On that day the LORD will punish the host of heaven, in heaven, and the kings of the earth, on the earth. They will be gathered together as prisoners in a pit; they will be shut up in a prison, and after many days they will be punished.

Next, Daniel reveals the Resurrection of the dead, "some to everlasting life and some to shame and everlasting disgrace".

Daniel 12:2 (NLT)
Many of those whose bodies lie dead and buried will rise up, some to everlasting life and some to shame and everlasting disgrace.

Lastly, we have the testimony of Jesus. In Luke 16, Jesus gives us a detailed look at the organization of *she'ol*. This is the story of Lazarus and the Rich Man. Poor, righteous, Lazarus dies, and is "carried by the angels to Abraham's side" in *she'ol*. The rich man also dies, and is in *she'ol* in torment.

Look at the vivid detail which Jesus gives us, as the rich man calls to Abraham:

Luke 16:24
And he called out, "Father Abraham, have mercy on me, and send Lazarus to dip the end of his finger in water and cool my tongue, for I am in anguish in this flame."

This doesn't leave much room for doubt about punishment in *she'ol*. Remember, *she'ol* is mentioned all over the Old Testament. It is upon the distinction between *she'ol* and Hell that many hang their doctrine that there is no Hell. But here we have a window into *she'ol*, and the unrighteous there are in anguish in the flame.

The great dividing line of all history is the resurrection of Jesus Christ. He not only conquered sin and death, and inaugurated His kingdom on Earth, but He radically altered the afterlife.

Have you ever wondered where Jesus' spirit was between His death on the Cross and His resurrection? This is sometimes called "Holy Saturday". Peter gives us a clue:

1 Peter 3:18b-19
...[Jesus,] *being put to death in the flesh but made alive in the spirit, in which he went and proclaimed to the spirits in prison.*

The "spirits in prison" were those in *she'ol*. Jesus went there, and made a proclamation. What do you think He proclaimed? Certainly, judgment to those on the hot side. But to those resting in the bosom of Abraham...Liberty!

Even for the righteous, in *she'ol* they were away from the presence of God (Psalm 6:5; 88:10-11; 115:17; Isaiah 38:18). Now, Jesus descends and liberates them! Pastor Joe Rigney describes it like this:

Following his death for sin, then, Jesus journeys to Hades [Greek for she'ol], *to the City of Death, and rips its gates off the hinges. He liberates Abraham, Isaac, Jacob...and the rest of the Old Testament faithful...After his resurrection, Jesus ascends to heaven and brings the ransomed dead with him, so that now Paradise is no longer down near the place of torment, but is up in the third heaven, the highest heaven, where God dwells .[11]*

So now, *after* the resurrection of Jesus, anyone who dies goes to one of two places: Paradise with God, or Hades. Both are temporary "waiting rooms"; places of conscious existence in a temporary body of some kind. One is a place of joy. The other a place of torment.

At the "End of the Age", when all the dead are resurrected, some will go to what we know of as Hell, others to the New Earth.

According to those who keep count, Jesus Himself spoke more about Hell than He did about Heaven.[12] Here are two examples:

Matthew 25:41b
Depart from me, you cursed, into the eternal fire prepared for the devil and his angels.

Matthew 13:41-42 (NLT)
The Son of Man will send his angels, and they will remove from his Kingdom everything that causes sin and all who do evil. And the angels will throw them into the fiery furnace, where there will be weeping and gnashing of teeth.

Jesus is not alone in the New Testament in affirming the existence and nature of Hell. Paul and James and Peter and John all confirm these undeniable facts in many places. Here are a few:

2 Thessalonians 1:9
They will suffer the punishment of eternal destruction, away from the presence of the Lord and from the glory of his might.

Revelation 20:15 (NLT)
And anyone whose name was not found recorded in the Book of Life was thrown into the lake of fire.

Revelation 21:8b
...their portion will be in the lake that burns with fire and sulfur, which is the second death.

Eternal destruction. The lake of fire. The second death. And worst of all, away from the presence of the Lord and from His glory. These things are difficult to accept. We could wish it were not so. But it is. And so we must ask. What will Hell be like? We can learn a great deal just by looking at who will *not* be there: *God.*

Whatever the joys of the New Heavens and the New Earth, Hell will be the polar opposite. Instead of the glory of God, dung. Instead of transformation into His likeness, an eternity of Self. Instead of God's presence, utter isolation from anything remotely good. Instead of swimming in a sea of Love, drowning in an ocean of selfishness.

Those in Hell will finally get what they wanted all along. Human ego, left to itself without any moderating influence from outside of Self, will always drift toward self-deification. We tend to think of ourselves as the center of the universe, whether we admit it or not.

And so those in Hell will finally realize their lifelong goal. To be a little god. But there's a problem. The problem is *where*:

Little gods in a universe of *one*.[13]

Can you imagine being completely alone with nothing but your ego? Completely self-absorbed. Nothing but your own sin to keep you company. For all eternity. Hell.

What are we to say to this? Is God cruel and unjust? The sad truth is, anyone who goes to Hell would be far more miserable in heaven. If they wanted God, they would have responded to Him long ago. If you find God unjust in all this, let us ask you a question.

What would you have God do?

Would you have Him erase their sins and give them a second chance? He already *did* that! He *died* for their sins, for heaven's sake! God has already forgiven them, but they will have none of it.

Would you have God just leave them alone, then? If they don't want eternity with God, then just leave them be? Well guess what? That's exactly what He does. He leaves them completely alone.[14]

And *that* is Hell.

Cast out from the presence of the Lord is the idea at the root of eternal death, the law of evil left to its unrestricted working, without one counteracting influence of the presence of God, who is the source of all light and holiness.[15]

God has revealed Himself to every human who ever lived in a way that they can perceive. At some level *everyone* has an unmistakable revelation of God. And at some level, every human being must respond to that revelation.

Either they honor Him as God, or they turn a blind eye. But make no mistake. Everyone has a conscious choice. They have no excuse. God will give them what they want.[16] Even if it is eternity without Him. Please don't skip this next quote. Read it carefully. God is just.

Romans 1:19-20
*For what can be known about God is plain to them, because God has shown it to them. For his invisible attributes, namely, his eternal power and divine nature, have been **clearly perceived**, ever since the creation of the world, in the things that have been made. **So they are without excuse.***

We are near to tears as we write this chapter. We have friends and family who, if the trajectory of their lives is not altered, will one day reside in Hell. They have heard the truth, and they have rejected it.

We love these people. We long to spend eternity on the New Earth with them. We long to explore the vast reaches of the New Universe with them. We long to see how they would uniquely reflect the glory of God.

That is our vision. That is our hope. May it be so, Lord. We have told them. They have heard. And now, we pray, and we weep.

Holy Dirt

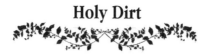

*The righteous shall inherit the land and dwell upon it **forever**.*
Psalm 37:29

The Hebrew word used above for "forever" means... *forever*.[17] How about that? We're going to inherit land and dwell on it *forever*! The Hebrew word for "dwell" is *shakan*. It means to dwell, settle down, abide.[18] When translated into Greek in the Septuagint, it is the exact same word Jesus used for "abide" in John 15:5 when He said, "Whoever abides in me and I in him, he it is that bears much fruit, for apart from me you can do nothing".

This promise from God of dwelling on the land forever is seen all over the Old Testament. Believing humans, those who have surrendered to King Jesus, are not the only things to be resurrected at Christ's coming.

This present earth, in fact the entire universe, is like a seed when it is planted. It is "but a bare kernel" of what it will eventually be.[19] It will be resurrected. It will be transformed. The Old Earth will be resurrected, just like we will be. All Creation will "join God's children in glorious freedom from death and decay"!

Romans 8:20-21 (NLT)
*Against its will, all creation was subjected to God's curse. But with eager hope, the creation looks forward to the day when **it will join God's children in glorious freedom** from death and decay.*

The land will be in perfect harmony with plants and animals and humans and God. Even the weather will join in harmonious equilibrium. Think of the most beautiful national park or natural wonder you've ever seen, and then multiply that beauty by billions.

And we will inherit it and dwell on it *forever*! The Bible never speaks of a disembodied spirit existence in eternity. We will have physical bodies on a physical earth, and it will be beyond anything our puny human minds can imagine!

So, what will we be doing while we're dwelling upon the transformed New Earth? What will be doing on the land forever?

Let's look at how it all started. The mandate which God gave to mankind in the very beginning was this:

Genesis 1:26b
*And **let them have dominion** over the fish of the sea and over the birds of the heavens and over the livestock and over all the earth and over every creeping thing...*

We were to take loving care of the land and everything which lived on it. Birds, deer, lions, whales, trees, shrubs...we were to have dominion over it all, and take care of it.

There's a specific word which God used over and over in the Old Testament in regard to humans and their relationship to the land: We were to *cultivate* the land. Look at these three examples:

Genesis 2:5b (NLT)
*For the Lord God had not yet sent rain to water the earth, and there were no people to **cultivate** the soil.*

Genesis 2:15 (NASB)
*Then the Lord God took the man and put him into the garden of Eden to **cultivate** it and keep it.*

Genesis 4:2b (NLT)
*When they grew up, Abel became a shepherd, while Cain **cultivated** the ground.*

The Hebrew word for "cultivate" used in all three of these verses is *abad*, which means to "serve, cultivate, enslave, work; to be a husbandman".[20] The Oxford English Dictionary defines "husbandman" as "A person who cultivates the land; a farmer".

The Hebrew word used for "keep" is *shamar*, which means "to keep, tend, watch over, retain."[21]

God's mandate to cultivate the land and be a husbandman will not end when the universe has been re-created, and we are living on the New Earth. The picture we get is that of us lovingly taking care of the land forever, so that it produces abundantly, and is brought into alignment with the purposes of God.

Will we *all* be dirt farmers, then? Probably not. But there will be a special connection to the land. As believers, we have an inheritance, which we look at in more detail in the next chapter. That inheritance starts with the land.

Margie wonders if, like Eden at the beginning of creation, the New Earth will be incomplete. God created the heavens and the earth. He then put mankind into His creation to tend it, to have dominion over it, and to *complete* it.

Could it be like that on the New Earth? We'll just have to wait and see!

The *land* of the New Earth is the stage on which the progressive unfolding of our inheritance will be played out.

What a glorious place it will be!

Life On The New Earth

*So then, there remains a Sabbath rest for the people of God,
for whoever has entered God's rest has also rested from
his works as God did from his.*
Hebrews 4:9-10

The first thing we may do when we inhabit our new bodies and set foot on the New Earth for the very first time is say, "Ahhh! No more sin! At last!". The Bible calls this our "Sabbath Rest". The verse quoted above tells us that we will rest from our works. Does that mean on the New Earth we'll all just be sitting around...eternal couch potatoes?

No. The "rest" this verse is talking about is this:

*Rest from weariness, sorrow, and sin; and rest in the
completion of God's new creation. The whole renovated
creation shall share in it; nothing will there be to break the
Sabbath of eternity...*[22]

Gone is the Land Where Everything is Small! In a world without sin, there will be no need for policemen or lawyers or soldiers. There will be no need for the IRS or the CIA, or Congress for that matter. There will be no politicians vying for your vote. There will be no psychiatrists or doctors or dentists.

There will be no scientists studying climate change or cancer. If there is something like NASA, they won't waste billions of dollars looking for (statistically impossible) life on other planets. Perhaps there will be something called NESA (New Earth Space Agency). They would study the glory of God throughout the New Universe, and schedule trips to distant galaxies. We'd sign up in a heartbeat!

The most noticeable difference we will see on the New Earth will be the presence and glory of Almighty God permeating everything. The second most obvious difference will be the complete and utter lack of sin.

The change will be stunning. It will not only affect us regenerated human beings. The absence of sin will affect the whole planet. It will affect the tectonic plates beneath our feet. It will affect the plants and trees. It will affect the animals and fish and birds. It will affect the climate. It will affect stars and galaxies.[23]

A universe without sin will be one of the most shocking changes we will see. Imagine stepping from an old-fashioned black-and-white silent movie into a 3-D IMAX theater. The sights, sounds, colors, smells, textures, detail, and depth will be far above anything we have ever seen on the Old Earth.[24]

Of course, the absence of sin will have its biggest impact on *us*. The rot of a slow death will be gone. Physical, emotional, and moral corruption will be extinct. With worldwide LDYL, anger will be turned into understanding, fear into courage, and lust into the purest love.

That will make way for an intimate connection between you and everyone else on New Earth. It will make way for an intimate connection between you and God.

We were created for that connection, with others, and with God. That's how we started out in Eden. On the New Earth, we will finally get back to that original design.

We will be fellow citizens, members of the household of God. We will be precisely fitted together with everyone and everything. And we will be wired into the Source of everything! God![25]

This intimate connection will not, however, include sex and marriage, at least as we know it. In Luke 20, Jesus said that there will be no marriage for those who attain to the resurrection.

Loving sex within marriage is one of the greatest joys God gave mankind. His very first command to Adam and Eve was to have sex ("be fruitful and multiply")[26]. But we won't need that on the New Earth. Whatever the joys of sex, the intimacy and connection we will enjoy on New Earth will be so much better it won't even compare.

That intimacy and connection will affect everything we do, including the houses we build. As the title of our book says, there are no mansions in heaven. There are no personal castles of individual sovereignty and isolation. The "mansions" Jesus spoke of will be our new eternal bodies.

But there *will* be buildings. To see what they might be like, we must first ask what buildings are for. On this Old Earth, we build houses to keep the rain off our heads. We build houses to protect us from the wind and snow and cold. We also build houses to mark out our private space.

On the New Earth, we will not need shelter from extreme weather, and we will not isolate ourselves with walls. But there *will* be houses. Jesus said so. In the "Parable of the Minas" in Luke 19, which is a "parable of the Kingdom of heaven", Jesus teaches that faithful servants will be given authority over many cities. Cities are made up of *houses*. The New Jerusalem, which John describes in Revelation 21, also has many *buildings*.

These houses may be one aspect of our personal expression of the glory of God. Did you ever want to design a dream house? You may get your chance. How would you design a house to reflect your unique personality, and also reflect God's glory?

But we will never need to retreat to a home for safety. There will be no fortresses holding back the attacking hordes, or preserving our sovereignty in a space we call "mine".

Our Father is going to give us the very very best. That means the buildings which will be at our disposal on the New Earth will be perfectly suited to us, and the activities there. They will never isolate us. They will be part of a radically new way of living in community.

Your awesome new body is not a standalone creation. You are going to be part of a living, organic community. It is hard for us, living on this fallen world where relationships have been broken, to imagine what it will be like to live in an organic, loving, community of redeemed human beings. The kind of community there will be in the Kingdom is a way of life unknown on this present planet.

But in the community of the redeemed, on a redeemed planet, in a redeemed universe, we will all be connected in marvelous ways.

Somehow we will each maintain our own unique personalities, with the gifts, talents, and imagination God has given us, but we will no longer operate as isolated units.

So, for all you doctors and policemen and lawyers, whose talents will no longer be needed — in fact, for all of us — what will we be doing on the New Earth? Well, given that we will have all of eternity, and all of the resources of Almighty God, and awesome resurrected bodies, and a regenerated planet at our disposal, the answer is:

Everything!

Everything not tainted by sin, that is. There will be things for us to do on the New Earth which haven't even been *imagined* on this Old Earth. In our discussion of the multiverse in Section Three, we said this:

Infinite is a hard concept to wrap you brain around. With infinite universes, every logical possibility becomes an inevitability. All possible options are continually and forever tried, so every remotely possible state eventually occurs.

The same logic applies to eternity. Eternity is *infinite time*. So with an infinite amount of time, every logical (non-sinful) possibility becomes an inevitability. Every possible activity will be enjoyed by the sons and daughters of the Most High God!

Obviously we don't have enough ink or paper to describe an eternity of options. So we shall limit ourselves to seven basic categories of the activities we will be engaged in on the New Earth:

1. Cultivate
2. Administer
3. Learn
4. Explore
5. Create
6. Celebrate
7. Worship

Cultivate refers to more than just digging around in the dirt. To cultivate is to nurture and care for everything around you. The Macmillan Dictionary gives these three definitions of "cultivate":

1. To make land suitable for growing crops or plants.
2. To develop something such as an attitude, ability, or skill.
3. To develop a friendship or relationship with someone.

We think all three types of cultivation will be taking place on the New Earth. We'll be making the lush, fertile land suitable for growing things. We'll be developing attitudes, abilities, and skills. And we'll be developing friendships and relationships with everyone else, and with God.

We will **Administer** much of what goes on. We will each have varying degrees of authority. The Bible says that we will be in charge of angels.[27] What a thought! The Bible also tells us that those who walk the New Earth will *reign* with Jesus Christ!

2 Timothy 2:12a
If we endure, we will also reign with him...

It is an amazing thought that we will someday be reigning with Jesus Christ. Do you grasp what that really means? You will have royal authority, power, and control over some aspect of heaven. That's the definition of "reign".[28] We are joint-heirs with Jesus; heirs of God.

Romans 8:16-17a
The Spirit himself bears witness with our spirit that we are children of God, and if children, then heirs—heirs of God and fellow heirs with Christ...

As "fellow heirs with Christ", we will all be, to varying degrees, in charge of the vast creative projects God has in store for the New Creation. How much authority you will have is directly proportional to how much treasure you have stored up. But this won't be independent authority. God will be right there with you. You will be *joint heirs*, not an independent lone-wolf.

Learning and **Exploring** are related. How long will it take to study all the wondrous facets of an infinite God? With a dazzling New Universe, and a lush New Earth, there will be much to explore and learn about. Every planet and galaxy will be reflecting His glory.

Will there be alien life forms on distant planets? We don't think so. Here's why. The human race is unique in all the universe. Only one man in all the universe brought the Curse down on everything. That man was Adam. Only one man broke the Curse. That man was Jesus. Both were men of planet Earth. They were not Vulcans or Klingons.

If there is intelligent life on other planets, then what part do they have in sin and redemption? It would be monstrously unfair for Adam's sin to cause the curse of death for aliens on faraway planets.

God's focus was on the Earth. That is where life was created, and that is where life will go on for all eternity. Remember, everything in the New Creation will be resurrected from the Old. There are no "aliens" now, and there will be none in eternity. God had one and only one plan for life, and that was on a pale blue dot called Earth.[29]

Our learning and exploration will lead directly to **Creativity**. What good is learning if it is never *expressed*? Creativity is the expression of learning. The arts give us a window into the depths of what we have learned as a culture about the world around us, and about the human condition.

The human capacity for creativity is God-given and ingrained. God is a Creator, and those created in His image will forever bear the stamp of His creativity. Behind all human creativity is the Self-Existent Cause, the Creator God. All human creativity, art, engineering, and accomplishment is powered by the Spirit of God.[30]

What an explosion of creativity there will be when all the shackles of sin, which twist and corrupt and discourage these gifts, have been crushed forever!

Michelangelo Buonarroti, the famous sixteenth century artist and sculptor, had an interesting take on creativity:

I saw the angel in the marble and carved until I set him free.[31]

The catalyst for our creativity will be the Glory of God. What facets of God's glory will we see in the New Creation? We will study them until we "see the angel in the marble". And then we will set him free in a blaze of creativity!

Our creativity will lead directly to **Celebration**. There is going to be a whole lot of partying going on! Each new discovery or finished creative project will trigger spontaneous celebration.

In the ancient land of Israel, the Jews celebrated seven annual festivals, or sacred feasts. Each one was meant to celebrate and give thanks to God.

Jesus told his disciples that at least one of these feasts, Passover, would continue on in the Kingdom (Luke 22:15-16). Jesus is going to "eat this meal again" in the Kingdom. He also said He would celebrate the Passover with us (Matthew 26:29).

There is no reason to believe that the Passover will be the only feast celebrated in the Kingdom. Taken as a whole, the sense we get from scripture is that at the drop of a hat, for the slightest reason, spontaneous celebrations will pop up all over the New Earth.

One of the first things we will do when we get to the New Earth is have a wedding feast.

Revelation 19:9a (NLT)
And the angel said to me, "Write this: Blessed are those who are invited to the wedding feast of the Lamb."

We will celebrate the wedding feast of the Lamb (Jesus) with Noah and Abraham and Moses and Ruth and King David and all the "cloud of witness" who have gone before[32], and with all our believing friends and relatives. What a joyous reunion! There is no reason to think that the wedding feast will be a one-time celebration, either.

The New Earth will be the ultimate party town!

Celebration will naturally flow into **Worship**. That's because anything and everything we could possibly celebrate will be from God and about Him. Worship is not a big at-a-boy slap on God's back. Worship is not just singing emotional songs about how He loves me.

Worship *always* starts with surrender.

Romans 12:1
*I appeal to you therefore, brothers, by the mercies of God, to present your bodies as a living sacrifice, holy and acceptable to God, **which is your spiritual worship**.*

Paul defined "spiritual worship" as presenting our bodies "as a living sacrifice". If we do not approach worship from an attitude of surrender, then something is wrong.

But worship is a two-way street. It is a feedback loop of blessing. As we bless God in worship, He blesses us with the very best blessing there ever could be...to "become partakers of the divine nature".[33]

This will continue on throughout all eternity. Our learning and exploration will lead to creativity, which will lead to celebration, which will lead to worship, which will lead to the blessing of His divine nature, which will lead to even more learning and exploration. On and on, "from one degree of glory to another".[34]

All of this is our inheritance. We are children of the Most High God, sons and daughters, princes and princesses, and the King, our Father, is going to share all that He has with us! This is a promise repeated all over the entire Bible.

Romans 8:16-17a
*The Spirit himself bears witness with our spirit that we are children of God, and if children, then **heirs**—heirs of God and fellow heirs with Christ...*

If you get nothing else out of this book, please get this. As a believer, you have an inheritance far more valuable than anything imaginable. Read through these verses, and let it sink in:

Colossians 1:12
*giving thanks to the Father, who has qualified you to share in the **inheritance** of the saints in light.*

Acts 20:32b
*...and to give you the **inheritance** among all those who are sanctified.*

Ephesians 1:11a
*In him we have obtained an **inheritance**...*

James 2:5a
*has not God chosen those who are poor in the world to be rich in faith and **heirs of the kingdom**,*

Ephesians 1:18b
*what are the riches of his glorious **inheritance** in the saints*

Galatians 4:7
*So you are no longer a slave, but a son, and if a son, then an **heir** through God.*

Titus 3:7
*so that being justified by his grace we might become **heirs** according to the hope of eternal life.*

1 Peter 1:4
*to an **inheritance** that is imperishable, undefiled, and unfading, kept in heaven for you,*

Colossians 3:24b
*...you will receive the **inheritance** as your reward.*

John, in his Revelation, starts out chapter 21 by talking about the New Heaven and the New Earth. Then in verse seven he says this:

Revelation 21:7a (NASB)
*He who overcomes will **inherit** these things...*

We will inherit these things. What "things"? The New Heaven and the New Earth! We will inherit *all* if it!

This is our "treasure in heaven". Jesus promised it. You can depend on it. What are you going to do about it?

Jesus wants us to get the most out of our life in eternity. He told us exactly how to do that:

Matthew 6:19-20
*Do not lay up for yourselves treasures on earth, where moth and rust destroy and where thieves break in and steal, **but lay up for yourselves treasures in heaven**...*

We highly recommend Randy Alcorn's books, *The Treasure Principle*, and *Heaven* for a more in-depth look at this subject.

With such an immense inheritance, with such a future guaranteed, how could anyone turn their back on it? How could anyone choose an eternity of Self over *this*?

And how can we who have the down-payment of the Spirit within us go on as we always have, consumed with lesser things? How can we go on gorging on mud pies when we have a banquet awaiting us?

How can we not lay up as many treasures as we possibly can? They will make our life on the New Earth so much richer. They will give us much greater authority and creativity and joy!

Jesus laid down the principle of varying degrees of reward in two parables. In the Parable of the Talents, Jesus tells the story of a master who went away on a journey, and entrusted money to three servants. To one he gave five "talents" of gold. A talent was about 130 pounds. To the others he gave two talents, and one talent, "to each according to his ability".[35]

When the master returned, the servants who had been given five talents and two talents had both used them well, and doubled the value. The master told them, "Well done, good and faithful servant. You have been faithful over a little; I will set you over much."

But the servant who had been given one talent had just hidden it in the ground. It had not produced anything. So the master says, "Cast the worthless servant into the outer darkness. In that place there will be weeping and gnashing of teeth."[36].

Likewise, in the Parable of the Minas, Jesus tells a similar story. This time there are ten servants, and they are given varying numbers of minas, which is another measure of gold. And just like the first parable, the servants produce varying results. To the most productive, he says, "Well done, good servant! Because you have been faithful in a very little, you shall have authority over ten cities."[37]

And again, to the servant who had produced nothing, the master says, "Take the mina from him, and give it to the one who has the ten minas".

The talents and the minas in both of these parables represent the faith we've been given. The servants who had produced nothing are like the wedding guest who had no wedding garments. In each case, their faith had produced no works of righteousness.

Such faith is dead.[38] Dead faith could not save them.[39] They were cast "into the outer darkness".

The servants in both of these parables who produced a good return represent faith which has produced abundant fruit. That fruit is their wedding garments, and *that* is their treasure. They were each given varying degrees of reward, The master will set them over much. They will have authority over many cities.

Both of these parables are parables of the Kingdom[40]. They are describing life on the New Earth. There are varying degrees of reward in eternity. There are different levels of authority and creativity. There are greater and lesser treasures and joy.

We saw a bumper sticker on an old beat-up car the other day, which we absolutely loved. This guy obviously gets it:

Don't let the car fool you. My treasure is in heaven.

You have a hand in designing what your life on the New Earth will be like. What happens now, while you are still alive and walking around on this planet, has massive consequences in eternity.

God wouldn't have said it seven times in the Bible unless He was very serious! Take Jesus' advice!

Lay up for yourselves treasures in heaven.

A Journey to New Jerusalem

And I saw the holy city, new Jerusalem, coming down out of heaven from God, prepared as a bride adorned for her husband.
Revelation 21:2

Imagine that you are now living on the New Earth, a citizen of the Kingdom.[41] Life with Jesus in the Intermediate Heaven was, well...*heavenly*. But New Earth is ten billion times more! Your spirit has joined your resurrected body, and you are NEW![42]

You have been here for about a thousand old-earth years, but somehow time is perceived differently in this wondrous place. Life moves much slower. It's hard to describe. The pace is much more leisurely, but that's not exactly the right word. You have taken to calling it "savory". You take the time (because you *have* the time) to savor everything and everyone, everywhere you go.

In the thousand years you've been here, you have memorized the entire Bible. It lives in your heart like a pilot-flame on an old gas stove. At the slightest provocation, it ignites a blaze of passion for the glory of God. As it always does, that passion fuels learning and exploration and creativity. For the past few years you've been exploring on the far side of the planet. Here, you have been learning about the culture of the ethnic group who live there, the Maori.

You see, human cultures from every time in history, in all their variety and uniqueness, have carried over to the Kingdom. Our own unique personalities have been preserved and purified in our new bodies, and it's the same with all the rich ethnic cultures. They have been preserved and purified in the Kingdom.

As you travel the new planet, each new ethnic group you meet reminds you of how it all began. God told the man and woman He had created to "fill the earth" (Genesis 1:28). But they did not.

Later, Noah's great-grandson Nimrod built the city of Babel, and all the people of the planet were gathered in one place. Still they were not scattering and filling the earth. And so God created 70 distinct language groups, and sent angels to lead each group to its own territory (Genesis 11). Over the long centuries, those original 70 blossomed to 7,000 unique ethnic language groups, each with its own rich culture.

That was the original design, and that design has carried over to the New Earth. God loves variety. He does not want homogenized legions of robots. He treasures our identities and our cultures.

And so now you have come to the Maori. They live on the far side of New Earth, not because they have been banished, but because the land there is best suited to their island ways.

In the Shadowlands, the Maori used to live in New Zealand. Long before the first Europeans arrived, they had enjoyed a rich culture.

An important part of that culture was *ta moko*. This was body and face markings, similar to tattoos. But the skin was carved with tiny chisels rather than being punctured, which left the skin with elaborate grooved filigrees and curls.

Moko carried the history of a person's achievements, and status. It was rather like a resume. Since coming to New Earth, the Maori have become adept at advanced technology. They have developed a holographic device which displays in mid-air the history of God's achievements and power. It's the *moko* of God. They jokingly called it "Holo-Moko", and the name has stuck.

The Holo-Moko fits in the palm of your hand, and millions of citizens around the planet now use them daily. It was this little device which first led you to visit the Maori.

You have been with them for a few years now, and some of the Maori are preparing for a journey. It is their pilgrimage to New Jerusalem to worship around the Throne. Each month one-twelfth of the Maori make the trek.

All over New Earth, some from every ethnic group and culture make the journey. The timing is staggered so that everyone has a chance to worship, and to savor the twelve kinds of fruit on the Tree of Life, and receive the healing from its leaves.[43]

You have decided to join this pilgrimage. Travel is on foot, the better to savor everything along the way. A legion of angels has been assigned to help. Everything is in order. And so the journey begins.

As they set out from their city, the Maori pilgrims begin to sing one of their traditional songs, called a *Karakia*.

He hōnore, he korōria ki te Atua
Whakatōngia to wairua tapu
Hei awhina, hei tohutohu i a mātou
Hei ako hoki i ngā mahi mō tēnei rā
Amine

You have learned enough of their language to answer back in song, echoing their words.

Honor and glory to God
Instill in us your sacred spirit
Help us, guide us
In all the things we need to learn today
Amen

After a few weeks travel you come to the land of the Chinese. This is a large province, divided into 56 different ethnic groups, each with its own city or group of cities. Han, Zhuang, Hui, and Manchu cities lie along your caravan's route. Many of these cities have suburbs populated by those who once met in underground house churches.

The Han have specialized in deep space travel. As you enter one of their cities, you hear excited chatter about the next launch. One of the citizens catches your arm.

"When you've done with your pilgrimage, come back to us," he says. "Next year will be our first trip to Centaurus A!"

You've learned enough about the New Heavens to know that Centaurus A is a nearby lenticular galaxy. It resembles a lens, with a beautiful glowing ring around the center. You'd love to see it up close.

"Maybe I will," you reply.

"Get your reservation in early," he says.

"Thank you. I will."

You shake his hand, and rejoin the caravan, which is making its way to the lavish accommodations the Han provide for pilgrims.

Your lodgings are situated at the head of a deep canyon called *Wulingyuan*. The view is spectacular. Hundreds of sandstone pillars are grouped like a forest of 600-foot tall greenish-white trees. A mist fills the the canyon, and the spires seem to float in mid-air.

You spend several days here, sampling the food and music, and getting to know the people. But soon the caravan moves on.

Over the next few months you travel through the territories of the Inuit, the Sioux, Aztec, and the Koreans.

Often Jesus will come walk with you, as He does with all pilgrims. He laughs and sings with you, and at times of rest He will tell stories which fill you with wonder. As you approach a Korean city, Jesus leaves to join another band of pilgrims.

You stop for a few days among the Koreans, whose leaders are mostly from the persecuted North Korean underground churches.

They have developed a unique way to explore the glory of God on a sub-atomic scale. Unlike the Han Chinese and their trips to distant galaxies, the Koreans have invented a way of shrinking human beings so that they may explore the incredible structure of molecules, atoms, quarks, and electrons.

A trip to the atomic world takes at least two weeks, so you add this to your list of adventures to try once your pilgrimage is done.

After three days among the Koreans, it is time to move on.

In your millennium of travel, most of the people you have met are what are called "Simple Citizens". They express their childlike faith in simple, yet beautiful ways, but they are not yet capable of comprehending or reflecting the deeper things of the glory of God. Their creativity is limited to more simple expressions.

They had not many treasures when they arrived here. But day by day, century by century, they are adding to what little they brought with them from the Shadowlands. They are not looked down upon. They are celebrated and cherished.

One of their favorite forms of expression is dance. Sometimes their simple joy is so infections that you join them, but you can never match their wild abandon.

As your caravan passes near one of their small villages, you notice a group dancing in a circle. Others come out to greet the pilgrims, and you turn aside to meet them.

Many of these were wealthy on the Old Earth. They didn't have to trust God much. They already had everything. One of them you recognize as a famous mega-church pastor. He had preached to tens of thousands, and knew all *about* God. But he never really *knew* God very well. He had missed the secret of storing up treasures.

One Simple Citizen runs up to show you the melon she has grown. She breaks it open, and you take a bite. Juice runs down your chin as you smile with delight. To your surprise, it tastes very much like one of the fruits which the Tree of Life produces. She explains that she has spent the last seventy years crossing various strains of fruit to get just the right flavor and texture.

You chat, enjoying her childlike excitement. Then you thank her, compliment her on her creation, and head back to the caravan.

"It tastes like the Father's smile!" she shouts as you depart.

"Ah," you think. "She's made the connection. One more inch of progress."

"And His smile is reflected in yours!" you shout back.

She grins from ear to ear, waves goodbye, and runs back to join her friends.

As you watch her go, you see something you hadn't noticed before. The man leading the dancing is familiar. You've seen him worshiping around the Throne. He always hangs back, bows his head, and worships with tears of joy. Everyone knows him by the name God Most High gave him long ago: The Man After God's Own Heart.

It is King David.

He is not one of the Simple Citizens, but ever since coming to New Earth, he has been working among them. They have almost nothing in the way of treasures, and his heart is to help them grow in the grace and knowledge of Jesus Christ. With his help, each day they reflect more and more, from one degree of glory to the next.

Seeing him dancing there with these simple people, a verse pops into your mind from the storehouse of your heart:

And David danced before the LORD with all his might.[44]

David has a unique way of dancing. He holds *nothing* back. When you see him, it is clear he is humbling himself before Almighty God. Another verse pops into your mind:

I will celebrate before the Lord. I will become even more undignified than this, and I will be humiliated in my own eyes.[45]

You wish that you could dance like that. But this is David's unique gift, and he is passing it on to those who need it most. It is a joy to stand at a distance and watch.

But something now catches your eye which astonishes you in the extreme. The man dancing next to David...oh tears well up in your eyes as you suddenly recognize him...tears of awe at the manifold goodness and grace of God.

It is Uriah the Hittite.

Bathsheba's husband. The man King David arranged to have killed so that he could steal his wife.[46] And here they are...dancing together...ministering to the least in the Kingdom!

As you watch this scene of forgiveness made alive, the grace of God floods over you like an ocean wave. You begin to sing as you return to the caravan:

> *Create in me a clean heart, O God,*
> *and renew a right spirit within me.*
> *Cast me not away from your presence,*
> *and take not your Holy Spirit from me.*
> *Restore to me the joy of your salvation,*
> *and uphold me with a willing spirit.*
> *Then I will teach transgressors your ways,*
> *and sinners will return to you.*[47]

As the caravan travels on, more and more pilgrims join in. You pass through the provinces and cities of many of the great cultures from different times in the history of Old Earth. Sumerians, Vikings, Mongols, and Egyptians now walk with you on the journey to New Jerusalem.

As you travel, the pilgrims sing the songs once sung by Jewish families as they went up to Jerusalem for the holy feasts. It was called the Song of Ascents. One group sings out:

> *I was glad when they said to me,*
> *"Let us go to the house of the LORD!"*[48]

Another group answers back:

> *Behold, as the eyes of servants*
> *look to the hand of their master,*
> *as the eyes of a maidservant*
> *to the hand of her mistress,*
> *so our eyes look to the LORD our God.*[49]

You and the Maori join in:

> *Come, bless the LORD, all you servants of the LORD,*
> *who stand by night in the house of the LORD!*
> *Lift up your hands to the holy place*
> *and bless the LORD!*[50]

On and on you go, month after month, city after city, singing and laughing and worshiping. Jesus often joins you, and the fellowship is sweet. There is little perception of time, but eventually the tip of the highest towers of New Jerusalem are visible far in the distance.

The caravan will soon pass through the outskirts of the vast region assigned to the Jewish people.

There is a particularly stunning Jewish province of glowing cities, but it is two days journey out of your way. The other ethnic groups want to press on, but the Maori have decided to take the short detour, and you are going with them.

As you approach the first city, it is clear why they are so famous. They actually do glow. But it isn't just a bright white light emanating from them. They seem to reflect all the colors of the rainbow.

You stop in the city square, and are greeted by the magistrate. He welcomes you, and says that you are all invited to join a delegation which is headed out tomorrow to the capitol of this province, a city called *Heirah*. Your Hebrew is a little rusty, but you think it means something like "luminous".

The Maori accept the invitation, and you spend a pleasant day in the city. Three days later you have traveled past the villages of Simple Citizens which dot the landscape between most cities, and are nearing Heirah.

The city is not just beautiful, it is majestic. Crystal spires rise over a thousand feet from its center. Every building, and even the streets, seem to be reflecting countless bright colors. Near the central spires sit the capitol buildings, which all appear to be made of clear cut diamonds, fitted together to form intricate patterns of light.

You and the Maori are invited to a banquet that night. It is a joyous affair, with lots of singing, and dancing lead by the Jewish Simple Citizens. The feast is sumptuous. Delicate flavors seem to stimulate taste buds you didn't even know you had.

At a raised table at the head of the hall sits the leader of this province. Nobody knows her true name. The citizens have given her the title, "The Lady of Light". The appellation is fitting, for her very being seems to glow. It is not just the glow of white light. White contains all the colors of the spectrum, and this beautiful lady seems to be reflecting all of them with near-perfect clarity.

"This one has learned to reflect the glory of God well," you think, as you study her. If it wasn't for a ribbon of lace made of pure gold, her long hair would be an unruly mane. It is jet black, yet it shines brightly as the sun.

Suddenly her dark eyes flash at you, and you quickly turn your gaze away. When you dare to look back, she is still staring at you.

"What could this mean?" You cannot take your eyes off of her. How strange and wonderful this is, and so confusing. She looks at you for a long while, and you can do nothing but look back in awe.

She finally looks away, and you enjoy the rest of the banquet in stunned silence, pondering why so high and glorious a being should notice a humble servant such as you.

The next morning, many of the Jewish citizens join you and the Maori on the journey. Everyone is surprised and pleased when the Lady of Light joins the pilgrims.

As the caravan leaves the city, she makes her way through the crowd, and takes up her place walking right beside you. Your heart quickens and your mind races.

She whispers as she walks close by your side.

"God Most High has bid me tell you the name He has given me. I know not why. He asks, and that is all I need to know. I have never spoken it to anyone before."

She looks at her feet and smiles. "It is Sarah El-Segullah".

She glances up to see your reaction.

"Princess of God's Possession," you whisper back.

"You know your Hebrew."

"I know but little Hebrew my Lady. But these words are precious to me. God Most High called me 'His possession' that first day when we all arrived on New Earth."

She seems pleased. "You also?"

You nod your head. "And now...I think I know why He bid you tell me your name."

She seems surprised. "He has spoken to you?"

"Yes...I am to ask you how...how you came to *be* His possession. What is your story?"

Her brow furrows as thoughts are transported thousands of years in the past. Her eyes dart back and forth as she searches the memories.

"My story? Do your really want to hear it? It isn't much."

"Yes, please. I think I need to know."

She takes a deep breath, and looks up at the sky. "My story...Well, you have probably already read it in the Bible."

You are astonished. "In the Bible?! You were one of the great saints of the Bible? I knew so great a lady..."

She places a finger on your lips, silencing you in mid-sentence.

271

"You misunderstand the ways of God. I was not great. In fact, I am the least of all. I was simply a little Jewish slave girl, handmaid to the wife of Naaman, commander of the army of the king of Syria.

"God lived in my heart and all I wanted was to glorify His name among the Syrians. All I ever did was to tell my mistress about the prophet Elisha, and how he could heal my master of his leprosy."[51]

She looks at you, studying your face.

"How can I explain?" she says, pausing to think. "Do you remember that first day, when we all arrived at New Earth?"

"Yes. Who could forget it!"

"Well...When I first arrived, Jesus met me and took me aside.

"'Well done, good and faithful servant,' He said. 'You have been faithful over a little; I will set you over much.'

"I was given authority over a hundred cities. I couldn't understand why. I asked Him. But all Jesus said to me was, 'Trust is gold.'"

You let out a laugh, and it startles her.

"What is so humorous?"

"Oh, please forgive me. I mean no offense. It's only...every leader of every city we've visited on this journey has told me the same thing, and I didn't know why...'Trust is gold,' they all said. I asked them what it meant, but all they did was repeat it. 'Trust is gold'."

She stops, takes your hand, and looks into your eyes.

"In the economy of God, trust is gold! You brought treasure with you from the Shadowlands, otherwise you would be among the Simple Citizens. But it is now time to take your place in the Kingdom. I can see it. God is about to place you over many cities. He..."

You stop her. "Please. I am no administrator."

She flings her dark hair back and looks sternly at you, speaking with passion and authority.

"It is far more than administration! We share in every joy, every creation, every discovery, every reflection of the glory of God within our cities! We help our people grow, and their growth propels ours. We have it all!"

She steps closer, now almost shouting.

"Whatever joys you have experienced thus far in your exploring are *nothing* by comparison!"

Her forcefulness has startled you, and she can see it. She cups a hand to your cheek, and whispers.

"To trust is to know that His ways and His purposes are best. To trust is to obey. God has been preparing you for this. He has given you great freedom. All you lack now is a greater measure of trust. Trust is gold!"

You step back from her, turning this over in your mind. Then you repeat it to yourself.

"Trust is gold."[52]

Sarah El-Segullah, the Lady of Light, the little slave girl of Naaman the Syrian, smiles at you. She turns and walks away, and as she goes you can hear her voice on the wind, a faint whisper.

"Trust is gold."

"Trust is gold," you recite one last time, as you run to catch up to the Maori.

Over the next three weeks, New Jerusalem looms larger and larger on the horizon. Soon you can make out the three gates on the Eastern wall. Your journey has been long, but not everyone travels this way on their annual pilgrimage to New Jerusalem.

There is a means of travel, invented by a partnership between the Germans and the Inuit, called the "Anfuhrschnell" (fast transport). With it, people can travel thousands of miles in the blink of an eye.

You acquired an Anfuhrschnell a few hundred years ago, and have used it often, whenever you decided not to take the "savory" route.

As you near New Jerusalem, your very last stop is in a city of the Basque people, one of the oldest cultures. Soon after God scattered the peoples from the Tower of Babel, the Basque split off from the main group settling in what was to become central Europe.

The Basque made their home in the western Pyrenees mountains, spanning the border between what later became France and Spain. Here on New Earth, they have become adept at taking technology from other groups and adapting it in amazing ways.

You have been looking forward to this stop, because you've had a plan ever since you first used a Holo-Moko. The Maori's device works by tapping into Time in an ingenious way. It can display holographic images from the past, but you can't actually *go* there.

Your idea is to marry the technology of the Holo-Moko and the Anfuhrschnell, and create a device which can be used for actual time-travel.

Your imagination races at the prospect of traveling to any point in history, and witnessing firsthand the grace of God in action.

The Maori plan to stay with the Basque people for three days in preparation for the last day's journey into the great city of New Jerusalem. That's just enough time to put your plan to the test.

As soon as you enter the city, you seek out a man named Argider. You first met him on a trip a hundred years ago, and were drawn to him by his name, which means "Beautiful Light". His countenance echoed his name. He reflected the glory of God in marvelous ways.

Argider is a master at adapting totally different technologies to produce something completely unique, and far greater. He greets you at the door of his workshop and invites you in. You are excited, and after brief greetings, you start to explain your idea.

"Ah, my friend, not so fast! First we have pintxos!"

Pintxos, sometimes called "pinchos", are a small snack which is a way of life among the Basque. You can seldom have a conversation in Basque country without munching on these little delicacies. They are made of bits of savory foods pinned with a little skewer to a delicious piece of bread.

Argider pours you a glass of Txakoli, and you both settle into chairs by his window. Like all wines on New Earth, Txakoli invigorates and inspires, but it never inebriates.[53]

You and Argider chat for an hour or so before he finally lets you tell him about your idea. When he hears about the possibility of time travel, he perks up.

"Do you have any idea what this could mean, my friend!? To actually go back in time and see God moving the events of history like great chess pieces! To see His sovereign plans unfold!"

"I thought you'd like the idea," you say, as you hand him your Holo-Moko and your Anfuhrschnell.

He turns them over, studying them.

"Alegiazko!" he exclaims. "Fantastic! Now get out of here, and let me work!"

He shoves you toward the door, and sets to work disassembling the two devices. You smile, and leave his workshop.

Your three days among the Basque are delightful. Their food and music and dance are renown, and it has all been purified and magnified to the glory of God.

On the morning of the fourth day, as the Maori are leaving, you hurry to Argider's workshop. He has completed a prototype of the new device, which he calls a "Denbora Bidaia". You have trouble pronouncing it, and it comes out, "Denbaia".

Argider laughs at your butchering of his language. But the name will stick when years from now the cities which you have been given authority over are manufacturing them by the millions.[54]

Argider explains that the Denbaia is not yet complete, and to come back when your worship at the Temple is done. For now, all it can do is *freeze* time. You can pause an instant in time, and savor everything. You have the ability to move about, while everything around you is frozen.

Argider hands you one of his Denbaia prototypes. You thank him, shake his hand and say goodbye. But that is not enough for this big bear of a man. He gives you a massive hug.

"Jainkoari aintza," he says.

"Glory to God," you repeat.

You must hurry to catch up to the Maori, who are already leaving the Basque city.

It has now been nearly a year since you left with the Maori from their lands. The high walls of New Jerusalem are just a day's walk. Halfway there, you stop to admire the massive city.

It is radiant, like a rare jewel, clear as crystal. The Eastern Wall, which you face, has three gates, each made of a single giant pearl, each guarded by ten-foot-tall angels, holding flaming swords.

Citizens from every tribe and tongue and nation move in and out through the giant gates. The Maori head for the center gate with their of entourage of angels.

As you pass through the gate, you see the city, New Jerusalem in all its glory. It is made of pure gold...so pure that it is like clear glass. Even the streets are pure gold, transparent as glass.

Down the middle of the main street flows the River of The Water of Life, bright as crystal. On either side of the river are planted the Tree of Life.[55]

Every ethnic group has come bringing their latest creations. These are shared and traded. In one quarter it is like a high-tech convention. Elsewhere it is like a fabulous street bazaar, with fruits and sweets and silks and delights of every kind.

The Maori have brought many cases laden with Holo-Mokos, carried by your angel companions. These are now shared with millions. As you look around at all of this, you recall a verse:

And the nations will enter New Jerusalem, and the kings of the earth will bring their glory into it.[56]

For a week there is feasting and dancing and trading and story-telling and symphonies. Groups of travelers meet in the towering buildings and share their discoveries, and encourage each other.

Jesus seems to be everywhere. He is fully God and fully Man. In His humanity, he joins in the celebration and fellowship and sharing. In His deity, Jesus is the *perfect* reflection of the glory of God.

Everything in this city is centered around that glory, and Jesus takes joy in celebrating it with you all in your own unique way. He will dance with the Simple Citizens. He will sing with those who sing. He will paint with those who paint. He will trade stories with those who are storytellers.

Jesus has the ability to meet everyone on an individual basis, even though there are millions. You haven't figured out if it's because He can slip in and out of time, or if He can be in more than one place at once. One way or another, Jesus makes you all feel as if you are beloved brothers and sisters.

On the fourth day of celebrations, as you sit under the Tree of Life feasting on its marvelous fruit, someone comes up behind you.

"May I sit with you, friend?" he asks.

You turn to look, and your heart skips a beat. It is Jesus.

"Yes, Lord," you reply.

He sits with you, but says nothing for several minutes. Then He turns and looks at you with His piercing eyes.

"You saw my servant David dancing with the Simple Citizens?" He speaks in His deity, and you answer reverently, "Yes, Lord."

"What did you see?"

"Lord, I saw a king using his gift to help others find Your glory."

"Very good," Jesus replies. "And did you see my servant Sarah El-Segullah?"

"Yes, Lord."

"And what did you see?"

"Lord, I saw a little slave girl who's heart was to help others find Your glory."

"Very good," Jesus replies. He now looks at you in a way which pierces to the depths of your soul. He calls you by the name which only He and you know, and asks one last question.

"Do you love me?"

You know what's coming next. This is the question He asked Peter three times, after His resurrection, by the Sea of Galilee.[57] You don't wait for Him to ask you twice again. You take His nail-scarred hand and place it over your heart.

"Yes, Lord, I love you and I trust you...and I will feed your sheep."

Jesus smiles. His tone changes, as He speaks now in His humanity. He is to you the Firstborn among many brothers and sisters, and you enjoy the sweet fellowship of beloved siblings for hours.

For the next three days you try to sample the creations of every one of the ethnic groups gathered in the city. What a joy it is.

On the seventh day it is time to go into the Temple of God Most High. Everyone is dressed in their most radiant robes, ready to reflect God's glory back when He reveals Himself in the Holy of Holies.

You enter the Holy Place. It is enormous. Massive enough to hold millions. A great purple curtain, which is ripped from top to bottom[58] down the center, is drawn across the Holy of Holies.[59]

God the Father is everywhere, and yet He delights in the special revelation of His glory in this holy place. "Holy" means "set apart", and this curtain is a reminder of that great truth.

Everyone has brought their new Holo-Mokos with them. As they take their places, all the millions of Holo-Mokos are now linked together (a new feature the Maori have added).

Above your heads, with detail beyond what physical senses could perceive, with razor-sharp spiritual detail, the moko of Jesus Christ, the glory of His Name and all that He has done, is played out.

Mighty angels stand about the perimeter, shouting back and forth to each other as the glorious deeds of God the Son are played out.

In the beginning was the Word, and the Word was with God, and the Word was God. All things were made through him, and without him was not any thing made that was made.[60]

All the worshipers join in, shouting hosannas and praise to God the Son. The images move on, showing the vast universe as it is stretched out by the mighty hand of God. Then Jesus, and His coming to earth as a man, and His ministry among the people, and His march to the Cross.

All but the angels are now silent as you witness the death of Jesus.

But he was pierced for our transgressions; he was crushed for our iniquities; upon him was the chastisement that brought us peace, and with his wounds we are healed.[61]

As the stone is rolled against His tomb, the images go black. All is still and utterly quiet for the space of an hour. From the depths of your heart, awestruck amazement at the immense sacrifice of God on your behalf fills your thoughts.

Then three million voices proclaim the glory of His name as you now see Jesus risen and exalted, standing above the earth as King of Kings and Lord of Lords. The angels shout with voices like thunder.

At the name of JESUS every knee will bow and every tongue confess that Jesus Christ is Lord, to the glory of God the Father.[62]

Every worshiper, man and angel alike, now kneel. For three full hours, the angels' last words echo from the massive walls, mixed with human-whispered prayers of surrender. Hearts are being prepared to meet the Infinite Almighty God, face to face.

The purple curtain then begins to stir. Everyone now rises to their feet, lifting hands in praise and surrender, some leaping wildly with joy. Shouts of worship grow to a crescendo. The sound is deafening.

The curtain begins to part. You can see flashes of lightning. The angels instinctively cover their faces with their wings.

As the curtain is slowly pulled back, you activate your Denbaia. Time is suddenly frozen. An instant, a Non-Existent Now, stopped in mid-flight.

You walk around the Holy Place, looking at the worshipers. Some are leaping, frozen in mid-air. You savor this interrupted scene... studying it for hours...memorizing every detail.

The first thing you notice is the angels. They cover their faces, not for awe of God alone. Their wings are shielding their view of you, the human worshipers as well. For them it is like intruding into the bedchamber of newlyweds on their wedding night.

There is an intimacy about to happen here which has no correlation to anything from Old Earth.

You can see it in the faces of your fellow humans.

Worship completes them. It completes them as love completes two lovers. It is ecstasy far greater than the greatest sexual orgasm. There is a giving of oneself. There is consummation in complete surrender to the greatest Love of all. There is oneness, and sweet communion with the One who is Infinite and All.[63]

You wander to the front, near the parting curtain. Those who have been forgiven much seem to gravitate here. You recognize a woman. She is the one who was caught in the act of adultery. The one to whose accusers Jesus said, "Let him who is without sin among you cast the first stone."[64]

She is weeping. This does not surprise you. It has been written, "He will wipe away every tear from their eyes".[65] But you have learned that there are *many* tears here. They are tears of joy, they are tears of gratitude, they are tears of awestruck wonder.

Scripture never said there would not be tears in heaven. It said He would wipe them all away. And those near the front seem to be weeping oceans.

You look around, taking it all in. Here are men and women you've read about in the Bible. Here are those from 21st century America, and from Ancient Greece, and medieval Europe. Here are those from all the centuries and all the continents and all the cultures, gathered together in worship.

There is a balcony at the back. You want to get a better view, and so you make your way there.

As you weave among the worshipers, you pass people from every imaginable ethnic group, each worshiping in their own unique way... the way of their culture...the way of their own God-created heart. Scripture comes to mind. You whisper as you walk:

After this I looked, and behold, a great multitude that no one could number, from every nation, from all tribes and peoples and languages, standing before the throne...[66]

You climb the stairs at the back, and mount the balcony. From here the perspective is breathtaking. A sea of worshipers stretching as far as the eye can see. The undiluted, unfiltered glory of God about to break out upon them.

It is as if all the wide universe is holding its breath.

This is joy...real joy. This is what we were created for. This is heaven come down to kiss the earth.

A verse leaps from your heart. You cannot contain it. You shout it out like a trumpet call, echoing from the stone walls:

> *For I know that my Redeemer lives,*
> *and at the last he will stand upon the earth.*
> *And after my skin has been thus destroyed,*
> *yet in my flesh I shall see God,*
> *whom I shall see for myself,*
> *and my eyes shall behold, and not another.*
> *My heart faints within me!*[67]

Holy! Holy! Holy!

*And one called to another and said: "Holy, holy, holy is
the LORD of hosts; the whole earth is full of his glory!"*
Isaiah 6:3

We have just seen what worship in heaven might look like. In the last chapter we saw joy and intimacy. Worship is what we were created for. God desires worship, not because He's on some huge ego trip. God desires worship because He knows that worship completes us.

The Bible gives us a picture of the worship that's going on in heaven *right now*. In the verse quoted above, and also in Revelation 4:8, we see the angels shouting, "Holy! Holy! Holy!". As we said before, "holy" means "set apart". God is everywhere, but He is also set apart. He is distinct from everything and everyone that ever was.

Jeremiah 10:6
*There is none like you, O LORD; you are great, and your
name is great in might.*

Notice that the angels repeat "Holy!" three times. Numbers were very important in ancient Hebrew culture. 6 is the number of mankind, and 3 is the number of the Triune God. The number of the Antichrist is 666[68]. It is the number of mankind repeated three times, thus attempting to masquerade as God.

The fact that the angels repeat "Holy!" three times not only emphasizes its importance, but also WHO is holy...God!

The Bible also tells us the *why* of worship in heaven. The angels are not worshiping because they've been forced to. The angels give us a concrete *reason* for their worship:

Revelation 4:11
*Worthy are you, our Lord and God, to receive glory and honor and power, **for you created all things**, and by your will they existed and were created.*

If God as Creator is not the foundation of your worship, then something is terribly wrong. You may not be worshiping God at all.

This puts the creation versus evolution debate in a new light. This is not just a debate about the finer points of science and theology. This is eternally significant.

All the things we have described as we have looked at eternity are mere shadows of what is yet to come. We have only been given a glimpse of future glory. We will all be overwhelmingly surprised when we finally set foot on the New Earth. All we can see now is a tiny fraction. We can only "see in a mirror dimly".

1 Corinthians 13:12
For now we see in a mirror dimly, but then face to face. Now I know in part; then I shall know fully, even as I have been fully known.

Until the time when we "shall know fully", we must all live out our lives on this planet in this time. Parents have children to care for. Husbands and wives have marriages to nurture. We go to our jobs and our schools, and we fulfill our responsibilities.

But along the way, as we walk this pilgrim path, there is fruit to bear, there is treasure to be stored up. May we not miss it. May God open our eyes to what His *Glory* can do, in this land where everything is small.

We may see in a mirror dimly now, but this much we know for certain. At the end of our journey, we shall see God, and we shall know, and be known. We shall see God as He is.

God is infinite. Yes, *infinite*. He is beyond all measure or comprehension. Far too many in the Western Church have too small a view of God. We often see Him as not much more than a Santa Claus, bringing us a bundle of presents if we've been nice and not naughty.

If your god is not way, way beyond anything your brain could ever conceive of, then he is not the Creator God of the universe. A lesser god could not create such things.

If your god is not both Infinite and Creator, then you are worshiping the wrong god. In that case, you may never get to explore the New Earth. You may never experience the pure joy of the worship we saw in the Temple at New Jerusalem. You may be off in a universe of one worshiping *yourself*.

It will take all of eternity to plumb the depths of God precisely because He is INFINITE!

Psalms 147:5 (NASB)
Great is our Lord and abundant in strength; His under-standing is infinite.

God's strength and understanding are *infinite*. *He* is infinite. Only an infinite Being has infinite understanding and strength.

Job 11:7
Can you find out the deep things of God? Can you find out the limit of the Almighty?

The "deep things of God" are beyond our knowing. He is simply too big for us. In our present state, we cannot comprehend. There is no limit to Almighty God. He is, therefore, infinite.

Ephesians 1:19
and what is the immeasurable greatness of his power toward us who believe, according to the working of his great might

God's greatness and power are "immeasurable" because *He* is immeasurable. He is *infinite*!

The greatness of God cannot be overstated. It is impossible. It is difficult for us to comprehend an infinite Being. We have nothing in our experience on this planet to compare. But when we see Him face to face, we will see Him in His infinity!

The thought of that makes us fall flat on our face in awe and worship even now. What will be our reaction *then*? The phrase "fear God" sounds archaic to our ears. But when we begin to understand how completely immense and awesome and powerful is our God, reverential fear is the only rational response!

The infinite greatness of God is the central truth of all time.

Margie ran an in-home daycare a few years ago. Following God's lead, we had stepped out in faith and built an addition onto our home for the play room.[69] It was a place of constant energy. Margie would often read Bible stories to the children, and sing songs about Jesus with them as they went about their activities.

I recall one little boy standing at the glass French doors one day looking out at the Olympic Mountains. It was late in the day. What filmmakers call "Golden Hour". The mountains stood in stark relief against a backdrop of dark turbulent clouds. The golden sunlight coming from the side, and the dark clouds behind, accentuated the rugged mountain features. It was *majestic*.

The four year old boy stood gazing at this awesome scene for a long time. He was not just looking at it, he was studying...connecting the dots. It was obviously stirring deep thoughts. I could almost see the gears turning in his little head. It seemed to me that, in his childlike simplicity, he was trying to make sense of something so big and so beautiful and so majestic.

Then he said something profound, which in a way sums up this whole book. I will always remember his five simple words. They are the central truth of all time:

"God must be really BIG!"

Amen.

[1] If you don't know what the Peoples Republic of Naturalism is, see our chapter on Scientific Naturalism in Section 3.

[2] *AppleTree 101* blog.

[3] *Interstellar*, Paramount Pictures, 2014; screenplay by Jonathan Nolan and Christopher Nolan.

[4] If you don't remember what LDYL stands for, see our chapter on Abiding Love in Section Six.

[5] For a good discussion of eschatology, see *Four Views of the End Times*, by Dr. Timothy Paul Jones (2011), and *The Oxford Handbook of Eschatology*, edited by Professor Jerry L. Walls (2010).

[6] *Jamieson, Fausett & Brown* commentary.

[7] *Jamieson, Fausett & Brown* commentary.

[8] *Jamieson, Fausett & Brown* commentary.

[9] From *The Divine Comedy: Inferno, Canto III*, by Dante Alighieri (1265-1321). Our chapter title is a common misquote.

[10] Vine's Complete Expository Dictionary.

[11] From *He Descended into Hell?*, by Joe Rigney, April 4, 2015.

[12] See *Jesus' Sermon on the Mount and His Confrontation with the World* by D.A. Carson; *The Ultimate Religious Decision* by John MacArthur; *Interview with John Piper* by Rick Warren.

[13] Randy Alcorn, in his novel *Deadline*, gives us a glimpse of Hell, and it is essentially what we have described, though he doesn't use our words for it: "a little god in a universe of one".

[14] These ideas about God's alternatives to Hell were discussed by C.S. Lewis in *The Problem of Pain* (1962).

[15] *Jamieson, Fausett & Brown* commentary.

[16] Romans 1:21-22.

[17] Vine's Complete Expository Dictionary.

[18] Vine's Complete Expository Dictionary.

[19] 1 Corinthians 15:37.

[20] Strong's Dictionary.

[21] Vine's Complete Expository Dictionary.

[22] *Jamieson, Fausett & Brown* commentary.

[23] Romans 8:19-23.

[24] Romans 8:18.

[25] Ephesians 2:19-22.

[26] Genesis 1:28.

[27] 1 Corinthians 6:3.

[28] Merriam-Webster..

[29] This is a tip-of-the-hat to Carl Sagan, and his oft-repeated description of the earth as a *Pale Blue Dot*.

[30] Exodus 35:30-33.

[31] This quote is a loose translation of a sentence in a letter from Michelangelo to Benedetto Varchi.

[32] Hebrews 11.

[33] 2 Peter 1:4.

[34] 2 Corinthians 3:18.

[35] Matthew 14:25-30.

[36] Matthew 25:30.

[37] Luke 19:17.

[38] James 2:17.

[39] James 2:14.

[40] Matthew 25:1; Luke 19:11.

[41] Most of this journey to New Jerusalem is, of course, imaginary. But we feel it is a culmination of all we have discovered thus far in this book. We like to think of it as "sanctified imagination". It is imagination illuminated by both scripture and the Holy Spirit.

[42] We will have temporary bodies in Paradise, while we're waiting for the Resurrection. See our discussion of the sequence between death and the New Earth in "The Big Sleep" chapter in Section One.

[43] Revelation 22:2.

[44] 2 Samuel 6:14.

[45] 2 Samuel 6:21-22 (NIV).

[46] Read 2 Samuel 11 & 12 for the whole story of David and Uriah.

[47] Psalm 51:10-13.

[48] Psalm 122:1.

[49] Psalm 123:2.

[50] Psalm 134:1-2.

[51] You can read Sarah's story in Second Kings chapter 5.

[52] "Trust is gold." This is what God told me (Stan) over and over and over again, during my long months of illness.

[53] This is taken from a line of dialog from the movie *The Bishop's Wife*, Samuel Goldwyn Studios, 1947.

[54] With an eternity of possibilities, anything not sinful will most likely become a reality sooner or later, even advanced technology.

[55] See Revelation chapters 21 & 22 for details of New Jerusalem.

[56] This is a paraphrase of Revelation 21:24.

[57] John 21:15-17.

[58] Matthew 27:51.

[59] There may or may not be a curtain across the Holy of Holies.

[60] John 1:1; 3-4.

[61] Isaiah 53:5.

[62] Philippians 2:10-11.

[63] Do you see now why God places such an emphasis on sexual sin in the Bible? Sex is an image of our union with Him! Over and over, God shares His heart about unmarried sex (fornication), adultery, homosexuality, transgender (effeminate), bestiality, incest, and prostitution.

[64] John 8:3-11.

[65] Revelation 21:4.

[66] Revelation 7:9.

[67] Job 19:25-27.

[68] Revelation 13:18.

[69] How this daycare began is a testament to the grace of God. Margie had done daycare twice before, as well as foster kids. By this point in our lives as "empty-nesters", we were glad to be done. One day God distinctly told Margie, "Add onto your house and do daycare for five years". She said, "No!". God repeated it. So she decided to take it to me, knowing that I was just as much "done" with kids as she was. To her astonishment, I said, "I like it!". We proceeded one step at a time as God opened impossible doors. There was no way we could afford to build an 800 square foot addition onto our home. But God did it. And because He did, a little boy heard about the big Creator God, and responded! And so did others, and their parents.

Appendix

Recommended Reading

N either of us has a seminary degree. We've never been pastors or elders. So we thought it would be helpful to let you know a little about where we're coming from. The best way to do that is to let you see the books we read. So here is a list of our favorite authors, in alphabetical order by author.

Almighty God
> *The Bible* — Our primary source is the Bible. This would be our first, and most important "recommended reading".

Randy Alcorn
> *Deadline* (novel)
> *Dominion* (novel)
> *Edge of Eternity* (novel)
> *Heaven*
> *Safely Home* (novel)
> *The Treasure Principle*

Kay Arthur
> *How to Study Your Bible*

Augustine of Hippo
> *City of God**
> *Confessions*

Richard Foster
> *Celebration of Discipline*
> *Freedom of Simplicity*
> *Spiritual Classics*

Ignatius of Loyola
A Pilgrims Journey

Saint John of the Cross
Dark Night of the Soul

Flavius Josephus
The Antiquities of the Jews
The Wars of the Jews*

Brother Lawrence
The Practice of the Presence of God

C. S. Lewis
Chronicles of Narnia (novel series)
Mere Christianity
The Screwtape Letters
Surprised by Joy

J. Vernon McGee
Through the Bible (radio broadcasts - www.ttb.org)

Stephen C. Meyer
Signature in the Cell

Watchman Née
The Spiritual Man

J.I. Packer
Knowing God

Eugene H. Peterson
A Long Obedience in The Same Direction

John Piper
Desiring God
Sermons (www.desiringgod.org/messages)

David Platt
  Radical
  Radical Together

Charles Spurgeon
  Sermons (www.spurgeongems.org)

J. Hudson Taylor
  Union and Communion

Teresa of Avila
  The Interior Castle

A.W. Tozer
  Knowledge of the Holy
  The Pursuit of God

Dallas Willard
  The Great Omission
  The Spirit of the Disciplines

N.T. Wright
  How God Became King: The Forgotten Story of the Gospels

* We have not read these two titles in their entirety.

Margie's Journey

S tan's journey of faith has already been told in this book. Margie's faith journey began at a much earlier age. Here is her story:

One of my earliest memories is going with my mother to the Good News Club that she taught for several years. Every week, I heard a Bible story and learned a Bible verse. Into each story, the gospel was woven. I heard how much God loved me. I learned that "all have sinned and fallen short of the glory of God". And that death was the consequence of sin.

But God loved me so much that He sent His Son, Jesus, who lived a perfect life without sin and died in my place. He came alive again on the third day proving that His death had paid the full price for sin. My responsibility was to receive the gift of eternal life that God offered me through His Son. Every week in every Bible story those truths were reiterated.

When I was about eight years of age, our family went to a revival meeting. When an invitation was given to go forward to receive Jesus, my father asked me if I wanted to go. I was very shy and did not want anyone to notice me, so I said no. But when my younger sister agreed to go, I followed. I knelt at that alter and no one noticed me.

I watched all the other people praying, some quietly, some with great emotion. And eventually, I decided that I should do what I came for. I bowed my own head and simply asked Jesus to come into my heart and wash away my sin.

The Bible teaches that when I receive Jesus, I am a new creation. Old things have passed away and the new has come. It says that the Holy Spirit comes to live in me to help me be what God wants me to be. I can look back into my eight year old life and see that demonstrated.

When we arrived home that evening, we were sent to get ready for bed. My sister was too short to reach the clothes hanger she needed to put her dress away. I reached up and took one down and handed it to her. I had never done that before. I was consumed with myself and had never desired to help her. But this night, things were new and I felt the nudge of God Himself to do a good thing.

When I was twelve years of age, on a family vacation, we attended the Church of t he Open Door in Los Angeles, CA. The pastor, J. Vernon McGee was preaching from Daniel chapter one. When he expounded the verse where "Daniel purposed in his heart that he would not defile himself" by eating food that was forbidden to the people of God, I knew in my heart that God was asking me if I was willing to make that same commitment.

It became the desire of my heart to be like Daniel.

In the half century-plus since I prayed those prayers, I have made many right choices and I have made a few huge wrong ones. But I have proven the truth of Romans 8 where Paul tells us that "nothing can separate us from the love of God". He has kept me all of these years. I am certain that He will keep every one of His promises and that we will not be separated for all eternity.

Romans 8:38-39
For I am sure that neither death nor life, nor angels nor rulers, nor things present nor things to come, nor powers, nor height nor depth, nor anything else in all creation, will be able to separate us from the love of God in Christ Jesus our Lord.

About The Authors

tan & Margie Osterbauer live on a rural acre near Sequim, on Washington's beautiful Olympic Peninsula. They have seven children and twenty grandchildren. They have taught preschool through sixth grade Sunday school for many decades. Margie has taught and mentored teen girls as well.

Margie grew up in the wheat country of eastern Washington. She served with Child Evangelism Fellowship for many years, teaching Good News Club. She did in-home daycare for many years.

Stan grew up in the Los Angeles area. He has a degree in English, but ended up with a career in computer programming, as a systems analyst. He likes to read about astronomy, physics, and history.

Margie and Stan have been through *Perspectives on the World Christian Movement*[1] several times, and Margie has served as grader and grading coordinator for the course in our county. Both Stan and Margie have done many *Precepts* Bible studies, which teach inductive study techniques.[2]

This book took over sixteen months of hard work. We have relied on God the Spirit every step. The concepts and Biblical truths were contributed and discussed by both of us. Stan did most of the writing, and Margie served as editor and fact-checker.

It started out as a personal study on what Jesus really meant by "treasures in heaven". As it became clear that this was bigger, we at first saw it only as an essay of encouragement for our friends and family. But as it grew, and we saw how universal these truths were, and how applicable to everyone who bows the knee to King Jesus, it became the book you now hold in your hands.

It has been a journey of discovery. We do not see ourselves as dispensing wisdom from on high. We are learning these truths right along with you. May God bless you in the reading of it, as He has blessed us in the writing.

As the authors of this book, we feel it is our responsibility to pray for those who read it. Here is our prayer for you:

> *We pray that the God of our Lord Jesus Christ, the Father of glory, may give you the Spirit of wisdom and of revelation in the knowledge of Him, having the eyes of your heart enlightened, that you may know what is the hope to which He has called you, what are the riches of His glorious inheritance for those who believe, and what is the immeasurable greatness of His power toward us, according to the working of His great might that He worked in Christ when He raised Him from the dead.*

Ephesians 1:17-20

---

[1] See www.perspectives.org for a class near you.

[2] See www.precept.org for a study group near you.

Made in the USA
Lexington, KY
25 July 2017